The Great Exposition of Secret Mantra

VOLUME ONE

The Great Exposition of Secret Mantra

VOLUME ONE
Tantra in Tibet

VOLUME TWO
Deity Yoga

VOLUME THREE
Yoga Tantra

The Great Exposition of Secret Mantra

VOLUME ONE

Tantra in Tibet

TSONGKHAPA

WITH A COMMENTARY BY THE

Dalai Lama

TRANSLATION, EDITING, AND
EXPLANATORY MATERIAL BY

Jeffrey Hopkins

ASSOCIATE EDITOR FOR
THE DALAI LAMA'S TEXT AND TSONGKHAPA'S TEXT

Lati Rinpoche

ASSOCIATE EDITOR FOR TSONGKHAPA'S TEXT

Geshe Gedun Lodro

SNOW LION
BOULDER
2016

Snow Lion
An imprint of Shambhala Publications, Inc.
4720 Walnut Street
Boulder, Colorado 80301
www.shambhala.com

The book was first published by George Allen & Unwin Ltd., London, England, 1977, and previously published as *Tantra in Tibet* by arrangement with Unwin Hyman Ltd., 1987. The translation has been updated for the 2016 edition.

9 8 7 6 5 4 3 2 1

Revised Edition

Printed in the United States of America

♾ This edition is printed on acid-free paper that meets the American National Standards Institute Z39.48 Standard.
♻ This book is printed on 30% postconsumer recycled paper. For more information please visit www.shambhala.com.

Distributed in the United States by Penguin Random House LLC and in Canada by Random House of Canada Ltd

Library of Congress Cataloging-in-Publication Data
Names: Bstan-'dzin-rgya-mtsho, Dalai Lama XIV, 1935– author. | Tsong-kha-pa Blo-bzang-grags-pa, 1357–1419, author. | Hopkins, Jeffrey, translator, editor.
Title: The Great Exposition of Secret Mantra / The Dalai Lama, Tsongkhapa; translated and edited by Jeffrey Hopkins.
Description: Boulder, Colorado: Snow Lion, 2016–2017. | Includes bibliographical references and index. Contents: volume 1. Tantra in Tibet — volume 2. Deity Yoga — volume 3. Yoga Tantra. | Includes translations from Tibetan.
Identifiers: LCCN 2016000757| ISBN 9781611803594 (v. 1) | ISBN 9781611803587 (v. 2) | ISBN 9781611803600 (v. 3)
Subjects: LCSH: Tantric Buddhism. | Buddhist mantras. | BISAC: RELIGION / Buddhism / Tibetan. | RELIGION / Buddhism / Rituals & Practice.
Classification: LCC BQ7935.B774 G74 2016 | DDC 294.3/444—dc23
LC record available at https://lccn.loc.gov/2016000757

Contents

Preface

Homage to Vajradhara.

The *Great Exposition of Secret Mantra* by Tsongkhapa (1357–1419), founder of the Gelugpa order of Tibetan Buddhism, presents the main features of all the Buddhist tantra systems as well as the difference between sūtra and tantra, the two divisions of Buddha's word. Tsongkhapa's text begins with an examination of the difference between the Buddhist vehicles, mainly analyzing a variety of earlier delineations of the difference between the Sūtra Great Vehicle and the Mantra Great Vehicle. Although Tsongkhapa does not mention Butön Rinchendrub[1] (1290–1364) by name, it is apparent that his prime source is Butön's encyclopedic presentation of the difference between Sūtra and Mantra in his *Extensive General Presentation of the Tantra Sets, Ornament Beautifying the Precious Tantra Sets.*[2] Butön lists presentations by several Indian scholars who delineate various numbers of ways the Mantra Great Vehicle surpasses the Sūtra Great Vehicle, or Perfection Vehicle[3] as it is commonly called:

- Tripiṭakamāla and his commentator Vajrapāṇi—four differences
- Jñānashrī—eleven differences
- Ratnākarashānti—three differences
- Nāgārjuna—six differences
- Indrabhuti—seven differences
- Jñānapāda—three differences
- Ḍombhiheruka—five differences
- Vajraghaṇṭapāda—four differences
- Samayavajra—five differences

In a radical departure from Butön's catalog of opinions, Tsongkhapa analyzes the structure of the path to Buddhahood and analytically chooses to emphasize a single central distinctive feature of the Mantra Vehicle,[4] deity yoga. His reason, in brief, is that method (compassion and the altruistic deeds it motivates) and wisdom are the central means of achieving the two Buddha Bodies, Truth Body and Form Bodies, and in deity yoga Mantra has a distinctive union of method and wisdom without which a Buddha's Form Bodies cannot be attained. This leads to Tsongkhapa's conclusion that even through the Perfection Vehicle alone, Buddhahood cannot be attained.

The main points Tsongkhapa makes in distinguishing the Lesser Vehicle and the Great Vehicle and, within the latter, the Sūtra and Mantra Vehicles, are:

- The difference between vehicles must lie in the sense of "vehicle" as that to which one progresses or as that by which one progresses.
- The Lesser Vehicle differs from the Great Vehicle in both. The destination of the lower one is the state of a Hearer or Solitary Realizer Foe Destroyer and of the higher one, Buddhahood.
- Concerning "vehicle" in the sense of means by which one progresses, although there is no difference in the wisdom realizing emptiness, there is a difference in method—Lesser Vehicle not having and Great Vehicle having the altruistic intention to become enlightened and its attendant deeds.
- Sūtra and Mantra Great Vehicle do not differ in terms of the goal, the state being sought, since both seek the highest enlightenment of a Buddha, but there is a difference in the means of progress, again not in wisdom but in method.
- Within method, Sūtra and Mantra Great Vehicle differ not in the basis or motivation, the altruistic intention to become enlightened, nor in having the perfections as

> deeds, but in the additional technique of deity yoga. A deity is a supramundane being who himself or herself is a manifestation of compassion and wisdom. Thus, in the special practice of deity yoga one joins one's own body, speech, mind, and activities with the exalted body, speech, mind, and activities of a supramundane being, manifesting on the path a similitude of the state of the effect.

As scriptural authority for the central distinguishing feature between the Sūtra and Mantra Great Vehicles, Tsongkhapa quotes a passage from the *Vajrapañjara Tantra,* rejects the commentaries of Kṛṣhṇapāda and Indrabodhi, and critically uses the commentary of Devakulamahāmati, accepting some parts of that explanation and rejecting others. He reinforces his presentation of deity yoga as the dividing line between the two Great Vehicles with citations from or references to works on Highest Yoga Tantra by Jñānapāda, Ratnākarashānti, Abhayākāra, Durjayachandra, Shrīdhara, Samayavajra, Jinadatta, and Vinayadatta.

Despite Tsongkhapa's many citations of tantras and Indian commentaries, it is clear that these are used only as supportive evidence for his presentation. Tradition is only supportive, not the ultimate authority. The arbiter is reason, specifically in the sense of determining coherence and consistency within a path structure. He refutes Ratnarakṣhita and Tripiṭakamāla, for instance, not because they differ from the aforementioned sources but because their presentations fail in terms of consistency with the path structure. By doing so, he moves the basis of the exposition from scriptural citation to reasoned analysis of a meditative structure.

Also, whereas Butön catalogs nine ways that Indian scholar-yogis differentiate the four tantra sets—by way of the four Indian castes, four schools of tenets, four faces of Kālachakra, four periods of the day, four eras, followers of four deities, four afflictive emotions to be abandoned, four levels of desire to be purified, and four levels of faculties—Tsongkhapa critically examines most of these, accepting only the last two, with modification. He differentiates the four tantra sets by way of their main trainees being of four very different types, since these trainees have (1) four different ways of using desire for the attributes of the desire realm in the path and (2) four different levels of capacity for generating the emptiness and deity yogas that use desire in the path.

In his systemization, the four tantras are not differentiated (1) by way of their *object of intent* since all four are aimed at bringing about others' welfare or (2) by way of the *object of attainment* since all four seek the full enlightenment of Buddhahood or (3) by way of merely having different types of *deity yoga* since all four tantra sets have many different types of deity yoga but are each only one tantra set. Rather, the distinctive tantric practice of deity yoga, motivated by great compassion and beginning with emptiness yoga, is carried out in different ways in the four tantra sets. Various levels of desire—involved in gazing, laughing, touching, and sexual union—are utilized by the respective main trainees in accordance with their disposition toward styles of practice, these being to emphasize external activities, to balance external activities and meditative stabilization, to emphasize meditative stabilization, or to exclusively focus on meditative stabilization.

Tsongkhapa's exposition represents an appeal to analysis, a carefully constructed argument based on scriptural sources and reasoning, with the emphasis on the latter. Consistency, coherence, and elegance of system are the cornerstones; his procedure is that of a thorough scholar, analyzing sources and counteropinions with careful scrutiny determining the place of the pillars of his analysis in the general structure of a system. His intention is clearly not to present a catalog of views as Butön mainly did, but to adjudicate conflicting systems of explication, thereby establishing a radically new one.

In 1972 when I was in Dharamsala, northern India, on a Fulbright Dissertation Fellowship, His Holiness the Dalai Lama asked me to translate the *Great Exposition of Secret Mantra,* the first section of which is the second part of this book. The first part is the Dalai

Lama's own commentary which he gave me in private in August 1974, upon my return to Dharamsala. His commentary, which I recorded, translated, and edited, provides valuable insight into tantra in general and Tsongkhapa's work in particular. Presenting the rich Tibetan oral tradition, his exposition reveals the highly practical and compassionate use of this ancient science of spiritual development.

The third part of the book is a supplement that I hope will clarify key points in the Dalai Lama's and Tsongkhapa's teachings. The supplement is also drawn from the oral teachings of Kensur Lekden (1900–71), abbot of the Tantric College of Lower Lhasa, and Professor Geshe Gedün Lodrö (1924–79) of the University of Hamburg as well as from general explanations of tantra found in all four orders of Tibetan Buddhism:

Nyingma
Longchen Rabjam's *Precious Treasury of the Supreme Vehicle* and *Treasury of Tenets;*

Kagyu
Padma Karpo's *General Presentation of the Tantra Sets, Captivating the Wise;*

Sakya
Sönam Tsemo's *General Presentation of the Tantra Sets;*
Butön's *General Presentation of the Tantra Sets*—condensed, medium length, and extensive versions;

Gelug
Lo-sang-chö-kyi-gyal-tshan's *Presentation of the General Teaching and the Four Tantra Sets;*
Long-dol Ngagwang Losang's *Terminology Arising in Secret Mantra, the Scriptural Division of the Knowledge Bearers;*
Pabongkha's *Miscellaneous Notes from Jonay Paṇḍita's "Explanation of the Great Exposition of Secret Mantra."*

I orally re-translated the first two parts into Tibetan for Lati Rinpoche, a philosophy master and tantric lama from the Dalai Lama's monastery in Dharamsala, for the sake of correction and verification. Geshe Gedün Lodrö, a Tibetan scholar of scholars who taught at the University of Hamburg, provided invaluable information and explanation for the translation of Tsongkhapa's text. Barbara Frye, a student of Tibetan Buddhism for several years, helped in editing the Dalai Lama's commentary.

A guide to Tsongkhapa's text, following his own mode of division of the contents, is given in tabular form in an appendix. The eight chapter divisions and their titles in the Dalai Lama's commentary and in Tsongkhapa's text were added to facilitate understanding. The transliteration scheme for Sanskrit names and titles is aimed at easy pronunciation, using *sh*, *ṣh*, and *ch* rather than *ś*, *ṣ*, and *c*. With the first occurrence of each Indian title, the Sanskrit is given, if available. Often Tsongkhapa refers only to the title or the author of a work, whereas both are given in translation to obviate the need for checking back and forth. The full Sanskrit and Tibetan titles are to be found in the bibliography, which is arranged alphabetically according to the English titles of sūtras and tantras and according to the authors of other works. The Sanskrit and Tibetan originals of key terms are given in a glossary at the end.

Jeffrey Hopkins
President and Founder, UMA Institute for Tibetan Studies
Emeritus Professor of Tibetan Studies
University of Virginia

Acknowledgment

We wish to thank Mr. Gerald Yorke for many suggestions that improved the rendering in English of Part II.

I

Essence of Tantra

The Dalai Lama

TRANSLATED AND EDITED BY

Jeffrey Hopkins

ASSOCIATE EDITOR

Lati Rinpoche

Tantra for Practice

It is essential to settle the meaning of the scriptures with stainless reasoning. The meaning of passages that are spoken only for certain trainees must be interpreted and the meaning of extremely subtle passages must be penetrated; this is difficult, and some are in danger of misunderstanding. Also, for many the countless books of sūtra and tantra do not appear as instructions for practice, and they are satisfied with seeing only a fraction of the path. Others are able to analyze a great many points but are unable, even though they are learned, to discern the important ones. They know, in general, how to practice but do not make any effort at practice. Those in these three situations cannot practice tantra properly.

Tsongkhapa saw that if the meanings of the countless scriptures were collected, settled with stainless reasoning, and set forth in the sequence of their practice, many sentient beings who had come under the influence of these bad circumstances would be helped. Captivated by the good explanations of the Indian and Tibetan tantrics such as Nāgārjuna, his spiritual sons, and the omniscient Butön, Tsongkhapa was enthused to gather together these explanations in order to rectify the faults and omissions existing in the presentations by earlier lamas.

Writing a book on Secret Mantra is not like writing a book on the Middle Way School or on the teachings of the paths contained in the *Perfection of Wisdom Sūtras* (*prajñāpāramitā*). The topics of Secret Mantra are not to be displayed like merchandise but practiced secretly. If they are not, instead of helping, there is a danger of harming many people due to generating misunderstanding. For instance, some who are unable to practice the four tantras in general and Highest Yoga Tantra in particular merely wish to play with

Mantra. Some, although they have faith, do not accurately know the Buddhist presentations of view, meditation, and behavior. Others know these topics accurately but do not have an ability to maintain vows, sustain faith, and be strong of mind. Without this knowledge and this ability, practice of the Mantra path is impossible.

In India fully qualified gurus taught the doctrines of Secret Mantra to only a few students, whose karma and aspirations were suitable and whom they knew well. The gurus passed the doctrines directly to their students, and when the students were able to practice with great effort the teachings that they received, the corresponding spiritual experiences and realizations were generated. In just that measure the Victor's teaching was furthered and the welfare of sentient beings was achieved. However, in the snowy country of Tibet these factors were largely absent. Secret Mantra was disseminated too widely, and people sought it because of its fame, without considering whether they had the capacity to practice it or not.

One is wise if, though wanting the best, one examines whether the best is fitting. The Tibetans wanted the best and assumed that they could practice the best. As a result of this, Secret Mantra became famous in Tibet, but the mode of practice was not like the proper hidden practice of the Indians, and thus we were unable to achieve the feats of Secret Mantra as explained in the tantras; the imprint of Secret Mantra practice did not appear. As it is said in the Tibetan oral tradition, "An Indian practices one deity and achieves a hundred; a Tibetan practices a hundred deities and does not achieve even one."

It is not good to begin many different works, saying "This looks good; that looks good," touching this, touching that, and not succeeding in any of them. If you do not generate great desires but aim at what is fitting, you can actualize the corresponding potencies and become an expert in this. With success, the power or imprint of that practice is generated.

Especially nowadays, Secret Mantra has become a topic of interest, but merely as an object of inquiry. From the viewpoint of a practitioner, it seems to have become an object of entertainment and to have arrived at a point where one cannot know whether it will help or harm. Many of the secrets have been disseminated; many lecturers are explaining tantra, and books are being translated. Even though Secret Mantra is to be achieved in hiding, many books have appeared that are a mixture of truth and falsity.

I think it would be good if the means and circumstances appeared which could clear away these wrong ideas. In general, translating a book of Mantra for sale in the shops is unsuitable, but at this time and in this situation there is greater fault in not clearing away wrong ideas than there is in distributing translations. Much falsely ascribed information about Secret Mantra has wide repute nowadays, and, therefore, I think that translating and distributing an authoritative book may help to clear away these false superimpositions. This is the reason for my explanation of Tsongkhapa's work.

If Secret Mantra is practiced openly and used for commercial purposes, then accidents will befall such a practitioner, even taking his or her life, and conditions unfavorable for generating spiritual experience and realizations in his or her continuum will be generated. With other books it is not too serious to make an error, but with books of Mantra it is very serious to err either in explanation or in translation. Furthermore, if the fault of proclaiming the secret to those who are not ripened is incurred, there is danger that instead of helping, it will harm. There are many stories of people who have begun treatises on Mantra but have been unable to complete their lifespan and of others whose progress was delayed through writing a book on Mantra.

A person who has practiced the stages of sūtra and wishes to attain quickly the state of a blessed Buddha should enter into the Secret Mantra Vehicle that can easily bestow realization of Buddhahood. However, you cannot seek Buddhahood for yourself, engaging in Mantra in order to become unusual. With a spiritual guide as a protector, you need to train in the common paths, engaging in the practices of beings of small and middling capacity—realizing suffering and developing a wish to leave cyclic existence. Then you must train in the compassion that is the inability to bear the sight of suffering in others without acting to relieve it. Beings want happiness but are bereft of happiness; they do not want suffering but are tortured by suffering. You must develop great compassion and empathy from the very orb of your heart for all sentient beings traveling in cyclic existence in the three realms—desire, form, and formless. You need to have a very strong mind wishing to free all sentient beings from suffering and its causes.

Through the force of having accumulated predispositions over many lifetimes, some persons have a good mind even when young; they have unbearable compassion for insects who are in danger of dying and for humans stricken with suffering; they have a keen sense of altruism. Such persons should enter the Mantra Vehicle in order to attain Buddhahood quickly.

Not all persons can practice tantra, but those who have performed good actions over many lifetimes, who even as children possessed a strong thought to help, and who have good predispositions should seek the aid of a spiritual guide. Through his or her quintessential instructions, these students should, with effort and over a period of months and years, raise this good mind to higher and higher levels. Finally, whether going, wandering, lying down, or staying still, they have a strong force of mind seeking to do whatever can be done to help others. They wish very strongly to bring vast help to others in a spontaneous manner, effortlessly, as a Buddha. Such persons are suitable to enter and *should* enter Secret Mantra in order to attain Buddhahood quickly.

If you are seeking a mere temporary sufficiency of food and clothing for yourself and others, seeking only the temporary purposes of this lifetime, avoiding temporary disease, attaining affluence of resources or a temporary good name or a great deal of money, certainly there are means for the temporary achievement of great wealth, for temporarily relieving sickness and disease, and for achieving temporary fame. You can be greedy and deceptive, sometimes being honest and at other times lying, sometimes fighting and at other times not. These are temporary means, and nowadays many people are proceeding in this way. If this is your intention, you have no need for Tsongkhapa's *Great Exposition of Secret Mantra*.

If, on the other hand, you do not take this system of the elders of the world to be sufficient, if you view such activities as senseless, pithless, if you know that these do not help future lives or higher aims, if you know that even in terms of this life no matter how wealthy you become, it is difficult to have peace of mind, and if you are seeking peace of mind for yourself and others, it is very important to improve your mind.

Many have given advice for this purpose, but we say that only the teacher Buddha taught forcefully that we should cherish others more than ourselves and that we should develop an intention definitely to establish sentient beings in a state free from suffering and the causes of suffering. All of the world's religious systems teach a means of bringing a little peace to the mind and cleansing coarser aspects of the mental continuum. They either directly or indirectly create improvement in terms of a good mind and of altruism, but among them it seems that only Buddhism presents, by way of a vast number of reasonings, scriptures, and views, the means of transforming the mind into ultimate goodness. I am not saying that Buddhism is best because I am a Buddhist. I think that if it is considered honestly one would think so, but even if it is the best, this does not mean that everyone should be a Buddhist. All do not have the same disposition and interest. All should have the best, but since not all are capable of practicing the best, it is necessary for each person to observe a path that accords with one's own disposition, interest, and ability.

If it were true that everyone should be a Buddhist, that everyone should be a Tantrist, and that everyone should follow Highest Yoga Tantra because it is the best, then Vajradhara would have taught only Highest Yoga Tantra. He would indeed have done so if everyone were capable of practicing it. But for those for whom Highest Yoga Tantra was not suitable he taught Yoga Tantra. For those for whom Yoga Tantra was not suitable he taught Performance Tantra. For those for whom Performance Tantra was not suitable he taught Action Tantra. Those for whom Action Tantra was not suitable he taught by way of sūtra in which not even the name of "Secret Mantra" occurs.

Within sūtra he taught the *Perfection of Wisdom Sūtras* setting forth the Middle Way (*madhyamaka*) view, and for those for whom this was not suitable, he taught sūtras presenting the view of Mind-Only (*cittamātra*). He set forth the Vehicle of Solitary Realizers which could help even more persons, and again, to help even more, he set forth the Hearer Vehicle, and within that there are vows for monks, nuns, novices, and two types of vows for laypersons. Within the lowest type of layperson's vow there is assumption of all five precepts or four or three or two or just one, or even just maintaining refuge; there are many who can do this.

Buddha set forth, in accordance with the dispositions and interests of those who could not practice the most profound aspects of his path, limitless forms of stages beginning from a layperson's vow of refuge and going through to training in the Vajra Vehicle of Highest Yoga Tantra. From the viewpoint of number of reasons, vastness, and depth, Buddhism has the most paths and techniques for the transformation of the mind into ultimate goodness.

In order to enter the profound vehicle of Secret Mantra one must know the essentials of the Vajra Vehicle, and for this reason Tsongkhapa explains the stages of its path. Among the eighteen volumes of his collected works, the *Great Exposition of the Stages of the Path Common to the Vehicles* and the *Great Exposition of Secret Mantra* are the most important. Many of his books are about selected topics in tantra—the stage of generation, the stage of completion, granting initiation, achieving special activities, and so forth—but that which presents in an ordered fashion the important essentials of all four tantras is his *Great Exposition of Secret Mantra* [the first section of which comprises Part Two of this volume].

When an oral transmission explaining the *Great Exposition of Secret Mantra* is given, listeners should have the initiations to the four tantras—for instance, of Mahākaruṇika for Action Tantra, of Vairochana for Performance Tantra, of Sarvavid for Yoga Tantra, and of Saṃvara, Guhyasamāja, or Bhairava in a maṇḍala of colored powders for Highest Yoga Tantra. At the least, one should have an initiation of Highest Yoga Tantra in a maṇḍala of colored powders or painted cloth. Also, when an oral transmission is bestowed, the lamas who form the continuum of the lineage should be identified. The full title of the *Great Exposition of Secret Mantra* is *The Stages of the Path to a Victor and Pervasive Master, a Great Vajradhara: Revealing All Secret Essentials*. It indicates the contents of the book. "Victor" generally means one who has conquered over coarse and subtle demons, and on this occasion of Mantra "Victor" refers to conquest over mistaken dualistic appearance. Extremely subtle obstructions to omniscience [which is the simultaneous and direct knowledge of all phenomena and their mode of being] are mentioned only in the teaching of Highest Yoga Tantra, the fourth and highest Mantra path. These are the stains of mistaken dualistic appearance that are called appearance, increase, and near attainment. Those who have conquered such sources of error by means of their antidotes are Victors. These beings have completely overcome the coarse and subtle obstructions both to liberation and to omniscience in their own continuum and are also capable of causing the conquest of these obstructions in other sentient beings, thereby overcoming the causes of suffering by which those beings are stricken.

A Victor is "pervasive" in that the emanator of all Buddha lineages, the Original Protector, Vajradhara, pervades all the lineages, such as those of Vairochana, Akṣhobhya, Ratnasambhava, Amitābha, and Amoghasiddhi. The excellent hundred, five, and three lineages are all included into one basis of emanation, the Body of Enjoyment, the great secret Vajradhara, who is therefore called the "Master." Because of pervading and being the master of all lineages, Vajradhara is the "Pervasive Master."

A "vajra" is the best of stones, a diamond; there are external symbolic vajras, as in the case of the vajra and bell used in ritual, and there are vajras that are the meanings symbolized. With respect to the latter, a vajra common to all four sets of tantras is an undifferentiability in one entity of method and wisdom. Method is observation of the vast—the body of a deity—conjoined with an altruistic aspiration to highest enlightenment. Wisdom is the knowledge of the suchness of phenomena just as it is. Also, according only to Highest Yoga Tantra, a vajra is the undifferentiability in one entity of method—great bliss—and wisdom—realization of emptiness. Because of bearing (*dhara*) such a vajra in his continuum, he is called "Vajradhara." He is "great" because there is none higher. Tsongkhapa's text is a presentation of the paths leading to the state of a great Vajradhara, not of assorted essentials of the path in unrelated groups but an arrangement in the order of practice. Since these essentials must be practiced in secret, hidden from persons who are not suited for them at this point, these are called the secret essentials of the Secret Mantra Vehicle.

Tsongkhapa gave this title to his book because it accurately presents in summary, through citing reasoning and scripture, the stages of the path by which one progresses to the ground of a great Vajradhara, pervasive master over all lineages.

The Homage

At the beginning Tsongkhapa pays homage in general to his vajra lamas—the chief of whom was Khaydrub Khyungpo Lhaypa (*mkhas grub khyung po lhas pa*)—and in particular to the revered Mañjushrī in dependence on whose kindness he realized the essentials of sūtra and tantra. The Sanskrit word for homage etymologically means "seeking the indestructible" and involves physical, verbal, and mental activities; it means, "I am placing my hope in you." He pays homage over his continuum of lives to the compassionate lamas who know the essentials of the path and then to his special guru, Mañjushrī.

Because Mañjushrī is the natural form of the wisdom of all Victors, one relies on him as one's special deity in order to increase the wisdom discriminating the truth. Discriminating wisdom thereby increases as it otherwise would not. Tsongkhapa and Mañjushrī met directly, like two people. Originally, Tsongkhapa meditated at Gawadong (*dga' ba gdong*) in central Tibet in order to achieve a meeting with Mañjushrī. At Gawadong there was a Khampa (*khams pa*) lama named Umapa Pawo Dorjay (*dbu ma pa dpa' bo rdo rje*) who had been under Mañjushrī's care for many lifetimes and who had repeated Mañjushrī's mantra, *oṃ a ra pa tsa na dhīḥ,* even in his mother's womb. He had been born into a poor shepherd family, and one day when he was out herding sheep he encountered a black Mañjushrī, after which his intelligence increased. When Tsongkhapa met Lama Umapa at Gawadong, he was able to ask Mañjushrī questions about the profound emptiness and the vast deeds of compassion of sūtra and tantra through Lama Umapa.

There was a painting of Mañjushrī on the wall of Tsongkhapa's Gawadong retreat, and upon improvement of his meditation a great light emitted from Mañjushrī's heart. That was the first time Tsongkhapa saw Mañjushrī, and thereafter at his wish he met with Mañjushrī, who taught him the difficult points of the stages of the path. Therefore, Tsongkhapa pays homage to the lowest part of Mañjushrī's body, his feet.

In ordinary refuge, once our temporary purpose has been satisfied, we no longer need that source of refuge. Here, Tsongkhapa takes refuge not for a trifling superficial purpose, but for the ultimate purpose of attaining the fruit of complete liberation from suffering and the causes of suffering, and, since this is not usually done in a few years or even in one lifetime, he pays respectful homage in all his lifetimes. This indicates that the path must be practiced within the context of refuge from lifetime to lifetime until becoming a Buddha.

The Expression of Worship

Books are generally divided into three parts, expression of worship, body of the text, and conclusion. Having paid homage to his lamas in general and Mañjushrī in particular, Tsongkhapa begins the expression of worship to spiritual guides. Usually expressions of worship are made to Buddhas and Bodhisattvas; however, Chandrakīrti took compassion as his object of worship in his *Supplement to the Middle* (*madhyamakāvatāra*), and Maitreya took the Mother, the perfection of wisdom, as the object of worship in his *Ornament for the Clear Realizations* (*abhisamayālaṃkāra*). Here, Tsongkhapa takes the lamas as his object of worship. This is because it is necessary to depend on a lama (*guru*) in order to complete the progression through the grounds and paths, and in particular it is extremely important to rely on a qualified spiritual guide in order to train in the paths of Mantra. If one relies on a lama over a long period of time with a union of faith and respect, one can learn quickly and easily the paths that are free from error and from the taints of seeking only one's own welfare. The spiritual guides teach out of great compassion, not out of desire for fame or wealth; they teach without confusion exactly as those paths were taught by Buddha.

Tsongkhapa next praises and pays homage to Vajradhara, the Original Protector. Vajradhara, without stirring from the state of the expanse of suchness, which is the extinguishment of all conceptual and dualistic proliferations, appears through his physical sport like a rainbow, emanating collections of deities to countless lands, pure and impure, in many forms, whatever is suitable for taming trainees. A Buddha's Truth Body has two aspects, a Wisdom Truth Body and a Nature Truth Body. Vajradhara's mind, the original innate wisdom, is the Wisdom Truth Body, remaining continuously in meditative equipoise on the expanse of suchness as long as space exists. The final expanse of suchness, the state of extinguishment of all proliferations—both naturally pure and purified of adventitious stains—is the Nature Truth Body.

A Bodhisattva generates a wish to attain Buddhahood for the sake of others; therefore, the purpose of actualizing the Truth Body is the welfare of others. However, that which directly appears to trainees is not the Truth Body but Form Bodies; thus, it is necessary to help migrators by way of Form Bodies, which a Buddha emanates without stirring from the nonconceptual, nondualistic Truth Body and without exertion, effort, or thought. Form Bodies appear spontaneously in accordance with the need of trainees.

The subtler of Form Bodies is the Body of Complete Enjoyment, and the coarser are Emanation Bodies, among which there are physically obstructive and nonobstructive types. Thus, this expression of worship indicates the Three Bodies: Truth Body, Complete Enjoyment Body, and Emanation Body, or Four Bodies: Nature Body, Wisdom Body, Complete Enjoyment Body, and Emanation Body. According to Highest Yoga Tantra, the Nature Body can also be considered compounded and not necessarily uncompounded, as it is considered in the sūtra systems, because the clear light wisdom of great bliss that is a Wisdom Truth Body is also said to be a Nature Body. The Complete Enjoyment Body is the sport of mere wind and mind. Emanation Bodies appear in countless pure and impure lands, sometimes with a coarse form. Tsongkhapa praises and makes an expression of worship to such a Vajradhara, the lord or principal of the maṇḍalas.

He next makes obeisance to Vajrapāṇi, master of the secret, leader of the bearers of knowledge mantras, and caretaker of the tantras. Vajrapāṇi collected all the secret essentials, the many and various teachings that Vajradhara set forth from the viewpoint of his exact knowledge of the trainees' disposition, interest, and potential. Tsongkhapa pays homage to Vajrapāṇi, arousing his compassion and suggesting that inner and outer demons beware.

Then Tsongkhapa takes Mañjushrī, who is the mother, father, and child of all Victors, as a special object of worship. He is the mother of all Victors in that he is the essence of all wisdoms; the father of all Victors in that he takes the form of spiritual guides and causes beings to generate an altruistic aspiration to highest enlightenment; and the child of all Victors in that he assumes the form of Bodhisattvas as he did within Shākyamuni Buddha's retinue.

When a trainee pleases him, Mañjushrī can, with merely a glance, bestow the wisdom discriminating the truth in the sense of quickly increasing realization, like lighting a flame. Tsongkhapa says that having heard such a marvelous account, he has relied on Mañjushrī as his special deity over a long time and will not forsake him in the future, there not being another refuge for him. Tsongkhapa pays homage to Mañjushrī as a treasure of wisdom, arousing his compassion through praise and asking him to bestow the fruition of his wishes.

Promise of Composition

At the request especially of Kyabchog Palsang (*skyab mchog dpal bzang*) and Sönam Sangpo (*bsod nams bzang po*), Tsongkhapa promises to compose the text for the reasons described above. To do this, he arouses the compassion of the Field-Born, Innate, and Mantra-Born Sky-Goers for the sake of bestowing feats on him, like a mother to her child. Field-Born Sky-Goers are born with bodies of flesh and blood; Innate Sky-Goers have attained realization of the stage of completion in Highest Yoga Tantra; Mantra-Born Sky-Goers have not yet generated the stage of generation. According to another explanation, Field-Born Sky-Goers have attained the subjective clear light [the third of five levels in the stage of completion]; the Innate have lesser realization but are still within the stage of completion; and Mantra-Born Sky-Goers are said to abide in the stage of generation. Tsongkhapa requests these feminine caretakers of tantra to be affectionate to him and overcome all obstacles to clear presentation of tantric doctrine and, seeing the purpose of his deeds, to grant the feats and activities benefiting all beings.

Refuge

We live in an ocean of cyclic existence whose depth and extent cannot be measured. We are troubled again and again by the afflictions of desire and hatred as if repeatedly attacked by sharks.

Our mental and physical aggregates are impelled by former contaminated actions and afflictions and serve as a basis for present suffering as well as inducing future suffering. While such cyclic existence lasts, we have various thoughts of pleasure and displeasure: "If I do this, what will people think? If I do not do this, I will be too late; I won't make any profit." When we see something pleasant we think, "Oh, if I could only have that!" We see that others are prosperous, and we generate jealousy, unable to bear their prosperity. We see an attractive man or woman, and we want a relationship. We are not satisfied with a passing relationship but want it to last forever. And then, once staying together with that person, we desire someone else. When we see someone we do not like, we become angry and quarrel after a single word; we feel we cannot remain even for an hour near this hated person but must leave immediately. Day and night, night and day we spend our lives in the company of the afflictions, generating desire for the pleasant and anger at the unpleasant, and continue thus even when dreaming, unable to remain relaxed, our minds completely and utterly mixed with thoughts of desire and hatred without interruption.

To what refuge should we go? A source of refuge must have completely overcome all defects forever; it must be free of all faults. It must also have all the attributes of altruism—those attainments which are necessary for achieving others' welfare. For it is doubtful that anyone lacking these two prerequisites can bestow refuge;

it would be like falling into a ditch and asking another who is in it to help you out. You need to ask someone who is standing outside the ditch for help; it is senseless to ask another who is in the same predicament. A refuge capable of protecting from the frights of manifold sufferings cannot also be bound in this suffering but must be free and unflawed. Furthermore, the complete attainments are necessary, for if you have fallen into a ditch, it is useless to seek help from someone standing outside it who does not wish to help or who wishes to help but has no means to do so.

Only a Buddha has extinguished all defects and gained all attainments. Therefore, one should mentally go for refuge to a Buddha, praise him or her with speech, and respect him or her physically. One should enter the teaching of such a being.

A Buddha's abandonment of defects is of three types: good, complete, and irreversible. Good abandonment involves overcoming obstructions through their antidotes, not just through withdrawing from those activities. Complete abandonment is not trifling, forsaking only some afflictions or just the manifest afflictions, but forsaking all obstructions. Irreversible abandonment overcomes the seeds of afflictions and other obstructions in such a way that defects will never arise again, even when conditions conducive to them are present.

Tsongkhapa's intention in praising Buddhism is not to insult other teachers such as Kapila. Statements of the greatness of Buddhism are made in order to develop one-pointedness of mind toward practice, because those who are able to practice Buddhism must generate effort to do so. It is necessary for them to have confidence in Buddha's teaching from the round orb of their heart. There is a Tibetan saying that one cannot sew with a two-pointed needle or achieve aims with a two-pointed mind. Similarly, if practitioners are hesitant, they will not put great force into the practice of any one system. Tsongkhapa states that Buddhism is the best in order that persons who would be helped more through engaging in the Buddhist path than through another system might not be diverted to another path.

Mere belief in a source of refuge is not firm; unless there is valid cognition, you are going only on the assertion that Buddhism is good. Refuge is not an act of partisanship but is based on analyzing what scriptures are reasonable and what scriptures are not. In order for the mind to engage one-pointedly in practice, there must be reasoned conviction that only the Buddhist path is nonmistaken and capable of leading to the state of complete freedom from defects and possession of all auspicious attainments. One should engage in honest investigation, avoiding desire and hatred and seeking the teaching that sets forth the means for fulfilling the aims of trainees.

The fruit of practice is the achievement of two types of aims: the temporary fruit of high status and the final fruit of definite goodness. High status refers to a life as a human or a god rather than as an animal, a hungry ghost, or a hell-being. Definite goodness is complete liberation from cyclic existence and the attainment of a Buddha's omniscience. Buddhism has teachings based on each as well as the means of achieving them. High status is achieved first, and definite goodness is achieved later because the attainment of liberation from cyclic existence and the attainment of the omniscience of Buddhahood depends on having a favorable life-support within cyclic existence; however, the validity of scriptures with respect to achieving definite goodness should be proven first. When the validity of scriptures presenting liberation and the means to achieve it has been proved with reasoning and when the conviction of valid cognition has arisen, it is possible to gain conviction with respect to the incontrovertibility of scriptures that teach high status and its means.

Buddha's teachings on nonmanifest phenomena, such as the extremely subtle presentations of actions and their effects—which are very hidden phenomena—cannot be proved with reasoning. How then can they be verified?

There is no need to verify manifest phenomena through reasoning because they appear directly to the senses. The slightly hidden, however, can be proved with reasoning that generates inferential understanding, and since emptiness is very profound but only slightly hidden, it is accessible to reasoning. Therefore, when conviction is generated in the incontrovertibility of Buddha's teaching on the very profound emptiness, conviction is gained in the validity of his teachings on very hidden phenomena that are not accessible to reasoning but are not so important.

For instance, with respect to accounts of the effects of actions that Buddha gives in sūtras such as the *Wise Man and the Fool* (*damamūkonāmasūtra*), we may wonder how it could possibly be so. Since these are very hidden phenomena, they cannot be proved with reasoning, and it seems that Buddha might say whatever he likes. However, through our own experience we can confirm Buddha's teachings on more important topics such as emptiness, the altruistic mind of enlightenment, love, and compassion, for no matter who analyzes—Buddhist or non-Buddhist—or how much one analyzes, if the person is not biased through desire or hatred, these teachings can bear analysis and serve as powerful sources of thought. When you see that Buddha does not err with regard to these more important phenomena, you can for the first time accept his other presentations.

Some wrongly think that the afflicted phenomena of cyclic existence and the purified phenomena of nirvāṇa cannot be proved by reasoning and that since liberation and omniscience cannot be directly seen, and are not manifest, they can be proved only through citation of scripture. They believe only in scripture and are displaying their own lack of foundation. Such a statement of refuge is only a proclamation of the weakness of that refuge. However, the process of cyclic existence and the eradication of it can be proved by the reasoning that establishes the misconception of inherent existence as its root cause and establishes the wisdom realizing emptiness as its antidote.

Even scriptures that present very hidden phenomena, inaccessible to both direct perception and inference, are proved to be valid through three modes of analysis. The three modes are establishment (1) that the passage is not damaged by direct valid cognition in its teaching of manifest phenomena, (2) that the passage is not damaged by evidential inference in its teaching of slightly hidden phenomena, and (3) that the passage is not damaged by scriptural inference in its teaching of very hidden phenomena in the sense of containing internal contradictions and so forth. Thus, even this process derives from reasoning.

Buddhist scriptures do not have inner contradictions whereas non-Buddhist scriptures do. This is not to say that non-Buddhist scriptures will not be valid with respect to certain meanings, but they do have contradictions with respect to the phenomena included within the afflicted realm and with respect to phenomena included within the realm of purification. The Forders' scriptures have non-mistaken explanations of how to generate the four concentrations and the four formless absorptions as well as small achievements of altruism; however, with respect to the chief aims of persons, their scriptures contain inner contradictions. For example, they assert that the creator of the world is permanent and then assert that the cyclic existence created by this permanent creator can be overcome. If the cause were permanent, the effect would have to remain permanent. However, since the effect is impermanent, the cause must be impermanent. It is the nature of things that if the cause is not overcome, the effect cannot be overcome; thus, there could not be an end to cyclic existence. As Dharmakīrti says:

> Because the permanent cannot be overcome,
> It is impossible to overcome its force.

It is necessary first to prove that the root of cyclic existence is the conception of inherent existence. Then it can be shown that a system asserting a view of self and thereby rejecting the view of selflessness would be self-contradictory when it asserts the attainment of liberation from cyclic existence.

This implies that from the viewpoint of the highest Buddhist philosophical system, the Middle Way Consequence School, the views of the lower systems—Autonomy School, Mind-Only School, Sūtra School, and Great Exposition School—also seem to contain inner contradictions. According to the system of the Middle Way Consequence School, the root of cyclic existence is the conception of the inherent existence of phenomena and the consequent misconception of the inherent existence of the "I," called the view of the transitory collection as a real "I." The other Buddhist systems assert an inherent existence of phenomena whereas the Consequentialists assert that inherent existence is the referent object of a mistaken consciousness conceiving self. Thus, the lower schools' assertion of liberation from cyclic existence involves a seeming inner contradiction which is resolved only through considering this teaching a nonfinal doctrine given to those who could not comprehend the highest view.

The path of liberation removes the adventitious defilements from the expanse of suchness which itself is intrinsically pure, and liberation is the state in which these adventitious defilements have been removed. It seems that some teachers did not know this liberation or the path to it and set forth systems in ignorance. The *Kālachakra Tantra* (*kālacakra*), after setting forth the various systems of Buddhist and non-Buddhist tenets and presenting with reasoning their relative superiority and inferiority, says, "It is not suitable to despise another system." The reason given is that often non-Buddhist systems have been taught through the empowering blessings of Buddhas.

There are cases of teachers' explaining paths in ignorance, but other teachers were emanations of Buddhas, free from all defects and endowed with all attainments. They knew the difference between the mistaken and nonmistaken paths, but because at that point there was no purpose in teaching the nonmistaken path, they set forth a nonfinal path, pretending not to know another.

One who has the ability should proceed on the nonmistaken path; however, in relation to one for whom another path is suitable, that path is right. For instance, for a person who can practice the Mind-Only view but not the Middle Way view, the Mind-Only view is unmistaken. The same is also true with regard to non-Buddhist teachings. Therefore, other teachers, their doctrines, and practitioners can be refuges, but not final refuges.

When conviction in the sources of refuge is generated through unbiased investigation and proper reasoning, faith is firm and powerful. Such faith cannot be generated in reliance on scripture alone. The means for generating such conviction are set forth in Dharmakīrti's Seven Treatises—three main works and four works of elaboration. Of the three main works, the extensive one is his *Commentary on (Dignāga's) "Compilation of Valid Cognition"* (*pramāṇavarttika*); the one of medium length is his *Ascertainment of Valid Cognition* (*pramāṇaviniścaya*), and the condensed is his *Drop of Reasoning* (*nyāyabindu*). The four works of elaboration are his *Drop of Reasons* (*hetubindu*), *Analysis of Relations* (*sambandhaparīkṣā*), *Principles of Debate* (*vādanyāya*), and *Proof of Other Continuums* (*saṃtānāntarasiddhi*). Inner conviction arises from reasoned investigation.

Lesser Vehicle and Great Vehicle

A Hearer's mode of practice accords with that of the Lesser Vehicle discipline, one-pointedly viewing the desire realm attributes of pleasant forms, sounds, odors, tastes, and tangible objects as faulty. Āryadeva says that those who engage in this practice which is free from desire have "an interest in the lowly" because this path accords with the nature of a mind lacking the strength of the unusual attitude that bears the burden of all sentient beings' welfare. Since they are unable to practice using the great power of desire in the path, they are taught a mode free from desire.

As long as you cannot use desire in the path there is a danger of coming under its influence, in which case it is better to proceed only on a path that is free from desire. Otherwise, if you attempt to use desire in the path, you will be harmed instead of helped. Prohibition is the only course. This is the mode of Lesser Vehicle practice.

For those having an interest in the vast, the Sūtra Great Vehicle practices of the grounds and the perfections are taught; these comprise the causal Perfection Vehicle. Those who, in addition to having an interest in the vast, have a special interest in the ultimate profundity, are taught practices wherein desire is used in the path. This is Tantra Great Vehicle.

The Indian scholar Tripiṭakamāla also includes all Buddha's teaching into these three modes, the Lesser Vehicle mode of the four noble truths, the Sūtra Great Vehicle mode of the perfections—giving, ethics, patience, effort, concentration, and wisdom—and the Tantra Great Vehicle mode of Secret Mantra. Thus, Buddha's word is divided into the two scriptural divisions of Lesser Vehicle and Great Vehicle; the vehicles or paths that are the subjects of expression by Buddha's words are also divided into the two, Lesser Vehicle and Great Vehicle.

The Lesser Vehicle is further divided into two vehicles, Hearer Vehicle (*śrāvakayāna*) and Solitary Realizer Vehicle (*pratyekabuddhayāna*). Solitary Realizers are of two types, congregating and rhinoceros-like. Congregating Solitary Realizers are a little more social, staying in a group or community for a longer period than the rhinoceros-like, who find it unsuitable to stay in society and therefore live alone. Hearers and Solitary Realizers equally abandon the conception of inherent existence, but Solitary Realizers amass more merit than Hearers and thus, when they actualize the fruit of their vehicle, are capable of becoming Foe Destroyers—destroyers of the foe, the afflictions, the principal of which is the conception of inherent existence—without depending on a teacher in that lifetime. They actualize the fruit of their vehicle "independently" through the force of accumulating merit for a hundred eons. Solitary Realizers are said to be very proud and independent-minded. They mostly attain their enlightenment in a dark age when no Buddhas appear—perhaps so that they will not be outshone by a Buddha's presence but more likely in order to be of greater benefit to others. As Nāgārjuna says in his *Treatise on the Middle* (*madhyamakaśāstra,* XVIII.12):

> Though the perfect Buddhas do not appear
> And Hearers have disappeared,
> A Solitary Realizer's wisdom
> Arises without support.

Both Hearers and Solitary Realizers seek the wisdom realizing the absence of inherent existence of all phenomena—persons and other phenomena. This is because the chief bond binding one in cyclic existence is the conception of inherent existence, the other bonds being the afflictions such as desire, hatred, and ignorance that depend on the conception of inherent existence. According to Mantra, the causes binding one in cyclic existence are two, ignorance and winds [currents of energy], and among them the chief is the ignorance conceiving inherent existence. The winds that serve as the mount of afflicted conceptual thought are cooperative causes in the process of cyclic existence.

Hearers and Solitary Realizers understand that without the wisdom realizing selflessness it is impossible to overcome cyclic existence. They understand that they need this wisdom and seek it in company with ethics, meditative stabilization, and so forth. Through this path all afflictions are extinguished.

There are four schools of Buddhist tenets:

1. Great Exposition School (*bye brag smra ba, vaibhāṣika*)
2. Sūtra School (*mdo sde pa, sautrāntika*)
3. Mind-Only School (*sems tsam pa, cittamātra*)
4. Middle Way School (*dbu ma pa, mādhyamika*)

The highest of these is the Middle Way School which is further divided into a Middle Way Autonomy School (*dbu ma rang rgyud pa, svātantrika-mādhyamika*) and Middle Way Consequence School (*dbu ma thal 'gyur pa, prāsaṅgika-mādhyamika*). The Middle Way Consequence School is considered to be the highest philosophical view, its teachers having been Nāgārjuna, Āryadeva, Buddhapālita, Chandrakīrti, Shāntideva, Atisha, and so forth. According to the Consequentialist system, those of the Lesser Vehicle—who are unable to bear the burden of all sentient beings' welfare but seek only their own liberation from cyclic existence—and those of the Great Vehicle—who are able to bear the burden of the welfare of all sentient beings throughout space—equally realize the subtle emptiness of both persons and other phenomena. They realize that both persons and other phenomena, such as mind and body, do not inherently exist, or exist in their own right.

However, the non-Consequence schools all say that those of the Lesser Vehicle—Hearers and Solitary Realizers—realize only a selflessness of persons which is a person's absence of substantial existence in the sense that a person does not have a character different from the character of mind and body. From the viewpoint of the Consequence School, however, this wisdom is not sufficient as a means of liberation from cyclic existence, and furthermore, the other schools have described not the innate form of the misconception of persons as substantially existent entities, but the artificial misconception. According to the Consequentialists, the innate form of this coarse misconception of self is the apprehension of a person as a controller of mind and body, like a master over servants, but it does not involve an apprehension of the person as having a character different from mind and body. Apprehension of the person as having a character different from mind and body occurs only through the intellectual acquisition of tenets of non-Buddhist systems and thus is called "artificial," not "innate." From the viewpoint of the system of the Middle Way Consequence School, the selflessness of persons that is set forth by the lower schools is thus only a *coarse* selflessness and is merely the negative of self as misconceived by an *artificial* misconception of the nature of a person.

The non-Consequentialist systems—Autonomy School, Mind-Only School, Sūtra School, and Great Exposition School—assert that Hearers and Solitary Realizers do not realize a selflessness of phenomena other than persons; they realize only the selflessness of persons—that the person is empty of substantial existence, or self-sufficiency. They assert that merely through this Hearers and Solitary Realizers attain liberation. Tsongkhapa's position is clear that according to the systems of the non-Consequence Schools, Hearers and Solitary Realizers attain liberation in this way. When he describes the type of selflessness that they realize, he says that they do not realize that persons are empty of establishment by way of their own character but realize that persons are empty of a substantial existence *as is imputed by the non-Buddhists*. He seems to be saying that according to the systems of tenets of the Great Exposition School and Sūtra School themselves, one need only realize that persons are empty of being a permanent, unitary, independent entity. However, we have to say that the Autonomists, Proponents of Mind-Only, Proponents of Sūtra, and Proponents of the Great Exposition do not assert that realization of a person's emptiness of being permanent, unitary, and independent opposes the *innate* misconception of self. In their own systems the conception of the person as permanent, unitary, and independent is only artificial, intellectually acquired, not innate.

The innate misconception of self—not involving reasoned affirmation—binds beings in cyclic existence, and according to these systems it is the conception that a person is a substantially existent or self-sufficient entity. The non-Consequentialist systems themselves say that no matter how much one meditates on a person's not being permanent, unitary, and independent, this cannot harm the conception of substantial existence or self-sufficiency. Therefore, according to them, Hearers and Solitary Realizers realize a selflessness which is the person's absence of a substantial or self-sufficient nature. They must train in such a path and proceed by this means.

Tsongkhapa here and in other places seems to say that in the lower systems themselves the subtle selflessness of the person is described as a person's not being permanent, unitary, and independent. Many scholars say that Tsongkhapa's reference is to the implications of the lower systems as seen from the viewpoint of the Consequence School. This means that when Consequentialists consider the reasons proving selflessness that are set forth in the lower systems, they find that persons' inherent establishment or establishment by way of their own character is taken for granted and that their reasoning for refuting self has the ability only to refute the existence of a person that has a character different from the character of mind and body.

According to the Consequentialist system, if one does not realize the absence of inherent existence of the person, one cannot eliminate the conception of a self of persons. Also, if the conception of inherent existence with regard to the mental and physical aggregates is not overcome, the conception of the inherent existence of the person cannot be overcome. Cyclic existence is achieved through the power of actions, and actions are achieved through the power of afflictions. Since this is so, ceasing actions meets back to ceasing afflictions. Ceasing afflictions, in turn, meets back to ceasing conceptions. Ceasing conceptions meets back to ceasing the proliferations of the conception of inherent existence which are ceased only by a mind realizing emptiness.

According to the final thought of the *Perfection of Wisdom Sūtras,* liberation from cyclic existence definitely involves realization of the selflessness of both persons and other phenomena. This is taught not only in the Great Vehicle but also in the Lesser Vehicle scriptures, though not in the Lesser Vehicle systems, the Great Exposition School and the Sūtra School. However, various ways of proceeding on the path are presented in the scriptures of both vehicles, and these must be distinguished to determine which scriptures require interpretation and which are definitive. For instance, it is taught that merely through realizing the coarse selflessness—the person's lack of substantial or self-sufficient existence—liberation can be attained whereas this realization, as well as that of impermanence, can only train the mental continuum, not liberate it.

In general, we are under the strong influence of the conception of inherent existence, and due to it we do not wish to be liberated from cyclic existence. However, when we see that all products are impermanent, this helps to advance us to the point where we can overcome the conception of inherent existence. Those who are vessels only for such paths, training the mental continuum but not liberating it, are trainees of dull faculties. Those who are also vessels for the path of liberation are suitable for the teaching of the selflessness of phenomena. Thus, among Lesser Vehicle trainees there are two types, dull and sharp, the latter being the main or special trainees of Lesser Vehicle, but not the majority.

The Mother, the perfection of wisdom, is the common cause of all four children, Hearer, Solitary Realizer, Bodhisattva, and Buddha Superiors; thus, Lesser Vehicle and Great Vehicle are not differentiated by way of view but by way of accompanying methods. In particular, these are the aspirational and practical minds of enlightenment and the deeds of the six perfections, found in the Great Vehicle but not in the Lesser Vehicle.

"Vehicle" (*yāna*) has two meanings: the means by which one progresses and the destination to which one is progressing. Great Vehicle in the sense of the vehicle by which one progresses means to be motivated by the mind of enlightenment—wishing to attain highest enlightenment for the sake of all sentient beings, one's objects of intent—and means to engage in the six perfections. These paths of training are the paths of the Great Vehicle in general, and even though the Middle Way School and the Mind-Only School have different views, these two are not different vehicles because the vehicles are differentiated by way of method, and the method—the altruistic mind of enlightenment and its attendant practices—is the same in the Mind-Only School and the Middle Way School. Still, those who are able to penetrate the subtle selflessness of phenomena, as presented in the Middle Way School, are the main trainees of the Great Vehicle. The Mantra division of the Great Vehicle, including all four tantra sets, has exactly the same motivation—altruistic mind-generation—and deeds—the six perfections.

Seeing reason and need, Buddha set forth many systems and vehicles, but these did not arise due to his being intimate with some and alien to others. The trainees who were listening to his teaching had various dispositions, interests, and abilities, and thus he taught methods that were suitable for each of them. For those who temporarily did not have the courage to strive for Buddhahood or who did not at all have the capacity of obtaining Buddhahood at that time, Buddha did not say, "You can attain Buddhahood." Rather, he set forth a path appropriate to the trainees' abilities. Buddha spoke in terms of their situation, and everything that he spoke was a means of eventually attaining highest enlightenment even though he did not always say that these were means for attaining Buddhahood.

Since the purpose of a Buddha's coming is others' realization of the wisdom of Buddhahood, the methods for actualizing this wisdom are one vehicle, not two. A Buddha does not lead beings by a vehicle that does not proceed to Buddhahood; he establishes beings in his own level. A variety of vehicles is set forth in accordance with temporary needs.

Question: Maitreya has taught that if those bearing the Great Vehicle lineage came temporarily to abide in a hell, this would not interrupt their progress to stainless enlightenment; however, if they were attracted to Lesser Vehicle practices, leading solely to peace, seeking to bring help and happiness only to themselves, this would greatly interrupt their progress to Buddhahood. Thus, according to Maitreya, generating a Lesser Vehicle attitude is a greater obstacle than taking birth in a hell; so, how can it be said that the Lesser Vehicle is a means leading to Buddhahood?

Answer: If those who have the ability to practice the Great Vehicle do not practice it, and instead assume Lesser Vehicle practices, this action will interrupt their progress to Buddhahood. It is not said that with respect to all people generation of a Lesser Vehicle attitude is an obstacle to Buddhahood. It is so only for those capable of practicing the Bodhisattva path. It depends on the individual.

Nevertheless, the Lesser Vehicle is not part of the Great Vehicle. Lesser Vehicle paths are subsidiaries of the path to Buddhahood but not actual Great Vehicle paths. The Great Vehicle has the complete paths for the attainment of Buddhahood; thus, there is a difference of incompleteness and completeness, and hence inferiority and superiority, between the Lesser Vehicle and the Great Vehicle. The Lesser Vehicle is a separate but not final vehicle because everyone has the Buddha nature that makes full enlightenment possible.

The teaching that the Buddha nature is present in all sentient beings, providing the "substantial cause" for the attainment of Buddhahood, inspires courage. This is the Buddha lineage of which there are two types, natural and transformational. The natural Buddha lineage is the emptiness of the mind, and, according to Mantra, the transformational Buddha lineage is the defiled mind of clear light which serves as the cause of Buddhahood.

In the Nyingma school of the earlier translations, it is said that Buddhahood exists primordially in oneself. This teaching refers to the very subtle mind of clear light that we presently have in our continuum; it is not different from the mind of a Buddha in terms of the entity of the basic innate mind. The continuum of our basic innate mind will become a Buddha's Wisdom Body; therefore, we presently have all the substances for achieving Buddhahood, and we should not seek for Buddhahood elsewhere. This is a very famous and meaningful instruction in the religious language of the Nyingma order.

If we think of the Buddha nature merely in terms of an emptiness of inherent existence, it is not so meaningful, for then it could be said that a pot's emptiness would be a Buddha nature because it is an emptiness of inherent existence. Here in this Nyingma teaching there is the strong suggestion that a positive phenomenon—the mind of clear light—is the Buddha nature.

Since the substances that make enlightenment possible are present in all sentient beings' continuums and since a Buddha knows the means of leading all these trainees through the stages of the path, if he hid that means from them, he would have the fault of miserliness. His mind would be biased. His compassion would not be unimpeded. On the contrary, the various vehicles that Buddha taught out of his unlimited compassion are all methods for achieving omniscience.

Shāntideva's *Engaging in the Bodhisattva Deeds* (*bodhisattvacaryāvatāra*) says that the truthful Buddha taught that even bees and donkeys can attain Buddhahood if they generate effort. Therefore, since we now have attained a human body and have met with the doctrine, if we generate the power of courageous effort, why could we not attain Buddhahood?

Vajrayāna

The Secret Mantra Vehicle is hidden because it is not appropriate for the minds of many persons. Practices for achieving activities of pacification, increase, control, and fierceness, which are not even presented in the Perfection Vehicle, are taught in the Mantra Vehicle but in hiding because those with impure motivation would harm both themselves and others by engaging in them. If one's mental continuum has not been ripened by the practices common to both Sūtra and Tantra Great Vehicle—realization of suffering, impermanence, refuge, love, compassion, altruistic mind-generation, and emptiness of inherent existence—practice of the Mantra Vehicle can be ruinous through assuming an advanced practice inappropriate to one's capacity. Therefore, its open dissemination is prohibited; practitioners must maintain secrecy from those who are not vessels of this path.

The word "mantra" means "mind-protection." It protects the mind from ordinary appearances and conceptions. "Mind" here refers to all six consciousnesses—eye, ear, nose, tongue, body, and mental consciousnesses—which are to be freed, or protected, from the ordinary world. There are two factors in mantra training, pride in oneself as a deity and vivid appearance of that deity. Divine pride protects one from the pride of being ordinary, and divine vivid appearance protects one from ordinary appearances. Whatever appears to the senses is viewed as the sport of a deity; for instance, whatever forms are seen are viewed as the emanations of a deity and whatever sounds are heard are viewed as the mantras of a deity. One is thereby protected from ordinary appearances, and through this transformation of attitude, the pride of being a deity emerges. Such protection of mind together with its attendant pledges and vows is called the practice of mantra.

In another way, the syllable *man* in "mantra" is said to be "knowledge of suchness," and *tra* is etymologized as *trāya*, meaning "compassion protecting migrators." This explanation is shared by all four tantra sets, but from the specific viewpoint of Highest Yoga Tantra, compassion protecting migrators can be considered the wisdom of great bliss. This explanation is devised in terms of a contextual etymology of the Sanskrit word for "compassion," *karuṇā*, as "stopping pleasure." When anyone generates compassion—the inability to bear sentient beings' suffering without acting to relieve it, pleasure, peacefulness, and relaxation are temporarily stopped. Thus, in Highest Yoga the word "compassion" (*karuṇā*) is designated to stopping the pleasure of the emission of the vital essence and refers to the wisdom of great bliss (*mahāsukha*). It is the mantra of definitive meaning and the deity of definitive meaning.

"Compassion protecting migrators" can be construed in a way common to all four tantras as an undifferentiable union of the wisdom realizing emptiness and great compassion, or a union of wisdom and method—wisdom conjoined with method and method conjoined with wisdom.

"Vehicle" can be considered in two aspects, an effect vehicle—the object to which one is progressing—and a cause vehicle—the means by which one progresses. Even though the Vajra Vehicle has both cause and effect vehicles, it is called the Effect Vehicle because a path of imagination is practiced wherein one believingly assumes the aspects of the four thorough purities—the *abode* where a One-Gone-Thus (*tathāgata*) resides after full enlightenment, the *body* that is a manifestation of the Wisdom Truth Body in the form of a residence and residents, the *resources* that are enjoyed in the high status of Buddhahood, and the supreme *activities* of a Buddha's ripening sentient beings. Similitudes of these four factors of the effect state are cultivated in meditation.

According to Highest Yoga Tantra the effect—the Mantra mode—is the wisdom of great bliss, and the cause—the Perfection mode—is the wisdom realizing emptiness as presented in the Middle Way scriptures. The indivisibility of these two is the meaning of "indivisibility of bliss and emptiness."

According to the *Kālachakra Tantra,* the cause is emptiness, but this emptiness is not a negation of inherent existence; it is a negation of physical particles. This is called "form of emptiness," form empty of physical particles, form beyond matter. This form of emptiness, adorned with the marks and beauties of a Buddha in father and mother aspect, is the cause, and the supreme immutable bliss, which is induced in dependence on various empty forms, is the effect. A union of these two is the Cause-Effect Vehicle. Such an indivisibility of the totally supreme form of emptiness and the supreme immutable bliss in the continuum of a learner is a vehicle in the sense of being the means by which one progresses. In the continuum of a nonlearner, a Buddha, it is a vehicle in the sense of being that to which one is progressing. Thus, there are two unions of the totally supreme form of emptiness and supreme immutable bliss.

This way of presenting the undifferentiability of method and wisdom is only from the viewpoint of Highest Yoga Tantra, and specifically that of the *Kālachakra Tantra*. Such an explanation does not apply to the three lower tantras—Action, Performance, and Yoga—because they do not have the means of generating the immutable great bliss. The *Kālachakra Tantra* has six branches: withdrawal, concentration, vitality and exertion, retention, mindfulness, and meditative stabilization. During the branch of mindfulness a form of emptiness is achieved, and in dependence on it, supreme immutable bliss is generated—this being the branch of meditative stabilization. The three lower tantras do not have all the factors included in the first five causal branches and thus, of course, do not have the sixth.

Indivisibility of method and wisdom indicates the necessity of proceeding with inseparable method and wisdom in order to attain the fruit of definite goodness, which is liberation from cyclic existence as well as omniscience. This mode of progress is common to all vehicles, Cause and Effect. In the Perfection Vehicle "inseparable method and wisdom" refers to method conjoined with wisdom and wisdom conjoined with method. When the altruistic mind of enlightenment is manifest, the mind actually realizing emptiness is not present, and when an actual realization of emptiness is manifest, an altruistic mind of enlightenment is not present. According to the Perfection Vehicle, it is unsuitable merely to stay in meditative equipoise on emptiness without also engaging at other times in the perfections of giving and so forth, and it is also unsuitable merely to engage in the practices of giving and so forth without engaging at other times in meditation on emptiness. Since this is the case, yogis of the Perfection Vehicle must cultivate a mind realizing emptiness and then, within nondiminishment of the force of reflection on all phenomena as a magician's illusions, train in giving, ethics, patience, and so forth. Also, within nondiminishment of the force of the altruistic aspiration, they must train in realizing emptiness. This is the inseparability of method and wisdom in the Perfection Vehicle.

In Mantra it is even deeper. Here, the inseparability of method and wisdom does not mean that wisdom and method are different entities conjoined in the sense of affecting each other; rather, method and wisdom are included in one entity. In Mantra these two are complete in the different aspects of one consciousness.

If, as in the *Kālachakra Tantra*, one posited method as the totally supreme immutable bliss, then this would not apply in general to all four tantras. Therefore, what is the meaning of inseparable method and wisdom, or "Vajra Vehicle," that applies to all four tantras? The six perfections are included in method and wisdom, and in Mantra, method and wisdom are considered as the one entity of the Vajrasattva meditative stabilization. This is a consciousness taking cognizance of appearance—the body of a deity—and realizing its emptiness of inherent existence. The yoga of nondual profundity and appearance is the Vajrasattva meditative stabilization. Being an indivisibility of method and wisdom, this is a vajra in the sense of being that to which one is progressing—in the continuum of a nonlearner—and in the sense of being the means by which one progresses—in the continuum of a learner.

Because the Mantra Vehicle has more varieties of methods or skillful means than the Perfection Vehicle, it is also called the Mantra Vehicle. Because the effect itself is taken as the path in the sense that one presently cultivates the four thorough purities—abode, body, resources, and activities of the effect state—it is called the Effect Vehicle. Because it must be practiced in extreme secrecy, it is called the Secret Vehicle. Because it contains the topics of training of Knowledge Bearers, it is also called the Scriptural Division of the Knowledge Bearers.

The tantras can be considered as a fourth scriptural division beyond the three scriptural divisions of sūtra—discipline, sets of discourses, and manifest knowledge—or as included in the three divisions. However, there is good reason to consider them as included in the sets of discourses. From among the three trainings, ethics, meditative stabilization, and wisdom, the tantras' feature of profundity is mainly concerned with the training in meditative stabilization. The discipline section of the scriptures mainly teaches the training in ethics; the sets of discourses mainly teach the training in meditative stabilization; and the manifest knowledge section mainly teaches the training in wisdom. Since the tantras contain extraordinary means for achieving meditative stabilization, the tantras that express these can be included in the sets of discourses.

In Tsongkhapa's miscellaneous works there is a question concerning this, to which he answers that the difference of profundity in the tantras occurs through meditative stabilization. There is also a difference with respect to the training in wisdom in terms of the type of consciousness realizing emptiness, but the main difference is found in the meditative stabilization that is a union of calm abiding and special insight. Let us discuss this.

As presented in the Perfection Vehicle, the achievement of Buddhahood involves at least three countless eons of practice; the first accumulation of merit over countless eons occurs on the paths of accumulation and preparation. The second occurs on the first seven

Bodhisattva grounds, which are called impure because the conception of inherent existence has not yet been fully abandoned. The third accumulation of merit over countless eons occurs on the eighth, ninth, and tenth grounds, which are called pure because the conception of inherent existence has been totally abandoned.

The three lower tantras present yoga with signs and yoga without signs which possess a special method for quickly generating a union of calm abiding and special insight that is a wisdom "arisen from meditation" realizing emptiness. Thereby, the first accumulation of merit over countless eons is accomplished in a shorter period of time. Then, from the first Bodhisattva ground on through to Buddhahood the three lower tantras present the path much as it is presented in the Perfection Vehicle.

A special trainee of Mantra initially generates an altruistic aspiration to highest enlightenment and then trains in the Mantra paths. For instance, according to Action Tantra, which is the lowest among the four tantra sets, a yogi engages in such practices as the four-branched repetition and subsequently practices the three concentrations—abiding in fire, abiding in sound, and bestowing liberation at the end of sound. During the concentrations of abiding in fire and abiding in sound, the capacity of meditative stabilization becomes powerful. Through this, a meditative stabilization that is a union of calm abiding and special insight is achieved in the course of the concentration that bestows liberation at the end of sound. This is a quicker path for the achievement of calm abiding and special insight than that found in the Perfection Vehicle.

Performance Tantra, the second of the four tantras, also has this distinguishing feature with regard to achieving meditative stabilization, while Yoga Tantra and Highest Yoga Tantra have even more profound techniques of meditative stabilization for achieving a union of calm abiding and special insight. Thus, even though there is a difference between the Perfection and Mantra Vehicles with regard to the training in ethics, the outstanding difference occurs with respect to the training in meditative stabilization.

Clear Light

"Tantra" means "continuum," like a stream, of which there are three types: base, path, and fruit. The base tantra is the person who is practicing. According to the *Secret Union Tantra* (*guhyasamāja*), a Highest Yoga Tantra, there are five lineages of persons—white lotus, utpala, lotus, sandalwood, and jewel, the last being the supreme person. The base continuum is also the naturally abiding lineage, the element, the Buddha nature, the One-Gone-Thus essence. It is called the base because it is the basis of the activity of the path.

The path tantras are the paths purifying that base. According to the lower tantras, these are the yogas with and without signs and, according to Highest Yoga Tantra, the stages of generation and completion that purify the defilements related with the suchness of the mind.

The fruit tantra is the state of the effect, the Truth Body, the state of complete extinguishment of all defilements as a Vajradhara. The three tantras—base, path, and fruit—contain the subjects and meanings of all tantra sets, and the continuums of words [texts] that express these subjects are called expressional word tantras that are divided into sets or groups.

The Perfection Vehicle is just the training in the altruistic mind of enlightenment and the six perfections; it does not clearly present any other mode of progress on the path. Mantra takes these as its basis but has other distinguishing paths. Since the Mantra Vehicle also has the practice of the altruistic mind of enlightenment and training in the six perfections, Tsongkhapa says that the Perfection Vehicle *only* has these paths.

There is no difference between the Perfection and Mantra Vehicles with regard to the two objects of altruistic mind-generation—

the field of intent which is the welfare of other sentient beings and the object of observation which is one's own attainment of Buddhahood. Trainees of Sūtra and Mantra wish for highest enlightenment for the sake of others and take cognizance of the same fruit, Buddhahood that is an extinguishment of all faults and endowment with all auspicious qualities.

There is also no difference in view, for Mantra does not explain a view of the middle way which exceeds that presented in the Perfection Vehicle by Nāgārjuna. Even if there were a difference in view, this could not serve to differentiate the two vehicles since the Mind-Only School and the Middle Way School, which have different views, are compatible in one vehicle.

The difference in vehicles must be determined through either wisdom or method. Because the wisdom realizing emptiness is the Mother common to all four children—Hearer, Solitary Realizer, Bodhisattva, and Buddha Superiors—Lesser Vehicle and Great Vehicle are differentiated by way of method, not by way of wisdom. For the same reason, the Perfection and Mantra Vehicles are differentiated by way of method, not wisdom.

Tsongkhapa says that there is no difference in view between the Lesser Vehicle and the Great Vehicle and, within the Great Vehicle, between the Perfection Vehicle and the Mantra Vehicle. He is referring to the "view" in terms of the object, emptiness—the objective clear light—not in terms of the wisdom realizing emptiness—the subjective clear light. Sakya Paṇḍita of the Sakya Order also held that Secret Mantra does not have a view different from the Perfection Vehicle and that if it did, that view would involve dualistic proliferations. Since the Middle Way view has passed beyond the limits of proliferations, a view different from it would have to involve such.

In the Old Translation School of Nyingma there is said to be a difference in view between Sūtra and Mantra, but this difference is primarily concerned with the subject. Nyingma does not make a clear distinction between the subject—wisdom—and the object—emptiness—because on the higher stages of the path, subject and object are mixed undifferentiably in one entity and can only be differentiated verbally. At the time of meditative equipoise on emptiness, subject and object become one inseparable entity, and since our ordinary expressions and conceptions cannot convey this state, it is called "unthinkable" and "inexpressible." This is an undifferentiability of method and wisdom passed beyond all limits of the proliferations of thought, an undifferentiability of bliss and emptiness, an indivisibility of the two truths, union. These are the best words of description and must be understood; without these most profound expressions any verbalization is insufficient. Within the context of not distinguishing between the objective clear light and the subjective clear light, Nyingmapas emphasize this undifferentiability when they speak of the view. Thus, in terms of this view there is indeed a difference between the Perfection Vehicle and the Mantra Vehicle.

As the Gelugpa Jamyang Shaypa says, the objective clear light—emptiness, the principal object—is taught in sūtra just as it is in tantra, but the subjective clear light—the extremely subtle fundamental innate mind of clear light—is taught only in Highest Yoga Tantra, not even in the three lower tantras and, of course, not in the Perfection Vehicle. Therefore, the view free of the proliferations of thought which is so frequently mentioned in the Old Translation School of Nyingma refers to the element of clear light without any differentiation of subject and object. This is called the essential purity, which is an affirming negative, not a nonaffirming negative as emptiness is.

In the books of the New Translation Schools this clear light is called the completion stage of ultimate clear light and is even called the ultimate truth. For example, in the Perfection Vehicle, the Middle Way Autonomists present a metaphoric ultimate truth referring to a mind that has emptiness as its object. Similarly, when Highest Yoga Mantra presents the conventional stage of completion—illusory body—and an ultimate stage of completion—clear light—the word "ultimate" does not refer to the object, emptiness, but to the subject realizing emptiness. The reason for this is that the mind has become undifferentiable from its object, emptiness, and thus is called an ultimate truth or a metaphoric ultimate truth. In this way the term "ultimate truth" is also used frequently in the books of the New Translation Schools to refer to more than just emptiness.

Within this context there is a difference in view between Sūtra and Mantra. Therefore, when Tsongkhapa says that with regard to the view of the middle way there is no presentation surpassing that of Nāgārjuna's *Treatise on the Middle,* he is referring to the objective clear light, emptiness. It is free of all dualistic proliferations, and, as Sakya Paṇḍita says, there can be no difference between Sūtra and Mantra with respect to this.

The Perfection Vehicle and the Mantra Vehicle also cannot be differentiated through practice of the six perfections. In Mantra it is necessary to train in giving, ethics, patience, and so forth during six sessions daily, dividing the day into six portions. Failure to do this is considered an infraction. Therefore, the presence or the absence of practicing the six perfections cannot differentiate the two vehicles.

The basic path for achieving a Buddha's Form Body is method—the altruistic mind of enlightenment induced by love and compassion. The basic path for achieving a Buddha's Truth Body is the wisdom realizing emptiness. In Sūtra and Mantra there is no difference with respect to these basic paths. Thus, from the viewpoint of the path that is practiced, its basis—altruistic mind-generation—and its deeds—the six perfections including the wisdom realizing emptiness—there is no difference. Also, small differences in path cannot be the differentiators of the Perfection and Mantra Vehicles.

The two vehicles cannot be differentiated by way of practitioners from the viewpoint of gradations in sharpness and dullness because if so, the Perfection Vehicle itself would have to be divided into many vehicles. The swiftness or slowness of practitioners' progress on the path also cannot serve as the differentiator since many differences in speed are set forth in the Perfection Vehicle.

How, then, are the two vehicles differentiated? Some say that the difference between Sūtra and Mantra is that Mantra was taught for those who can use desire as an aid in the path whereas the Perfection Vehicle was taught in order to tame beings within the context of separation from desire. This opinion is wrong because both the Perfection Vehicle and the Mantra Vehicle have modes of advancing on the path without having abandoned desire and both have modes of progress by cultivating paths to abandon desire. For, in Sūtra it is said that just as the filth of a city is helpful to the field of a sugarcane grower who knows how to utilize a substance which itself is not helpful, so the afflictions can be useful in the path. If one knows how to use the afflictions for the welfare of others, they can serve as aids in amassing the accumulations of merit, and in this sense desire is not one-pointedly to be avoided although, from the viewpoint of the entities of the afflictions, they are indeed to be abandoned. Sūtra Bodhisattvas who have not yet thoroughly abandoned the afflictions of desire and hatred can use them for the benefit of others, as in the case of Bodhisattva kings who have fathered many children in order to further the welfare of the country through the work of their children. Here the afflictions act as secondary causes in the aiding of others.

Just as within Sūtra practice there are occasions when Bodhisattvas intentionally do not abandon afflictions but use them as aids, so in Mantra practice, according to the time and the situation, Bodhisattvas use the afflictions. However, on the occasions when there is no purpose for desire or hatred, a Mantra practitioner must intentionally seek to abandon them. If in order to be a practitioner of Mantra one necessarily had to have not abandoned desire and hatred, there would be no opportunity to become a Buddha through the Mantra path.

Others hold the more refined position that the division between Sūtra and Tantra is determined by the special or main trainees initially engaging in those vehicles who either cannot or can use desire as an aid to the path. In general, it is true that using four types of joy arising from four types of desire—gazing, laughing, holding hands and embracing, and union—as favorable circumstances for cultivating the path occurs in the four tantra sets. Thus, with regard to initial practitioners of the Perfection and Mantra Vehicles it can be said that the one is not able and the other is able to use such desire in the path. However, this cannot be posited as the differentiator between the paths of the two vehicles. Although it indicates a difference in the capacities of the two types of persons, it is not the profound and complete distinction between the Perfection and Mantra Vehicles.

Others say that the bliss arising from concentration on the channels, winds, and drops [see note 81, section II] differentiates the two vehicles, but this is a feature only of Highest Yoga Tantra, not of Mantra in general. Thus, it cannot serve as the distinction between the two vehicles.

Greatness of Mantra

The difference between the Perfection and Mantra Vehicles must apply to one of the two meanings of "vehicle": the means by which one proceeds or the fruit to which one proceeds. There is no difference in the fruit, Buddhahood; hence, the difference rests in the sense of "vehicle" as the means by which one progresses to that fruit.

The Great Vehicle surpasses the Lesser Vehicle in terms of method, the altruistic aspiration to highest enlightenment for the sake of all sentient beings, and the division of the Great Vehicle into a Perfection Vehicle and a Mantra Vehicle is also made by way of method. In general, the paths included within the factor of method are the means for achieving a Buddha's Form Body, whereas the paths included within the factor of wisdom are the means for achieving a Buddha's Truth Body. To achieve a Truth Body one needs to cultivate a path similar in aspect to a Truth Body, and both the Perfection and the Mantra Vehicles have a path of wisdom in which one cultivates a similitude of a Buddha's Truth Body: the realization of emptiness in space-like meditative equipoise.

In order to achieve a Form Body, one needs to cultivate a path that is similar in aspect to a Buddha's Form Body. Only Mantra has the special method for achieving this feat by cultivating paths that are similar in aspect to a Buddha's Form Body. The presence of meditation that utilizes a similitude of a Form Body is the greatness of the Mantra method; such is not set forth in Sūtra.

In order to remove mental defilements it is necessary to meditate on emptiness, but this is not a complete method for achieving Buddhahood because meditation on emptiness only removes the conception of inherent existence and all the afflictions that are based on it; other practices are needed in order to achieve the physical perfection of a Buddha. The complete method capable of bestowing Buddhahood quickly is the cultivation of a path of deity yoga in which the pride of being the deity of the effect state is established.

The attainment sought is the state of a Buddha endowed with the marks and beauties. To achieve this state one must train in the path of a divine body similar in aspect to the body of a Buddha. Therefore, cultivation of a divine body is not used merely for the achievement of common feats but is essential for achieving the uncommon feat of a Buddha's Form Body.

According to the Perfection Vehicle, in order for the wisdom realizing emptiness to serve as an antidote to the obstructions to omniscience, it must be conjoined with altruistic mind-generation and practice of the perfections. The vast methods such as giving, ethics, and patience help limitless sentient beings, and their imprint at Buddhahood is the achievement of Form Bodies which perform limitless altruistic activities.

The wisdom penetrating the depth of the suchness of phenomena is the means for actualizing the nonconceptual wisdom of a Buddha. Thus, the special imprint of the collection of wisdom is the attainment of the Wisdom Truth Body coupled with the abandonment of all contaminations.

Neither a Truth Body nor a Form Body is attained singly because they both depend on completion of these causal collections of method and wisdom. The two collections act as cooperating cause and special cause of the Truth and Form Bodies. For example, an eye consciousness is generated in dependence on three causes, an object, an eye sense, and a former moment of consciousness; the ability of an eye consciousness to apprehend color and shape rather than sound is the imprint of the eye sense; its being a conscious entity is the imprint of an immediately preceding moment of consciousness; and its being generated in the image of a particular object is the imprint of the object. Just as each of the three causes is said to have its own individual imprint in the generation of the eye consciousness, the imprint of wisdom is a Truth Body and the imprint of method is a Form Body.

Because the Perfection Vehicle sets forth a method for achieving the nonconceptual Wisdom Body of a Buddha and the Form Bodies effecting limitless maturations of other beings' minds, it is *said* to have unsurpassed method. However, in the path of the Perfection Vehicle, the causes of highest enlightenment are explained as only the six perfections. These are not sufficient because through cultivating causes such as giving, ethics, patience, and so forth—that are different in aspect from Form Bodies, the fruit—one cannot actualize the enlightenment of a Buddha. One would be attempting to actualize an effect that is different in aspect from the causes. The effect of Buddhahood, which has a nature of profundity—a Truth Body—and vastness—a Form Body adorned with the marks and beauties—in one undifferentiable entity, is achieved from causes that have a similar nature. Just as one meditates on the meaning of selflessness that is similar in aspect to a Truth Body, so one should cultivate paths of vastness that are similar in aspect to a Form Body.

In the Mantra Vehicle the "vast" refers to the appearance of a divine body. There is a vastness at the time of the path—cultivation of the vivid appearance of a divine body coupled with divine pride—and a vastness at the time of the fruit—an ultimate vastness that achieves the welfare of others. Deity yoga is "vast" because deities such as Vairochana, who are qualified by emptiness and included within the factor of appearance, are inexhaustible, continual, limitless, and pure. Even though both pure and impure phenomena are qualified by emptiness, there is said to be a difference due to the phenomena qualified by it.

In Mantra, conjunction of method with wisdom and vice versa means not that method and wisdom are individual entities which are merely compatible with each other but that they are complete within the entity of one mind. Based on cultivating this union of method and wisdom, at Buddhahood the Truth Body of nondual wisdom itself appears as the features of a deity. Therefore, prior to meditating on a divine body it is necessary to establish through reasoning the absence of inherent existence of oneself; then, within the context of meditating on this emptiness, just that mind which has one's own emptiness as its object serves as the basis of appearance of the deity.

Induced by ascertaining the emptiness of one's own inherent existence, this consciousness itself appears in the form of the face, arms, and so forth of a deity. Wisdom vividly appears as a divine body and at the same time ascertains its absence of inherent existence. These two—wisdom realizing the absence of inherent existence and the mind of deity yoga—are one entity, but posited to be different from the viewpoint of their imprints. Thus, from a conventional point of view method and wisdom are different within the context of being one entity. They are said to be different in that method is the exclusion of nonmethod and wisdom is the exclusion of nonwisdom.

Based on the appearance of a divine body, the pride of being that deity develops, having ultimate and conventional aspects. Some scholars say that the appearance of a mind ascertaining emptiness in the form of a deity means that this one mind has emptiness as its referent object and a divine body as its appearing object. Thus, the consciousness has a factor of ascertainment—the understanding of a negative of inherent existence—and a factor of appearance—the vivid reflection of a divine body. In this way, divine pride has two aspects, observing the ultimate—emptiness—and observing the conventional—a divine body.

Among the sūtra explanations there are two systems with regard to whether a phenomenon qualified by emptiness appears to a mind that inferentially realizes that emptiness. Some say that an object qualified by an empty nature appears during inferential realization of its emptiness, and others say that the appearance of the object is no longer present when its emptiness is being understood. In Tsongkhapa's *Great Exposition of the Stages of the Path Common to the Vehicles,* it seems that the phenomenon qualified by emptiness does appear to an inferential consciousness realizing emptiness, but in some monastery textbooks the opposite is held. In any case, initially one meditates on an emptiness, and then, within the context of the mind's continuous ascertainment of emptiness, meditators believe that they are using this mind as the basis [or source] of appearance. At that time, the sense of a mere "I" designated in dependence on the pure resident—the deity—and residence—the palace and surroundings—is a fully qualified divine pride. As much as one can cultivate such pride, so much does one harm the conception of inherent existence that is the root of cyclic existence.

This composite of method and wisdom—the appearance of a deity empty of true existence, like an illusion—is an affirming negative, an absence of inherent existence as well as a positive appearance. One gradually becomes accustomed to this mind, and finally when one arrives at high levels on the stage of completion as explained in Highest Yoga Tantra, the union of a learner is attained in which a continual similitude of a Form Body and a Truth Body is actualized. These are a "Form Body" on the occasion of the path and a wisdom of clear light, which are the actual substantial causes of Buddhahood.

Thus, Mantra is distinguished from the Perfection Vehicle through its superior method for the achievement of a Form Body. Mere meditation on a divine body that is not related with meditation on emptiness is not sufficient. On the other hand, mere meditation on emptiness is also not sufficient. Even though it is not possible to attain Buddhahood in dependence on the paths of the Perfection Vehicle alone, the Perfection Vehicle does set forth paths for the achievement of Buddhahood. If one engages in these paths, meditating on emptiness and cultivating the features of method as explained in the Perfection Vehicle, then it is said that one will attain Buddhahood only after many countless eons; one cannot attain Buddhahood quickly. Actually, one cannot attain Buddhahood through causes that do not have an aspect similar to the effect, a Form Body. In brief, the Body of a Buddha is attained through meditating on it. One should meditate on a divine body until its features appear clearly and steadily, until it seems that one can touch it with one's hand and can see it with one's eye.

Someone might think that in the Perfection Vehicle one cultivates a Buddha's Form Body through meditation involving prayer petitions to attain such. However, if that were the case, one would not need to meditate on emptiness in order to attain a Truth Body; planting prayer petitions would be sufficient. However, Buddhahood is attained through the nondual yoga of the profound and the manifest; without it Buddhahood is impossible.

This is established not only in Highest Yoga Tantra but also in the other three tantras. In Action and Performance Tantra a Truth Body, which is said to be thoroughly pure in the sense of being free of all dualistic proliferations, is achieved through the yoga of signlessness—meditation on emptiness—and a Form Body, which is said to be "impure" in the sense that it is involved in duality, is achieved through the yoga with signs—deity yoga. In Yoga Tantra deity yoga is presented in conjunction with five factors, called the five manifest enlightenments.

This yoga of the union of the profound and manifest is the path of all the *chief* trainees of the Vajra Vehicle but not necessarily of *all* trainees of the Vajra Vehicle. For those who cannot imagine themselves as deities, the practice of contemplation of a deity in front of oneself is set forth in conjunction with repeating mantra, making petitions, and so forth. The chief trainees in terms of whom the Vajra Vehicle was taught are those capable of practicing the full Mantra path, and generating oneself as a deity is definitely taught for all chief trainees. The modes of meditation for the achievement of feats, such as the techniques for meditating on the winds (*prāṇa*), are all for the sake of either making deity yoga more firm or enhancing realization of suchness.

Clarification

Mantra uses the effect as the path in the sense that a path similar in aspect to the effect is cultivated. In both the Perfection and Mantra Vehicles one cultivates a path similar in aspect to a Truth Body, but in the Mantra Vehicle one also cultivates a path similar in aspect to a Form Body. In this way, the Mantra Vehicle surpasses the Perfection Vehicle.

Wrong idea: Deity yoga is unnecessary

Someone might object: To achieve a body adorned with the auspicious marks of a Universal Monarch, it is not necessary to cultivate a path of meditation that is similar in aspect to the body of a Universal Monarch [see note 69, section II]. Thus, it is not established that in order to achieve an effect one must cultivate a cause that accords in aspect with that effect. What is the reason for singling out Buddhahood as requiring a cause similar in aspect to the effect?

Answer: According to the Perfection Vehicle, in general a Form Body is achieved through the amassing of merit. In particular, when Bodhisattvas arrive on the eighth among the ten grounds, they newly achieve a mental body that has similitudes of a Buddha's marks and beauties and that arises in dependence on the stage of latent predispositions of ignorance [the motivation of wishing to assume a mental body] and noncontaminated action [the mental factor of intention which is the subtle exertion involved in the motivation of wishing to assume a mental body]. This body gradually improves and eventually turns into the Form Body of a Buddha. Thus, even the Perfection Vehicle does not say that merely amassing the collections of merit is sufficient, or that at Buddhahood one newly achieves a Form Body, the continuum of which did not exist before. In the systems of both Sūtra and Tantra it is necessary to achieve a similitude of a Form Body prior to attaining Buddhahood.

According to Highest Yoga Tantra, some persons attain Buddhahood in one lifetime, and because these persons are not born with a body adorned with the marks and beauties they must achieve such a body through the practice of deity yoga. These are not cases of taking birth as a Form Body and thus are not similar to the accumulation of causes that impel one into a rebirth as a Universal Monarch or as an animal, hungry ghost, or hell-being. In the case of rebirth it is not necessary to accumulate causes that are similar in *aspect* to the particular type of rebirth being impelled. There is a great difference between a cause projecting rebirth and a cause of similar type.

Meditation on oneself as undifferentiable from a deity is the special cause of similar type for attaining Buddhahood. If one meditated only on emptiness and did not cultivate any method—either that of the Perfection or that of the Mantra Vehicle—one would fall to the fruit of a Lesser Vehicle Foe Destroyer. In order to attain the definite goodness of the highest achievement, Buddhahood, deity yoga is needed. Also, in order to attain the common achievements, the eight feats and so forth, one must view one's body clearly as a divine body and train in the pride of being a deity. Without deity yoga the Mantra path is impossible; deity yoga is the essence of Mantra.

Meditating on oneself as having a divine body seems to be childish play, like telling a story to a child to stimulate his or her imagination. However, in conjunction with the view of emptiness, altruistic motivation, and knowledge of its purpose, it is a very important psychological training—viewing one's body in the form of a deity, generating the pride of being a deity, temporarily performing the activities of pacification and so forth, and ultimately achieving Buddhahood. There is a difference in force between merely repeating a mantra and repeating that mantra within the context of deity yoga; there may in time be a scientific explanation of this difference.

Wrong idea: The Buddhahood of the Perfection Vehicle and the Buddhahood of the Vajra Vehicle are different

Although there is a difference between the Perfection and Mantra Vehicles in terms of method and many forms of paths, there is no difference in the fruit, the Buddhahood that is sought by both. In some scriptures Buddhahood and Vajradharahood seem to be different, and thus some have thought that the fruits of the Perfection and Mantra Vehicles must be different and that Vajradharahood is higher than Buddhahood. This confusion sometimes arises because tenth ground Bodhisattvas are often referred to as a "Buddha" although they are not yet an actual Buddha.

Although practice of only the Perfection Vehicle is not sufficient to achieve Buddhahood, the Buddhahood described in the Perfection and Mantra Vehicles is the same. It is incorrect to say that Buddhahood can be achieved solely though the paths of the Perfection Vehicle and that upon attaining Buddhahood one must enter into the Mantra Vehicle to achieve an even higher fruit. Even though one must finally engage in Mantra in order to become a Buddha, it can be said in general that the Perfection and Mantra paths achieve the same fruit, with their difference lying in the speed with which the fruit is attained.

It cannot be said that *in general* Buddhahood can be achieved through Mantra in the one lifetime of this degenerate age without depending on practice over countless eons because this cannot be done following the paths of the lower tantras alone. One must finally enter Highest Yoga Tantra in order to achieve Buddhahood without practicing for countless eons. According to Tsongkhapa's *Great Exposition of Secret Mantra* the attainment of Buddhahood in one lifetime is a distinguishing feature of Highest Yoga Tantra.

The paths of the three lower tantras are faster than the Perfection path in that the paths of accumulation and preparation do not require one period of countless eons of practice in the three lower tantras, but their mode of procedure on the paths of seeing and meditation is similar to that of the Perfection Vehicle. However, it must be taken into account that Action, Performance, and Yoga Tantras say that Buddhahood can be achieved in one lifetime. For instance, the continuation of the *Vairochanābhisaṃbodhi Tantra* (*vairocanābhisaṃbodhi*), a Performance Tantra, says, "Those Bodhisattvas engaging in practice from the approach of Secret Mantra will become completely and perfectly enlightened in just this lifetime." Such statements that enlightenment can be achieved in one lifetime by means of the three lower tantras should be taken as an exaggerated expression of the greatness of that particular tantra.

Practitioners of the three lower tantras attain many common feats through which they see Buddhas and Bodhisattvas, hear their teachings, and under their care complete the practices for enlightenment quickly, but aside from proceeding faster on the paths of accumulation and preparation, the rest of the path is still protracted. According to the oral tradition, attainment of Buddhahood in the one short lifetime *of this degenerate era* [which nowadays is roughly sixty years] is a distinguishing feature of Highest Yoga Tantra but the attainment of the enlightenment of Buddhahood in one lifetime is also a feature of the three lower tantras. The latter is not the one short lifetime of the degenerate era but refers to the ability gained by yogis through the practice of deity yoga, repetition of mantra, and so forth to extend their lifetime over many eons. During such a lifetime one can attain highest enlightenment, relying on the paths of the three lower tantras and eventually engaging in Highest Yoga. The passage in the *Vairochanābhisaṃbodhi Tantra* may refer to such a long lifetime.

Wrong idea: The stage of generation is just deity yoga

Shāntideva says in his *Engaging in the Bodhisattva Deeds* that when Bodhisattvas who have attained a ground give away their own body they have no physical suffering and thus no mental suffering and thereby can easily give away even their body if needed. Also, the *Meeting of Father and Son Sūtra* (*pitāputrasamāgama*) says that Bodhisattvas can maintain a blissful feeling in all situations, even during torture. Based on such teachings, Ratnarakṣhita mistakenly propounds that the great bliss generated in the Perfection Vehicle is the same as that generated in Highest Yoga Tantra. Nevertheless, he correctly asserts that both the Mantra and Perfection Vehicles involve meditation on emptiness and also correctly points out that in the Perfection Vehicle Bodhisattvas on certain occasions use the desire realm attributes of pleasant forms, sounds, odors, tastes, and tangible objects and that, therefore, the usage of desire in the path is not a distinguishing feature of the Mantra Vehicle. He cites the *Kāshyapa Chapter Sūtra* (*kāśyapaparivarta*):

> Just as the filth of city-dwellers
> Helps the field of a sugarcane grower,
> So the manure of a Bodhisattva's afflictions
> Assists in growing the qualities of a Buddha.

He also correctly notes that an altruistic aspiration to highest enlightenment, induced by love and compassion, is common to both the Perfection and Mantra Vehicles. However, he mistakenly concludes that the distinctive feature of tantra is the stage of generation. He wrongly assumes that the stage of generation in Highest Yoga Tantra is primarily deity yoga and that the stage of completion is primarily meditation on emptiness, whereas the very foundation of deity yoga is meditation on emptiness, and deity yoga also occurs in the stage of completion.

Wrong idea: Usage of desire in the path is for low trainees

Tripiṭakamāla says that even though the aim of the two vehicles—Buddhahood—is the same, the Mantra Vehicle surpasses the Perfection Vehicle by way of four features:

> The first feature is that practitioners of Mantra are not obscured whereas those of the Perfection Vehicle are obscured. Practitioners of Mantra realize that the completion of a perfection is a fruit of meditative stabilization and that one cannot complete a perfection through actually giving away one's own body and so forth. Practitioners of the Perfection Vehicle do not realize this and thus are obscured.

This explanation is wrong because in the Perfection Vehicle itself Shāntideva says that since we see that there are still beggars in the world and since we know that the earlier Buddhas and Bodhisattvas achieved a perfection of giving, the perfection of giving could not involve eliminating all poverty in the world. Rather, the perfection of giving is the full development of an attitude of generosity—the completion of the attitude to give away all of one's possessions, along with all effects that might arise from them, to all sentient beings. According to Shāntideva, a perfection depends on the mind. Therefore, Tripiṭakamāla's explanation of the feature of nonobscuration is not feasible.

> The second feature is that the Mantra Vehicle has many methods whereas the Perfection Vehicle does not. In the Perfection Vehicle one proceeds only by peaceful means, but the Mantra Vehicle has four divisions which each have many techniques to counter one problem. For instance, for the desirous and the proud Mantra

> has many methods such as imagining oneself as any of a great number of deities.

Tripiṭakamāla's explanation of this feature appears to be correct, but it cannot serve as a reason for dividing the Great Vehicle into a Perfection Vehicle and a Mantra Vehicle because Highest Yoga Tantra, for instance, has many techniques which the other three tantras do not have, but these do not make it a separate vehicle.

> The third feature is that the Perfection Vehicle involves asceticism whereas the Mantra Vehicle does not. Jñānakīrti and Tripiṭakamāla explain that Mantra has two types of trainees: those without desire for a Knowledge Woman [see note 86, section II] and those with desire. Those without desire for a Knowledge Woman are the highest trainees, and they meditate on the actual great seal which is a union of method and wisdom. Those with desire are divided into two groups: those without desire for an external Knowledge Woman and those with desire for an external Knowledge Woman. The former meditate on an imagined Knowledge Woman, and the latter use an actual Knowledge Woman.

This explanation is wrong because among the trainees of Highest Yoga Tantra those having the sharpest faculties use desire for an external Knowledge Woman in the path. It is through this means that "jewel-like persons" achieve Buddhahood in one lifetime. Since both vehicles have cultivation of paths free of desire and paths using desire, this feature cannot distinguish the two vehicles.

Tripiṭakamāla's explanation of the fourth feature, sharpness of faculties, is also incorrect because if he means nonobscuration with respect to method his explanation of the difference in method has already been shown to be inadequate. If he means that in Mantra desire for the attributes of the desire realm is used in the path, then he is also wrong because according to his faulty explanation the best of sharp trainees do not have such, whereas they actually do.

Wrong idea: The four tantra sets correspond to the four castes

There are four tantra sets: Action, Performance, Yoga, and Highest Yoga. Some also divide Highest Yoga into father tantra, mother tantra, and nondual tantra, making six. According to Tsongkhapa, "nondual tantra" refers to a nonduality of method and wisdom—great bliss and emptiness; therefore, he says that all Highest Yoga Tantras are nondual tantras. The translator Tagtshang, however, asserts that the *Kālachakra Tantra* is a nondual tantra because it emphasizes the fourth initiation which is concerned with a union of supreme immutable bliss and totally supreme emptiness. For him dualistic tantras emphasize either of these two.

Practitioners of the four tantras have the same intention in that they all are seeking others' welfare. The object of attainment—Buddhahood, which is the extinguishment of all faults and fulfillment of all auspicious attributes—is the same for all. Therefore, the four tantras cannot be divided from the viewpoint of field of intent or object of attainment. All four have deity yoga, and variations of deity yoga are not sufficient to serve as the difference between them because each of the four also has many forms of deity yoga. Although there are sources in Indian texts that say that the four tantras are for the four castes or those dominated by particular afflictions, these cannot serve as the differentiators of the four tantras or even indicate a predominance among their trainees.

The tantras were mainly expounded for those of the desire realm and specifically for those seeking enlightenment by way of using desire in the path. The tantra sets are differentiated by way of four modes of practice and four types of trainees whose abilities correspond to these four types of practice; these are four ways of using desire in the path based on differing capacities for generating the emptiness and deity yogas.

Among the seven branches—complete enjoyment, union, great bliss, absence of inherent existence, compassion, uninterrupted continuity, and noncessation—three are found only in tantra—complete enjoyment, union, and great bliss—and the other four are common to both sūtra and tantra although the absence of inherent existence can also be put in the group specific to tantra when it is considered as the object ascertained by a bliss consciousness. The three lower tantras do not set forth the branch of union; also, in the lower tantras one does not take cognizance of an external Knowledge Woman and then use desire in the path, but takes cognizance only of a meditated Knowledge Woman. In Yoga Tantras the bliss arising from holding hands or embracing is used in the path; in Performance Tantras, from laughing; and in Action Tantras, from gazing. In brief, the four tantras are similar in that they all use desire for the attributes of the desire realm on the path.

In Action Tantras external activities predominate. In Performance Tantras external activities and internal yoga are performed equally. In Yoga Tantras internal yoga is predominant. In Highest Yoga Tantras a path unequalled by any other is taught. These etymological descriptions of the names of the four tantras apply to their main trainees but not to all of their trainees, because, for instance, it is said that even some Yoga Tantras were taught for those frightened by meditation on oneself as a deity.

The four tantras are distinguished by way of their main trainees' abilities and not by way of those who merely have an interest in them, because, as is the case nowadays, there are many who take an interest in a path for which they have no capacity.

Initiation

A maṇḍala is said to be extremely profound because meditation on it serves as an antidote, quickly eradicating the obstructions to liberation and the obstructions to omniscience as well as their latent predispositions. It is difficult for those of low intelligence to penetrate its significance.

There is a difference between entering a maṇḍala and receiving initiation. In order merely to enter a maṇḍala it is sufficient to have faith; it is not necessary to have generated the altruistic mind of enlightenment. Also, one may enter a maṇḍala and receive initiation without having fully generated the altruistic mind of enlightenment, but it is necessary for one who is training in the two stages of Highest Yoga Tantra to have done so.

In the past, entrance into a maṇḍala and granting initiation were used very carefully, discriminating between the two, but nowadays Tibetans tend to initiate anyone. Vajradhara set forth a complete system with different levels—those who could just enter a maṇḍala, those who could also receive the water and head-dress initiations, and so forth. When it is done systematically, the lama, prior to granting initiation, analyzes the student to determine whether he or she can engage in the three trainings [ethics, meditative stabilization, and wisdom] and keep the vows. The lama allows those who are not qualified but who have great faith to enter a maṇḍala but does not allow initiation. These systematic restrictions, which when followed make initiation effective and practical, are often not followed nowadays, causing trouble for both lama and initiate.

There is a story about Drugpa Kunleg who was visiting an area where a lama was bestowing initiation. When the lama passed by, all thereabouts rose and paid him respect, but Drugpa Kunleg did not. The lama playfully asked him what he was doing. "When I pass by, other people pay respect. Why are you displaying this ill behavior?" Drugpa Kunleg answered by asking, "Are you giving many initiations? Are you causing many to fall from their vows and pledges? Are you opening the way to hell for many?"

If you are able to think about the meaning of cyclic existence in general and human life in particular, then it is possible to discipline the mind through religious practice which is the process of becoming peaceful and anxiety-free. Otherwise, if too much emphasis is put on the sufferings of the hells and the imminence of death, there is a chance of falling into paralyzing fear. There is a story in Tibet about an abbot of a monastery who went to give a discourse. A fellow asked the abbot's servant where the abbot had gone, and the servant said, "He has gone to frighten old folks." If you fulfil the value of a human lifetime through engaging in religious practice, then there is no point in worrying about death.

Initially, you should take refuge in the Three Jewels from the round orb of your heart, then take a vow of individual emancipation, and after that generate the aspirational and practical minds of enlightenment. Then, when you arrive at the point where it is suitable to hear tantra, you should receive teachings on Ashvaghoṣha's *Twenty Stanzas on the Bodhisattva Vow* (*bodhisattva-saṃvaraviṃśaka*) and *Fifty Stanzas on the Guru* (*guru-pañcāśikā*). Then you may receive initiation.

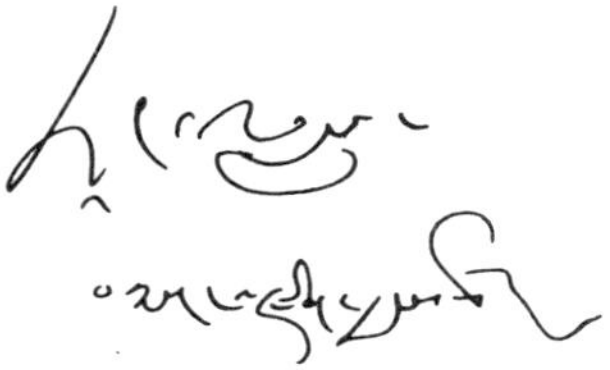

The Buddhist monk, Tenzin Gyatso 2518 B.C.E., 1974 C.E.,
the Tibetan year of the Fire Tiger

II

The Great Exposition of Secret Mantra

The Stages of the Path to a Victor and Pervasive Master, a Great Vajradhara: Revealing All Secret Essentials

Part One

Tsongkhapa

TRANSLATED AND EDITED BY

Jeffrey Hopkins

ASSOCIATE EDITORS

Lati Rinpoche and

Geshe Gedün Lodrö

Reasons for Faith

I bow down and go for refuge with great respect in all my births to the lotus feet of the excellent gurus and the Foremost Holy Mañjughoṣha.

Homage to the Spiritual Guides

Homage to the feet of the excellent guides
Who through their mind of empathy give exact advice,
By respectfully taking their lotus feet to the top of one's head,
About the stainless path removing the troubles of cyclic existence and solitary peace.

Homage to Vajradhara

May I be protected by the sovereign of maṇḍalas
Who like a captivating rainbow in the stainless sky
Without stirring from the state of complete quiescence of all proliferations
Emanates countless hosts of deities through physical creations of his sport.

Homage to Vajrapāṇi

Through my respectfully bowing to the powerful protector,
The master bearing the knowledge mantras, the collector of all
Whatsoever secret topics spoken by him,[1]
The groups of demons should now take heed.

Homage to Manjughoṣha

O Manjughoṣha, sole father of all the Victors,
Treasure of wisdom such that having heard
That you bestow the superior gift of discrimination even with a glance
Upon having been pleased, granting realization of the profound thought of the Victors,

I have relied on you continuously for a long time
As my special god and still further will not forsake your lotus feet,
For me there is never another refuge.
O Manjughoṣha, grant the fruit of my wishes.

Reasons for Composing the Book and Promise to Compose the Book

I have long been beseeched by many wishing to practice
The meaning of the tantras properly as they are expounded by the wise
And by one speaking the two languages
With extensive knowledge of countless books,[2]

And have been strongly beseeched again and again by one
Resplendent with many merits at the forefront of all beings,
A good being of unusual thought bearing the burden of spreading
The glorious Vajra Vehicle in all directions,[3]

And seeing that those satisfied with but a portion for whom the great systems
Do not dawn as practical instruction and that those who cannot analyze
With stainless reasoning what the scriptures mean, and those who have heard a lot
But make no effort at practice cannot please the Victors,

And with my mind greatly affected
By the behavior of the excellent beings
Of the past who properly trained in the teaching
I will strive here to clarify their systems.

For this may the hosts of Sky-Goers—
Field-born, Innate, and Mantra-born—regard me
With empathy like a mother for her child, granting all the feats
And bestowing the kindness of removing all obstacles.

There are those whose capacity of the supreme vehicle lineage is not meager, whose minds are strongly moved by great compassion through having trained in the common path sustained by a spiritual guide, an excellent protector, due to which they are in great haste to free from cyclic existence the kind mothers wandering there. They should enter the short path, the profound Vajra Vehicle that quickly bestows the state of a Supramundane Victor Buddha, the sole refuge of all sentient beings. Hence, I will explain here the stages of the path to the state of a great Vajradhara.

The explanation has two parts: showing that only the Victor's teaching is the entrance for those wishing liberation and indicating the doors of the different stages for entry to the teaching.

Only the Victor's Teaching Is the Entrance for Those Wishing Liberation

Since having engaged in analyzing the greater aims of oneself and others, there is no satisfaction with merely the system revealed by the elders of the world—the achievement of happiness and avoidance of suffering as long as one lives—the entrance for those seeking the higher features of future lives and above [namely, liberation from cyclic existence and the attainment of omniscience] is only the teaching of the Buddha. For, he attained a supreme amazing state through having trained in the aspiration to highest enlightenment for the sake of all sentient beings—a cherishing of others more than oneself—and through having trained in the great waves of the deeds of Buddha Children induced by this altruistic mind of enlightenment, which most other persons find it difficult even to take delight in from the depths of their heart and which are topics of discourse that accord not at all with the world. Thereby he became a great foundation of the welfare of all beings, the mere movement of his breath in and out being a great means providing medicine for sentient beings, such that a banner of renown as the Supramundane Victor flies over the three realms. It is as Mātṛcheta's [or Ashvaghoṣha's] and Dignāga's *Interwoven Praise* (*miśrakastotra*)[4] says:

> I thoroughly dwell in an ocean
> Of cyclic existence of limitless depth.
> The frightful sea monsters of desire
> And so forth are eating my body.
> Where will I go for refuge today?
>
> If one has intelligence,
> It would be right to take refuge
> In the one who completely does not have
> Any of all the defects
> And in whom in every way
> All auspicious qualities reside
> And to praise and to venerate
> And to abide in his teaching.

Nevertheless, Kapila and so forth—even though they did not know the path of release—were maddened by the poison of pride and claimed to be teachers. Wishing to teach a suchness of phenomena in a way other than that taught by the Ones-Gone-to-Bliss (*sugata*),[5] they put together many different texts that were made to appear like correct paths and advised those wishing liberation. Therefore, you must gain conviction in the sources of refuge such that your mind does not waver elsewhere: "Only the completely perfect Buddha, his teaching, and those properly learning it are the teacher, the path, and friends progressing to liberation for those wishing liberation. Teachers, teachings, and their students other that these are not." Thereby you will realize that only the Subduer's teaching is the entrance for those wishing liberation. Those with less force of mind will determine this merely through a correct assumption, but those with stronger minds should seek firm conviction induced by valid cognition, since otherwise it will only be an assertion.

Moreover, Shaṃkarapati's *Praise of the Supra-Divine* (*devātiśayastotra*)[6] says:

> Though I am not a partisan of Buddha
> And do not hate Kapila and so forth,
> I hold as teachers only those
> Whose words are endowed with reason.

Accordingly when, having forsaken partisanship and hatred for the systems of your own and others' teachers' systems, you analyze which of these two is explained well and which is explained poorly, you should adopt only that which has correct proofs for teaching the means of accomplishing the two aims of trainees [high status within cyclic existence and the definite goodness of liberation and omniscience]. At that time, the scriptures of the two systems are what are to be analyzed to find which does or does not bear the truth; hence, it would not be suitable to cite the matter under debate as a proof [of their own truth]; therefore, only reasoning distinguishes what is or is not true.

The manner of reasoning is this: It is indeed the case that in terms of the order in which they are generated in a person's continuum the temporary attainment of high status is achieved first and definite goodness is achieved later. However, when scriptures showing the two aims of beings are analyzed to find whether they are incontrovertible or not, one first establishes through reasoning that a system is not deceptive about the principal aim of definite goodness; then one can infer from this that the system is not deceptive with respect to the secondary attainment of high status. This is the assertion of the mighty scholars, like what Dharmakīrti's *Commentary on (Dignāga's) "Compilation of Valid Cognition" (pramāṇavarttika)*[7] says:

> Because [the Buddha's word] is nondeceptive about the
> principal meaning,
> It is to be inferred with regard to the others.

and Āryadeva's *Four Hundred (catuḥśataka)*[8] also says:

> Whoever has generated doubt
> In what Buddha has said about the obscure
> Will believe that only Buddha [is omniscient]
> Based on [his teaching about] emptiness.

Therefore, one must establish through reasoning the stages of cyclic existence—the continuation of the aggregates of suffering through the source that is the apprehension of self [inherent existence]—and the stages progressing to liberation, achievement of the state of freedom through the wisdom realizing selflessness. These should be proven with reasoning as they are in the systems of logic.

The proposition that "Since these are extremely obscure for a limited being, the proof is reduced to only scripture," would make the statement "I go for refuge to you, O Supramundane Victor, having abandoned other teachers," turn into a proclamation of the weakness of one's own refuge: "It is exhausted as only my own wish; there are no correct proofs," for at this point citation of scripture is not suitable as a proof, and you also assert that there are no proofs by reasoning. Furthermore, when our own great schools and others' schools debate about whether the scriptures taught by our own and others' teachers that disagree about whether or not there is rebirth, whether the mental and physical aggregates are permanent or impermanent, whether self exists or not, and so forth, are correct or not, we also would not be able to prove that the scriptures of our own teacher are correct [without relying on reasoning].

Scriptures teaching very obscure topics, which are not proved by valid cognition by the power of the fact, are proved to be incontrovertible with respect to their contents by reasoning purified through the three analyses.[9] The establishment of the modes of the process also is performed through reasoning; one does not rely on asserting scripture as proof. Here I have indicated only a little; I will treat it at length elsewhere.[10]

The scriptures of other schools teaching the chief aims of persons are just internally contradictory. For example, they propound that a permanent factor, such as the Principal (*pradhāna*) or Lord (*īshvara*), is the creator of cyclic existence, and then they assert that those seeking liberation also overcome cyclic existence at the end of cultivating the path, but without overcoming the main cause of cyclic existence, cyclic existence could not be overcome, and if it is a permanent cause, it could never be susceptible to being overcome. Similarly, it is also contradictory to reject the view of selflessness and to take as an object of attainment a liberation that cuts the bonds to cyclic existence.

As explained above, if you have not induced conviction that the three refuges—our Teacher [Buddha] and so forth [the Doctrine and Spiritual Community]—are refuges for those wishing liberation, but teachers and so forth who do not accord with them are not at all [final] refuges, a firm single-pointed awareness with respect to your own sources of refuge will not arise. The arising of such a firm awareness relies on seeing, through reasoning, the faults and advantages of the two systems.

Therefore, whether or not a [non-Buddhist] Forder (*tīrthika*) is actually present [to refute in debate], if the intelligent wish to generate a special awareness of refuge, they should do as was explained above. Therefore, know that the treatises on reasoning such as Dharmakīrti's *Seven Treatises*[11] are a superior means of generating great respect, not merely verbal, for our teacher Buddha, for his teaching—both verbal and realizational—and for those properly practicing them.

Paths to Buddhahood

Indicating the Doors of the Different Stages for Entry to the Teaching

This has two parts: divisions of the vehicles in general and divisions of the Great Vehicle.

Divisions of the Vehicles in General

This has four parts: how the vehicles are divided, reasons for the divisions, nature of the individual divisions, and a teaching that even all of them in the end are branches of the process of fullest enlightenment.

How the Vehicles Are Divided

In Āryadeva's *Lamp Compendium of Practice* (*caryāmelāpaka-pradīpa*),[12] the vehicles are divided through gathering practices into three types from the viewpoint of the three types of trainees' interests. Practices free from desire are taught to those interested in the lowly; practices of the grounds and perfections are taught to those interested in the vast; and practices of desire are taught to those specially interested in the profound. Similarly, Tripiṭakamāla's *Lamp for the Three Modes* (*nayatrayapradīpa*)[13] also says:

> The meanings of the modes
> Of the truths, of the perfections,
> And of the great secret mantra
> Through abridgement have been taught here.

Thus, the master Tripiṭakamāla includes all within three modes—the mode of the yoga of the four truths and so forth, and Jñānakīrti also gathers them the same way in his *Abridged Explanation of All the Word* (*tattvāvatārākhyasakalasugatavacastātparyavyākhyāprakaraṇa*).[14]

Maitreya's *Ornament for the Great Vehicle Sūtras* (*mahāyānasūtrālaṃkāra*) says, "The scriptural collections are either two or three." Thus, there are said to be two scriptural collections, Supreme Vehicle and Lesser Vehicle [or three, discipline, discourses, and manifest knowledge]. It is permissible to use these explanations with reference both to divisions of scriptures and divisions of paths or vehicles.

Reasons for the Divisions

Let us explain the reasons for saying that there are two divisions [of vehicles]. There are two types of trainees, low and supreme:

- low trainees who seek a low object of intent which is a low attainment solely for their own sake—the state of the mere quiescence of the suffering of cyclic existence
- supreme trainees who seek an elevated object of intent, the supreme attainment—the state of Buddhahood—for the sake of all sentient beings

Since there are these two types of trainees, low and supreme, the two vehicles by which these two go to their own state are called the "Lesser Vehicle" (*hīnayāna*) and the "Great Vehicle" (*mahāyāna*). Doctrines taught in accordance with these are called the scriptural divisions of the Lesser Vehicle and of the Supreme Vehicle.

The Lesser Vehicle has two types, Hearers and Solitary Realizers, and since the paths that lead them to their respective states are divided into the two, a Hearer Vehicle and a Solitary Realizer Vehicle, there are three vehicles [the Hearer, Solitary Realizer, and Great Vehicles].

Nature of the Individual Divisions

This has two parts: presentations of the Lesser Vehicle and of the Great Vehicle.

Presentation of the Lesser Vehicle

It is said in Asaṅga's *Actuality of the Grounds* (*bhūmivastu, yogācārabhūmi*) that although Hearers and Solitary Realizers differ in inferiority and superiority with respect to their faculties and fruits [of practice, Hearers being inferior to Solitary Realizers], the presentations of their paths are mostly the same. Because I fear that the fine details would run to too many words, I will just summarize the coarse general features of both Hearers and Solitary Realizers.

Since those who have Hearer and Solitary Realizer lineages have turned away from bearing others' welfare, they are engaged only in their own liberation. The chief cause of attaining liberative release is the wisdom realizing the meaning of selflessness because the chief cause of being bound in cyclic existence is the conception of self [inherent existence]. Therefore, [not just Bodhisattvas but] also Hearers and Solitary Realizers, understanding this fact, seek this wisdom, and through having cultivated it while accompanying it with other paths such as ethics and meditative stabilization, they extinguish all afflictions.

Proponents of Sūtra, Kashmiri Proponents of the Great Exposition, Proponents of Mind-Only, and certain Proponents of the Middle Way [namely, Middle Way Autonomists] explain that Hearers and Solitary Realizers do not realize that persons, even though from the start empty of inherent existence in the sense of lacking establishment by way of their own character, appear like a magician's illusion to exist inherently; rather, they say that realization that persons do not have the substantially existent self that is imputed by non-Buddhists is the meaning of realizing the selflessness of persons. The glorious Chandrakīrti says that if that were so, then Hearers and Solitary Realizers would not in the least overcome the conception of true existence with respect to persons, and, therefore, such does not have the meaning of realizing the selflessness of persons:

- because as long as persons are conceived to truly exist, the conception of a self of persons has not been overcome
- and because just as a realization of a mental or physical aggregate or the like as not inherently existing must be put as the meaning of realizing the selflessness of phenomena [other than persons], so a realization of a person as not inherently existing must be put as the meaning of realizing the selflessness of persons.

Therefore, Chandrakīrti considered that as long as the aggregates are conceived to truly exist, the conception that persons truly exist also operates, and as long as this operates, one cannot entirely overcome the afflictions, and due to this it would have to be asserted that, no matter how much Hearers and Solitary Realizers strove at it, they could not be liberated from cyclic existence, and [thus he concluded that] this is not reasonable. Chandrakīrti says in the *Supplement to the Middle* (*madhyamakāvatāra,* VI.131):

> According to you, yogis who have seen selflessness
> Would not realize the suchness of forms and so forth.
> Thus desire and so forth would be generated because of
> engaging in forms
> With apprehension [of inherent existence], for they have
> not realized their nature.

And Chandrakīrti's own commentary also says:

> Because they have gone astray through apprehending an inherent existence of forms and so forth, they would not realize even the selflessness of persons. For they are apprehending [the inherent existence of] the mental

and physical aggregates that are the cause of the imputation of a self.

This is the assertion of the protector Nāgārjuna because his *Precious Garland* (*ratnāvalī*, 35) says:[15]

As long as the aggregates are conceived,
So long thereby does the conception of "I" exist.
Further, when the conception of "I" exists, there also is action,
And from action (*karma*) there also is birth.

And his *Fundamental Treatise on the Middle, Called "Wisdom"* (*prajñānāmamūlamadhyamakakārikā*, XVIII.5) says that one is bound in cyclic existence through conceiving the aggregates to exist inherently, and in order to be liberated from cyclic existence one must overcome its root, the proliferations of conceiving true existence, and those are overcome through realizing the meaning of the emptiness of inherent existence:

Through extinguishing actions and afflictions, there is liberation.
Actions and afflictions arise from conceptualizations.
These arise from proliferations.
Proliferations are ceased through emptiness.[16]

Also, Nāgārjuna's *Praise of the Nonconceptual* (*nirvikalpastava* [?]) says:

The path of liberation relied upon
By Buddhas, Solitary Realizers,
And Hearers is only you.
None other, it is definite.

Thus, Nāgārjuna says that only the Mother—the nonconceptual wisdom realizing that phenomena do not inherently exist—is the path of liberation of all three vehicles; he is summarizing the meaning of the statements in the *Mother of the Victors* (the *Eight Thousand Stanza Perfection of Wisdom Sūtra, aṣṭasāhasrikāprajñāpāramitā*)[17] which says, "Even those who want to train in the grounds of a Hearer must train in just this perfection of wisdom," and the statement of the same also with respect to the levels of a Solitary Realizer and of a Buddha, and the *Condensed Perfection of Wisdom Sūtra* (*prajñāpāramitāsañcayagāthā*),[18] which says:

> Those who think to become Hearers of the
> Ones-Gone-to-Bliss
> And those who wish to become Solitary Realizers or
> Monarchs of Doctrine
> Cannot achieve [their aims] without depending on this
> endurance.

Also, in the Hearer scriptural collection[19] it is said:

> Forms are like balls of foam.
> Feelings are like bubbles.
> Discriminations resemble mirages.
> Compositional factors are like banana tree trunks.
> Consciousnesses resemble magical illusions.
> Thus the Sun Friend Buddha said.

Indicating the same meaning, Nāgārjuna's *Fundamental Treatise on the Middle, Called "Wisdom"* (XV.7) says:

> In the Advice to Kātyāyana
> "Exists," "does not exist," and "both"
> Are rejected by the Supramundane Victor,
> Knower [of the nature][20] of things and nonthings.

Hence, it is not that a selflessness of phenomena [other than persons] is not also taught in the Lesser Vehicle scriptural collections.

However, in the Hearer scriptures there are many explanations that through the view of the sixteen attributes of the four truths—impermanence and so forth—one can progress to the state of a Foe Destroyer, and even in the Great Vehicle both modes of progress are taught, one through realization that phenomena do not inherently exist and one through the paths of impermanence and so forth. Nevertheless, about the statements, for example, even in Great Vehicle sūtras that there are two ways of progressing to omniscience through the views of the Mind-Only School and of the Middle Way School, the master the Superior Nāgārjuna certified through his *Collections of Reasoning*[21] that sūtras teaching the Middle Way are not suitable to be interpreted as other than as taught, whereby sūtras elucidating the Mind-Only way must be interpreted as other than as taught, so in the same way here also such a procedure should be asserted.

Even the tantras also frequently say that Hearers and Solitary Realizers have not realized the suchness of phenomena; however, they also frequently state that without realizing the suchness of things one cannot pass beyond cyclic existence and frequently state that conceptuality apprehending things as truly existent binds one in cyclic existence. Therefore, you must know how to explain these without contradiction [through accepting as nonliteral the teaching that Hearers and Solitary Realizers have not understood the suchness of phenomena].

Question: If the teachings of the paths of impermanence and so forth do not release one from cyclic existence, what is the purpose of teaching them?

Answer: It is to be known in accordance with the statement in Nāgārjuna's *Sixty Stanzas of Reasoning* (*yuktiṣaṣṭikā*):

> The paths of production and disintegration
> Were expounded for a meaningful purpose.
> Through knowing production one knows disintegration,

> Through knowing disintegration one knows impermanence.
> Through knowing impermanence
> One knows also the excellent doctrine.
> Those who know how to abandon wholly
> The production and disintegration
> Of dependent-arisings cross the ocean
> Of cyclic existence with its [bad] views.

In this way you should know the purpose of teaching impermanence, for a wish to leave cyclic existence does not arise in a mind thoroughly attracted to products, and thus as an antidote to this the paths of impermanence and suffering are taught, whereby a wish to leave cyclic existence arises. Then, if one realizes—by way of the reason of production and disintegration—the excellent doctrine that dependent-arisings lack inherently existent production and disintegration, one will be released from cyclic existence. Therefore, the path of release is the realization itself that persons and other phenomena do not inherently exist, and the paths of impermanence and so forth are to be taken as means of generating this realization, paths training the mental continuum.

Other masters [Autonomists, Proponents of Mind-Only, Proponents of Sūtra, and Proponents of the Great Exposition] also do indeed assert that the paths of emptiness and selflessness are the means of release and that cultivating the paths of the remaining aspects of the four truths, such as impermanence, are means for training the continuum for the sake of realizing selflessness. However, they identify the realization of emptiness and selflessness among the sixteen aspects of the four truths as an ascertainment only that the self imputed by non-Buddhists does not exist, and hence such realization is not suitable as an antidote to the innate conception that persons exist by way of their own character; therefore, all the paths of the sixteen aspects are similar in not being liberating paths, only being techniques to train the mental continuum.

Thus, those of the Lesser Vehicle of dull faculties for the time being are suitable vessels for paths that train the continuum, but not for a path that liberates, and those of the Lesser Vehicle of sharp faculties are also suitable as vessels of a path that liberates. The main or special trainees for whom Lesser Vehicle scriptural collections were spoken are the latter; the former are subsidiary trainees.

Even though among Lesser Vehiclists there are those who realize that phenomena do not inherently exist, it is not that the Lesser Vehicle and the Great Vehicle do not differ because the Great Vehicle teaching does not just clarify the selflessness of phenomena; it also teaches the grounds, perfections, aspirational wishes, great compassion, and so forth, and dedications, the two collections, and also the inconceivable nature free from all defilements [a Buddha's Nature Body]. Nāgārjuna's *Precious Garland* (stanzas 390 and 393) also says:[22]

> Bodhisattvas' aspirational wishes, deeds, and dedications [of merit]
> Were not described in the Hearers' Vehicle.
> Therefore how could one become
> A Bodhisattva through it?
>
> The subjects concerned with the Bodhisattva deeds
> Were not mentioned in the sūtras [of the Hearer Vehicle],
> But were explained in the Great Vehicle.
> Hence the wise should accept it [as Buddha's word].

Therefore, Lesser Vehicle and Great Vehicle are not differentiated through their view [of emptiness]; the Superior Nāgārjuna and his spiritual sons assert that the two vehicles are differentiated by way of the deeds of skillful method. Just as a mother is a common cause of her children, but the fathers are the causes of individually differentiating the children's lineages [Tibetan, Mongolian, Indian, and so forth], in the same way, the Mother—the perfection of wisdom—is the common cause of all four children [Hearer, Solitary Realizer, Bodhisattva, and Buddha Superiors], but the causes of their being individually differentiated into the individual lineages of Great Vehicle and Lesser Vehicle are methods, such as the generation of an aspiration to highest enlightenment for the sake of all sentient beings.

Presentation of the Great Vehicle

Wanting to attain highest enlightenment for the sake of all sentient beings and thereupon training in the Bodhisattva deeds—the six perfections—is the general meaning of being a person of the Great Vehicle (*theg pa chen po pa*) in the sense of vehicle as the means by which one progresses because it is said many times in tantras that also in the Mantra Vehicle one proceeds by this path. However, within this context there are many distinctive attributes of different paths.

The path of these persons is the Great Vehicle proceeding to omniscience. The general body of the path is just this for those of the Great Vehicle of the Perfection Vehicle; however, when those of the Perfection Vehicle within the Great Vehicle are divided by way of their view of emptiness, there are Proponents of the Middle Way and Proponents of Mind-Only. Even so, those two are not described as stages of different vehicles; therefore, both are one vehicle. Since there is a difference of whether or not they have penetrated the depth of suchness, Proponents of the Middle Way are of sharper faculties and Proponents of Mind-Only are of duller faculties. Here also Proponents of the Middle Way are the main special trainees for whom the Perfection Vehicle was set forth; Proponents of Mind-Only are subsidiary, or secondary, trainees of that Vehicle.

Even those of the Perfection Vehicle (*phar phyin gyi theg pa pa*) are said in the *Introduction to the Forms of Definite and Indefinite Progress Sūtra* (*niyatāniyatagatimudrāvatāra*)[23] to be of five types when differentiated from the viewpoint of their speed on the path: two Bodhisattvas who progress carried respectively in an ox chariot and in an elephant chariot, one Bodhisattva borne by the moon and the sun, and two others by the magical creations of Hearers and Solitary Realizers or by the magical creations of Buddhas. Though they, like their examples, differ very greatly in their speed of progress on the path, they do not have individual vehicles. Therefore, the vehicles cannot be individually differentiated only by sharpness or dullness of faculty or by great or small progress over the path.

Hence, individual vehicles are posited (1) if there is a great difference of superiority or inferiority between them in the sense that a vehicle is a fruit or goal toward which one is progressing; or (2) if there are different stages of paths that give a different body to a vehicle in the sense that a vehicle is a cause by which one progresses. However, if the bodies of the path have no great difference in type, then a series of vehicles cannot be assigned merely because the paths have different internal divisions or the persons who progress by means of them differ in superiority or inferiority.

Even All the Divisions in the End Are Branches of the Process of Fullest Enlightenment

Though those of the Lesser Vehicle do not engage in their own paths with an aim to attain Buddhahood, their paths are methods leading those persons to Buddhahood; therefore, it should not be strictly held that Lesser Vehicle paths are obstacles to fullest enlightenment; the *White Lotus of the Excellent Doctrine* (*saddharmapuṇḍarīka*) says:

> So that they might realize a Buddha's pristine wisdom
> I taught these methods on my own.
> Still, I never said to them,
> "You will become Buddhas."
> Why? The Protector sees the time.

And:

> So that they might realize a Buddha's pristine wisdom
> The sole Protector appears in the world.

> There is one vehicle, there are not two,
> Buddhas do not lead with a Lesser Vehicle.
> I set sentient beings in the powers,
> Concentrations, liberations, forces,
> And paths like those in which a Buddha,
> An independent being, abides and realizes.
> If, having attained the special pure enlightenment,
> I set some beings in a Lesser Vehicle, I would have
> The fault of miserliness, thus it would not be good.
> There is one vehicle, not two, never a third except
> For the various vehicles taught in the world
> Through the skillful means of supreme beings.

The meaning of this is that the purpose of Buddha's coming to the world was for the sake of sentient beings' attaining the pristine wisdom that he achieved; hence, the paths that he taught are only means leading to Buddhahood; he does not lead sentient beings with a Lesser Vehicle that is not a method leading to Buddhahood. Therefore, he also sets sentient beings in the powers and so forth that exist in the state in which he resides. If, having attained enlightenment, he set some beings in a Lesser Vehicle that was not a means leading to Buddhahood, he would have a miserliness that is a holding back of doctrine because since there is one final vehicle, even those having the lineage of a Lesser Vehicle are capable of being led to Buddhahood, and while knowing the methods to do this, he would have hidden from them the doctrines leading to Buddhahood in the sense that he would not teach these to them.

The *Chapter of the True One Sūtra* (*satyakaparivarta*) also expresses it clearly:[24]

> Mañjushrī, if the One-Gone-Thus taught the Great Vehicle to some sentient beings, taught the Solitary Realizer Vehicle to some, and taught the Hearer Vehicle to others, the mind of the One-Gone-Thus would be very impure. His mind also would be without equa-

> nimity. It also would have the fault of attraction. It also would have partial compassion. It also would have the fault of different discriminations. I would also be enacting a teacher's miserliness with regard to doctrine.
>
> Mañjushrī, all the doctrines that I teach to sentient beings are for the sake of attaining omniscient wisdom. Flowing into enlightenment and descending into the Great Vehicle, they are means of achieving omniscience, leading completely to one place. Therefore, I do not set up different vehicles.

The meaning of "If the One-Gone-Thus taught individual vehicles" is as explained above.

Question: Well then, how should the statement be taken in Maitreya's *Ornament for the Great Vehicle Sūtras* that generating a Lesser Vehicle attitude interferes [with attaining highest enlightenment] and that being born in a hell does not?

> If the intelligent dwell in a hell, it never interferes
> With their [progress to] enlightenment broad and stainless.
> Through a thought that takes delight in another vehicle
> One helps oneself and lives in happiness, but it interferes.

Answer: This passage means that if the intelligent—that is, Bodhisattvas—generate an aspiration for the Lesser Vehicle, they remove themselves far from Buddhahood, but they do not do so by dwelling in a hell. Hence, there is no fault because there is not any contradiction in the fact that for those of the Great Vehicle the Lesser Vehicle is an obstacle to full enlightenment but for one having the Lesser Vehicle lineage it serves as a means toward full enlightenment. Furthermore, just previous to that stanza such is said in reference to Victor Children [Bodhisattvas]; therefore, the stanza is not a source of debate [as it would be if the reference were to all practitioners].

Also, the statement in the *Compendium of All the Weaving Sūtra* (*sarvavaidalyasaṃgraha*)[25] that it would be an abandonment of doctrine if the Victor's word were divided into the good and the bad, the suitable and unsuitable, or if what is taught for Hearers and Solitary Realizers and for Bodhisattvas referred to taking some of [Buddha's] words as means for fullest enlightenment and some as obstacles to fullest enlightenment. In that sūtra[26] it is said that if the abandonment of doctrine explained there occurs through a sinful friend, the sin can be cleansed by disclosing it three times a day for seven years, but in order to attain endurance [which is the facility to advance to the next level] one needs ten eons even at the quickest. Therefore, if time passes in wrong understanding, one is yoked to great misfortune; however, if unmistaken understanding [of the compatibility of the vehicles] is found, through merely finding it these faults [of abandonment of doctrine] do not occur.

Therefore, like the statement in the *Chapter of the True One Sūtra* that just as many rivers flow to a great ocean from different approaches, so all the water of the three vehicles also flows into the great ocean of a One-Gone-Thus, you should understand that all doctrines taught by Buddha are, in relation to the trainees at those specific points, only means leading to Buddhahood. Still, it is feasible that these means differ in terms of completeness and incompleteness and in terms of the speed of their paths and so forth due to the superiority or inferiority of the trainees, whereby the two, a path that is a branch of the process leading to Buddhahood and a Great Vehicle path, are not one and the same. Seeing the impact of this, the *Expression of the Ultimate Names of the Wisdom-Being Mañjushrī* (*mañjuśrījñānasattvasya paramārthanāmasaṃgīti*)[27] also says:

> The deliverance of the three vehicles
> Abides in the fruit of the one vehicle.

Vajra Vehicle

Divisions of the Great Vehicle

This has two parts: division of the Great Vehicle into two and a detailed explanation of the forms of entry to the Vajra Vehicle.

Division of the Great Vehicle into Two

This has three parts: the number of divisions of the Great Vehicle, the meaning of the individual divisions, and the reasons for dividing the Great Vehicle this way.

Number of Divisions of the Great Vehicle

According to the explanation by Shraddhākaravarma in the *Introduction to the Meaning of Highest Yoga Tantras* (*yogānuttaratantrārthāvatāra*):[28]

> Bodhisattva vehicles also are twofold, a [Cause] Vehicle of the grounds and perfections and an Effect Vehicle of Secret Mantra.

"Secret Mantra Vehicle," "Effect Vehicle," and "Vajra Vehicle" are synonyms of Mantra Vehicle, which is also called "Method Vehicle." The term "Cause-Effect Vehicle" is an enumeration of the two vehicles [of Perfection and Mantra]. The *Superior Sūtra Revealing the Secret,* as quoted in Jñānashrī's *Eradication of the Two Extremes in the Vajra Vehicle* (*vajrayānakoṭidvayāpoha*),[29] says:

> Once the wheel of the cause doctrines
> Acting on the causes has been turned,
> The Effect Vehicle, the short path [...]

In the texts of the Vajra Vehicle it is also renowned as the "scriptural collection of the Knowledge Bearers" and the "tantra sets."

Meaning of the Individual Divisions of the Great Vehicle

With respect to the "Secret Mantra Vehicle," it is secret because it is achieved secretly and in hiding, and since it is not in the province of those who are not proper vessels for it, it is not taught to them. In the [Sanskrit] original of the word "mantra" *man* means mind, and *tra* (*trā / trāya*) means protection. The continuation of the *Guhyasamāja Tantra* (*guhyasamājatantra,* chap. XVIII)[30] says:

> Minds arising dependent
> On a sense and an object
> Are said to be *man,*
> *Tra* means protection.
>
> Protection by means of all vajras
> Of the pledges and vows explained
> Free from the ways of the world
> Is called "the practice of Mantra."

You should know that in another way *man* is also said to be taken as knowledge of suchness and *trāya* to be compassion protecting those migrating [in the six types of cyclic existence].

About "vehicle," there is an effect vehicle which is that to which one is proceeding and a cause vehicle which is that by which one proceeds. Due to proceeding it is called a vehicle. With respect to "Effect Vehicle," the word "Effect" refers to the four thorough purities—abode, body, resources, and deeds, which are a Buddha's palace, body, fortune, and activities. In accordance with them one meditates on oneself as presently having an inconceivable mansion, divine companions, sacred articles, and deeds such as purification of environments and beings. Hence, it is called the "Effect Vehicle" because one is progressing through meditation in accordance with the aspects of the effect [or fruit, Buddhahood], like the explanation in Shraddhākaravarma's *Introduction to the Meaning of the Highest Yoga Tantras:*[31]

> It is called "Effect" because one enacts the ways of thoroughly pure body, resources, abode, and deeds.

The *Stainless Light* (*vimālaprabhā*) [a commentary on the *Kālachakra Tantra* by Kalkī Puṇḍarīka (*rigs ldan pad ma dkar po*) an Emanation Body of Avalokiteshvara] speaks of the meaning of the name "Vajra Vehicle" through taking the meaning of "Vajra" as an indivisibility of the two, the effect—the Mantra mode—and the cause—the Perfection mode:

> "Vajra" is the indivisible and the great unbreakable; its being the Great Vehicle is the Vajra Vehicle; it is a mixture as one entity of the Mantra mode and of the Perfection mode, effect and cause.

Here, "cause and effect" are emptiness endowed with all supreme aspects and supreme immutable bliss in accordance with the statement in the *Brief Explication of Initiations* (*śekhoddeśa*) [included in the *Kālachakra* cycle]:

> That bearing the form of emptiness is the cause,
> That bearing immutable compassion is the effect.
> Emptiness and compassion indivisible
> Are called the mind of enlightenment.

Within these two—emptiness endowed with all supreme aspects and supreme immutable bliss indivisible—are a Cause Vehicle in the sense of being the means by which one progresses and an Effect Vehicle in the sense of being that to which one is progressing. Such Vajra Vehicles have reference to Highest Yoga Tantra and are not suitable on the occasion of the lower tantra sets because if supreme immutable bliss must be posited upon having attained the branch of meditative stabilization [in the system of *Kālachakra*][32] and hence the branches of mindfulness and those below must be the means of achieving it, the three lower tantras do not have the full complement of those causal branches. Therefore, here on the occasion of identifying the general meaning of "Vajra Vehicle" it is too narrow, and also positing the meaning of the Vehicles of Cause and Effect through this way does not cover a general presentation. Therefore, here these should be taken in accordance with what is said in Ratnākarashānti's *Handful of Flowers, Explanation of the Guhyasamāja Tantra* (*kusumāñjaliguhyasamājanibandha*):

> With regard to "Vajra Vehicle," those which include all the Great Vehicle are the six perfections; those that include them are method and wisdom; that which includes even them as one taste is the mind of enlightenment; that moreover is the Vajrasattva meditative stabilization; just this is a vajra. Because it is a vajra and also a vehicle, it is the meaning of "Vajra Vehicle," "Mantra Vehicle."

As it says, the Vajrasattva yoga that indivisibly unites method and wisdom is the Vajra Vehicle; it exists on both occasions of the path and of the fruit.

Because the Vajra Vehicle has more skillful means than the Perfection Vehicle, it is called the Method Vehicle. Jñānashrī's *Eradication of the Two Extremes*[33] also says:

> Because of indivisibility, it is the Vajra Vehicle. Because just the effect becomes the path, it is the Effect Vehicle.

> Because of the greatness of its methods, it is the Method Vehicle. Because of its extreme secrecy, it is the Secret Vehicle.

"Scriptural division of the Knowledge Bearers" should be taken as teaching the topics of training and the tenets of those who bear the knowledge mantras, in accordance with the explanation in Buddhaguhya's *Condensation of the "Questions of Subāhu Tantra"* (*subāhuparipṛcchānāmatantrapiṇḍārtha*). Although in Shraddhākaravarman's *Introduction to the Meaning of the Highest Yoga Tantras*[34] the scriptural division of the Knowledge Bearers is described in two ways—one in which it is a fourth scriptural division not included in the three scriptural divisions [discipline, sets of discourses, and manifest knowledge] and one in which it is included in the three scriptural divisions, the *Questions of Subāhu Tantra* (*subāhuparipṛcchā*) says, "I will explain this in accordance with the sets of discourses (*mdo sde, sūtrānta*) of Secret Mantra. Listen!" and, moreover, in many tantras [the scriptural division of the Knowledge Bearers] is described as sūtras (*mdo*) and sets of discourses (*mdo sde*); therefore, it is good [to take this] in accordance with Ratnākarashānti's assertion that because of teaching profound meanings in abridged form, [the scriptural division of the Knowledge Bearers] is sets of discourses (*mdo sde, sūtrānta*). About them, moreover, in terms of internal divisions, they teach meanings also of the other scriptural divisions [discipline and manifest knowledge]; therefore, Abhayākara's assertion [that the scriptural division of the Knowledge Bearers] is included in all three scriptural divisions is also feasible.

A "tantra" is a "continuum," and in the continuation of the *Guhyasamāja Tantra*[35] tantras are said to be of three types:

- a "base continuum" that is the base on which the paths are acting [to purify it of obstructions],
- a "path continuum" that purifies this base,
- and a "fruit continuum" that is the fruit of purification,

these being continuums (tantras) on the level of the meanings that are discussed. A scripture taking any of these as its object of discussion is a text continuum (tantra) discussing [such topics]. The word "set" in "tantra set" (*tantrānta*) means a collection or group of tantras.

The "Perfection Vehicle" is to be taken as the vehicle that has as the foundation of its practices altruistic mind-generation [that is, an aspiration to highest enlightenment for the sake of all sentient beings], proceeds by way of its practices—the six perfections—and does not have other paths such as the two stages [of Highest Yoga Tantra] and so forth. If the Perfection Vehicle were taken as that which has altruistic mind-generation and proceeds by way of the six perfections [without qualifying that it does not have other paths such as the two stages and so forth], then the Vajra Vehicle would also be a Perfection Vehicle.

"Cause Vehicle" is to be taken as not meditatively cultivating a path that accords in aspect with the four fruits mentioned earlier [abode, body, resources, and activities of a Buddha] and only meditatively cultivating their causes.

Reasons for Division of Great Vehicle into a Perfection Vehicle and a Vajra Vehicle

This has two parts: the statement of points generating qualms in the discriminative and a response.

Statement of Points Generating Qualms in the Discriminative

Why is the Great Vehicle divided into two vehicles? It is not from the viewpoint of generating an aspiration to highest enlightenment for the sake of all sentient beings because even both Bodhisattvas practicing by way of Mantra and by way of the Perfection Vehicle are equally engaged toward attaining complete Buddhahood for the sake of all sentient beings. Hence, since there is also no difference of superiority and inferiority in the enlightenment that they seek for this purpose, it is not reasonable to divide the Great Vehicle into two vehicles also from that viewpoint.

The division is also not from the viewpoint of whether or not they have the view realizing the suchness of phenomena because there is no view surpassing the Superior Nāgārjuna's delineation in his *Treatise on the Middle* of the thought of the definitive sūtras, such as the *Perfection of Wisdom Sūtras* and so forth, and even if there were, it could not establish the existence of individual vehicles—just as even though the Perfection Vehicle has a Middle Way School and a Mind-Only School, these two do not constitute individual vehicles. Also, practice of the six perfections exists in both the Perfection and Vajra Vehicles. Hence, a difference with respect to the main paths—method and wisdom—for achieving the Form and Truth Bodies of a Buddha is not seen, and though the Vajra Vehicle does have some features of paths that do not exist in the Perfection Vehicle, these are not features of the main paths; therefore, merely through these the vehicles cannot be posited as separate.

Also, separate vehicles cannot be posited by the mere existence of a difference of sharpness or dullness of faculties in persons [who train in these paths] or in the speed of progress on the paths, just as even though the Perfection Vehicle has many of those differences, it does not have separate vehicles. Otherwise, within the Mantra Vehicle itself many separate vehicles would have to be posited.

Response

The response is in two parts: refutation of positions conjectured by others and presentation of the well-grounded position.

Refutation of Positions Conjectured by Others on the Reason for Dividing the Great Vehicle into a Perfection Vehicle and a Vajra Vehicle

Some say, "Mantra was propounded for the sake of taming desirous trainees, and the Perfection Vehicle for the sake of training trainees free from desire; therefore, meditative cultivation of a path without abandoning desire or of a path that abandons desire is the reason dividing the Great Vehicle into two vehicles."

About this let me explain: If the Great Vehicle were divided into two vehicles because among the trainees of these two vehicles there are those who cultivate the path without having abandoned desire and those who cultivate a path abandoning desire, then since both vehicles have both, this feature cannot distinguish the vehicles:

- because there are many householder Bodhisattvas who have entered the path of the Perfection Vehicle but have not abandoned impure deeds, and there are also many skilled in method who out of great altruism act impurely, as in the case of the Brahmin Khyiu Karma (*khyi'u skar ma / khye'u skar ma*)
- and because among the trainees of the Mantra Vehicle there also are many who have abandoned attachment to the attributes of the desire realm; otherwise, there would be the fault that one could not be freed from the desires of the desire realm until Buddhahood, or the fault that, having attained Buddhahood, one would still not have abandoned the desires of the desire realm.

Objection: This is not to be applied to any and all trainees of the Mantra and Perfection Vehicles; it is to be taken within the framework of the special or main trainees who are initially entering these paths. Furthermore, a trainee of the Mantra Vehicle is not just someone who is suitable for cultivating the paths of that vehicle without having intentionally abandoned desire for the attributes of the desire realm; whether someone is or is not a trainee of the Mantra Vehicle is determined by whether or not one has the good fortune [of having formerly accumulated meritorious actions] such that desire can become a cause of liberation through its being able to act as an aid in the path.

Answer: In accordance with the explanation below[36] of the statement [in the *Saṃpuṭa Tantra*[37]]:

> The four aspects of laughing, gazing,
> Holding hands and the two embracing
> Reside as the four tantras
> In the manner of insects.

it indeed must be asserted that the trainees of the four tantras each have a particular usage of pleasure in the path in dependence on four types of desire for the attributes of the desire realm [that is, the desire involved in laughing, gazing, holding hands, and union], but although such is suitable if it is used as a difference between persons who are initially entering the Mantra Vehicle or Perfection Vehicles, it is not a means of differentiating the vehicles.

Similarly, the Great Vehicle also cannot be divided into a Mantra Vehicle and a Perfection Vehicle through the features of whether their paths are or are not adorned with bliss or whether concentration occurs on essential points in the body and mind. "Adorned with bliss" might [mistakenly] be taken to mean that through having cultivated the path a special bliss arises in the body and a special joy in the mind and through the power of these the mind abides steadily on its object. [However,] Asaṅga's Treatises on the Grounds says that for all those who initially achieve calm abiding, first a pliantly serviceable physical wind is generated [in the body], and it produces great bliss in the body, and then in dependence upon the generation—through its power—of a special joy in the mind, the mind comes to calmly abide on its object of observation. Therefore, because those [that is, special physical bliss and special mental joy] exist in calm abiding for both Outer or Inner [non-Buddhist or Buddhist], how then could these differentiate the Mantra and Perfection paths! Since I have explained this extensively in my *Stages of the Path Common to the Vehicles,* I will not elaborate on it here.

If you think that the meaning of "adorned with bliss" is to be taken as realizing the meaning of suchness in dependence on a "melting bliss" relying on advice for achieving the special essential of the meeting and staying together of the white and red minds of enlightenment,[38] this is not reasonable for separately positing the general Vajra Vehicle and the Perfection Vehicle because it is a feature only of Highest Mantra [Highest Yoga Tantra]. Through this reasoning, you should understand that focusing on essential points in the mind and body also is not feasible as a feature differentiating the two vehicles.

Presentation of the Well-Grounded Position on Dividing the Great Vehicle into a Perfection Vehicle and a Vajra Vehicle

This has two parts: the actual reason for dividing the Great Vehicle into two vehicles and indicating that though the paths differ, their fruits do not differ as to superiority and inferiority.

Actual Reason for Dividing the Great Vehicle into a Perfection Vehicle and a Mantra Vehicle

This has three parts: indicating the reason for the division, citing its sources, and dispelling objections to it.

Indicating the Reason for Dividing the Great Vehicle into a Perfection Vehicle and a Mantra Vehicle

With regard to "vehicle" in the sense of being the fruit to which [trainees] progress, the Mantra and Perfection Vehicles do not differ as to superiority or inferiority because the objects of attainment for both paths are equally the Buddhahood that is an extinguishment of all defects and a completion of all auspicious qualities. Hence, the two differ with respect to the sense of "vehicle" as the causes by which [trainees] progress, and furthermore, concerning this there is no difference in:

- their realization, the view [of emptiness],
- their attitude, mind-generation [an aspiration to highest enlightenment for the sake of all sentient beings],
- or their behavior, mere training in the six perfections;

therefore, they cannot be divided from these points of view.

Question: From what viewpoint are they differentiated?

Answer: The chief aims sought by both types of those of the Great Vehicle are the aims of others, not the enlightenment that is the aim of one's own attainment because seeing Buddhahood as a means to achieve others' aims, they seek it as a branch of the aims of others, because Maitreya's *Ornament for the Clear Realizations* (*abhisamayālaṃkāra,* I.18ab) says:[39]

> Mind-generation is a wish for thoroughly
> Complete enlightenment for the sake of others.

and because altruistic mind-generation is the same [for both Great Vehicles].

The Buddha who, actually appearing to trainees, achieves their aims is not the Truth Body but the two aspects of the Form Body [the Complete Enjoyment Body and Emanation Bodies]. A Truth Body is achieved through the wisdom realizing the profound [emptiness], and Form Bodies are achieved through vast methods. Also, the Two Bodies cannot be achieved with wisdom lacking method or with method lacking wisdom; therefore, the statement "Inseparable wisdom and method are needed," is a general tenet of those of the Great Vehicle.

Without realizing the mode of abiding of phenomena, one cannot cross to the other side of the ocean of cyclic existence upon having extinguished all afflictions; therefore, the wisdom realizing the profound [emptiness] is in common even with the two lower types of Superiors [Hearers and Solitary Realizers]. Hence, the main distinctive feature of Great Vehicle paths must be taken as the methods serving as causes of becoming a protector and refuge for sentient beings as long as cyclic existence lasts, through appearing in Form Bodies to fortunate trainees.

Although those of the Perfection Vehicle have meditation of paths that accord in aspect with the Truth Body through meditating on the suchness of phenomena free of the proliferations [of conventionalities, duality, and the conception of inherent existence], they do not have paths of meditation that are similar in aspect to a Form Body adorned with the marks and beauties, whereas Mantra does. Consequently, there is a great difference in the corpus of the Perfection and Mantra paths with respect to the method for achieving Form Bodies for the welfare of others; due to this, [the Great Vehicle] is treated as two vehicles because:

- in general the Lesser Vehicle and the Great Vehicle must be divided not by the wisdom of emptiness but by method,
- in particular the differentiation of the Great Vehicle into two also is not made on account of the wisdom realizing the profound emptiness but must be made on account of method,
- the chief method also is from the viewpoint of the achievement of Form Bodies,

- and for the achievement of Form Bodies deity yoga—meditation on oneself as having aspects similar to a Form Body—surpasses the methods of other vehicles.

Deity Yoga

Citing Sources [for the Reason for Dividing the Great Vehicle into a Perfection Vehicle and a Vajra Vehicle]

This has two parts: how [the reason for dividing the Great Vehicle into a Perfection Vehicle and a Vajra Vehicle] is explained in the texts of Highest Yoga and how it is explained in the texts of the lower tantras.

How [the Reason for Dividing the Great Vehicle into a Perfection Vehicle and a Vajra Vehicle] Is Explained in the Texts of Highest Yoga

This has two parts: how [the reason for dividing the Great Vehicle into a Perfection Vehicle and a Vajra Vehicle] is explained in [Highest Yoga] tantras and how it is explained in commentaries on their thought.

How [the Reason for Dividing the Great Vehicle into a Perfection Vehicle and a Vajra Vehicle] Is Explained in Highest Yoga Tantras

The first chapter of the *Vajrapañjara Tantra* (*vajrapañjara*)[40] clearly says:

> If emptiness were the method,
> Buddhahood could not be.

Since other than a cause there is no other fruit,
The method is not emptiness.

To overcome the conceptions of self
In those who from [right] views have turned away
And in those who seek the view of self
The Victors teach emptiness.

Therefore through the "circle of a maṇḍala,"
A binding of the blissful method,
The yoga of Buddha pride,
Buddhahood will not be distant.

The Teacher is endowed with thirty-two marks
And possesses the eighty beauties,
Therefore through this method it is achieved.
The method is to have the Teacher's form.

One by one these four stanzas (1) refute the assertion that merely meditating on emptiness is the method, (2) indicate the purpose of teaching emptiness, (3) indicate the uncommon method as well as its greatness, and (4) indicate the reason why [Buddhahood] must be achieved through this method.

First stanza

Concerning this, the first line means: Stemming from the earlier teaching in the *Vajrapañjara* that "Since the mind is polluted with the defilements of one's own conceptuality, one should with all striving purify the mind," one might think, "In that case, to cleanse defilements, one should meditate only on emptiness because the wisdom realizing the suchness of selflessness is itself contradictory in aspect with conceptuality conceiving self [inherent existence], whereas other paths are not contradictory with it. Therefore, the method for developing into the full purity [of a Buddha] is exhausted as only meditation on emptiness, and of what use are other proliferations?"

If that were the case, no matter how one strove at such a method, one could not become a Buddha because other than a cause that is a meditation on emptiness, such is without a method [to achieve] the fruit [of Buddhahood], whereby the branch of method is lacking, and thus the causes are not complete. Therefore, familiarizing only with emptiness is not a complete method. Devakulamahāmati's explanation[41] that this is the system not only of Mantra but also of the Perfection Vehicle is good.

SECOND STANZA

Question: Then what is the purpose of teaching emptiness?

Answer: Emptiness—selflessness—is taught for the sake of overcoming the two conceptions of self in those who have turned away from the views of the selflessness of phenomena and so forth and in those who seek the view of a self [of persons] in the sense that they strongly adhere to a conception of it. This shows that in order to cleanse the defilements of conceptualizations of the two types of self [inherent existence of persons and of phenomena] one definitely must seek and thereupon meditatively cultivate the view realizing suchness—selflessness; these points are similar in the Perfection [Vehicle]. This explanation of the two lines "In those who from [right] views have turned away/And in those who seek the view of self," accords with the thought of Devakulamahāmati's commentary on the *Vajrapañjara*.

THIRD STANZA

Question: If the method is not complete in mere meditation on emptiness, what is the special method?

Answer: Because mere meditation on emptiness is not feasible as the method, the special method is that said to be "the circle of a maṇḍala" [a "resident maṇḍala" which is a divine body and a "residence maṇḍala" which is the deity's abode]. This is how the stanzas should be connected.

In Devakulamahāmati's commentary on the *Vajrapañjara*[42] the next line is translated [into Tibetan] as "The method is a blissful binding" (*thabs ni bde ba'i sdom pa ste*); this is a better translation [than the one given above, "A binding of the blissful method" (*bde ba'i thabs kyi sdom pa ste*)]. Here, this is an occasion of teaching a method surpassing that of the Perfection Vehicle, and since it has been shown that mere meditation on emptiness is not a complete method, the method to be added to meditation on emptiness is said to be deity yoga, whereby meditation on a maṇḍala circle [divine resident and residence] is known to be the main method for [achieving] a Form Body. The features of this method are two, blissfulness and binding. Blissfulness is nonreliance on asceticism. Although many modes of binding are set forth in the *Hevajra Tantra,* on this occasion binding should be taken as an indivisibility of method—appearing in aspect as a divine circle—and wisdom—realizing its nature as empty of inherent existence.

The statement that "Through such a yoga of method and wisdom in which one cultivates the pride of a Buddha such as Vairochana, one attains the state of a Buddha without the passage of a long time as in the Perfection Vehicle," is an expression of the greatness of this path. The description of deity yoga as a quick path refutes wrong conceptions that deity yoga is useless for achieving the supreme.

Fourth stanza

Question: Well then why is it that in order to achieve a Form Body one needs a yoga bearing the pride of a Buddha having the aspect of a maṇḍala circle?

Answer: The *Vajrapañjara* says:

The Teacher is endowed with thirty-two marks
And possesses the eighty beauties,
Therefore through this method it is achieved.
The method is to have the Teacher's form.

Taking as the reason that the object of attainment—a Form Body—is adorned with the marks and beauties, it is said that the fruit must be achieved through a method that has the form, or aspect, of a Teacher [Buddha].

In the other two commentaries on the *Vajrapañjara* [by Kṛṣhṇapāda[43] and by Indrabodhi[44]] it does not appear that qualms are eradicated and [that the topic is] clearly explained, but such is done in Devakulamahāmati's commentary[45] [even though not all of it is correct]. The explanation in his commentary—at the point of refuting the assertion in the first two lines that mere meditation on emptiness is the method—that "If one cultivates only an emptiness lacking method, one will be born in an unfortunate existence such as in Limitless Space and so forth," is not seen to be feasible [because one actually could become a Lesser Vehicle Foe Destroyer].

Then, in answer to the proposition that "On the occasion of the path emptiness is the method and on the occasion of maturation emptiness is the fruit," Devakulamahāmati explains that since the emptiness both of the cause, or path, and of the fruit, or maturation, would have no other distinctive features, emptiness—while it was being asserted as the fruit—could not also be the method. He explains that since the cause is an elaborative entity involving apprehension [of inherent existence] and the effect is the opposite, the cause and the effect are established as different; therefore, the method is not solely emptiness.

[His explanation of] the purpose for teaching emptiness is the same as that given above. Then, to clear away the qualm, "If it is taught in the Perfection Vehicle that enlightenment is achieved through the practice—for three countless eons—of the perfection of wisdom conjoined with the other five perfections, what is the use of methods such as a maṇḍala circle and so forth?" Devakulamahāmati explains the four lines:

> Therefore through the "circle of a maṇḍala,"
> A binding of the blissful method,
> The yoga of Buddha pride,
> Buddhahood will not be distant.

[He explains] bliss here is as it was above. He says that "binding" is to experience the bliss of the union of the two organs [which actually is limited to Highest Yoga Tantra], and "Buddha pride" he [correctly] explains as being free from the pride of ordinariness, and "not be distant" he explains as attaining [Buddhahood] in this life [but this is also limited to Highest Yoga Tantra].

Then to clear away the qualm wondering whether "A Buddha Body is to be cultivated in the mode of a Truth Body [in meditative equipoise on emptiness alone]," it appears that Devakulamahāmati explains the four lines:

> The Teacher is endowed with thirty-two marks
> And possesses the eighty beauties,
> Therefore through this method it is achieved.
> The method is to have the Teacher's form.

He explains that the method is the three meditative stabilizations having the form of the Three Bodies.

That here many Tibetan lamas have applied the teaching of deity yoga—a maṇḍala circle—only to the first stage of Highest Yoga Tantra [the stage of generation] is the fault of not discriminating between the respective greater and lesser extent of deity yoga [which actually occurs in the three lower tantras and in both stages of Highest Yoga] and the stage of generation [which occurs only in Highest Yoga and is the first of its two stages]. Hence, deity yoga should be taken as occurring in both stages [generation-stage and completion-stage in Highest Yoga Tantra].

The greater basis of wrong ideas that reject deity yoga as a method for achieving the supreme [state of Buddhahood] is this wrong conception that meditation on emptiness itself is the means for achieving both Bodies. I have quoted the *Vajrapañjara* because it clearly appears to plainly eliminate this qualm and thereupon say that deity yoga must be meditatively cultivated as a cause of a Form Body. Hence, with this as an illustration, the teachings of the other tantras also should be understood. Fearing it would be too much, I will not cite them here.

How [the Reason for Dividing the Great Vehicle into a Perfection Vehicle and a Vajra Vehicle] Is Explained in Highest Yoga Commentaries

This has two parts: how [the reason for dividing the Great Vehicle into a Perfection Vehicle and a Vajra Vehicle] is explained in the master Jñānapāda's texts and how [the reason for dividing the Great Vehicle into a Perfection Vehicle and a Vajra Vehicle] is explained by other masters.

How [the Reason for Dividing the Great Vehicle into a Perfection Vehicle and a Vajra Vehicle] Is Explained in the Master Jñānapāda's Texts

A very clear affirmation in accordance with what is taught by the tantra quoted above is set forth by the great master Jñānapāda in his *Engaging in the Means of Self-Achievement* (*ātmasādhanāvatāra*). Concerning this, first he sets out the way of the Perfection Vehicle[46] saying:

> If cultivation of selflessness lacks the specifics of method,
> it cannot generate a pristine wisdom of omniscience free
> from all taints of conceptuality and aiding all migrators;

> therefore, one should intensively strive at a very manifest method. The nature of helping all beings is an omniscient pristine wisdom, and help moreover arises from vastness that has reached consummation. Its cause also is only cultivation of method because cultivation of selflessness has the fruit of only forsaking conceptuality. Further, [Maitreya's *Ornament for the Great Vehicle Sūtras*] says:
>
> > Because of profundity and because of vastness
> > These two [wisdom and method] are taught for the two,
> > Nonconceptuality and full maturation,
> > Therefore, they are the unsurpassed method.
>
> Hence, nonerroneous activities of mind, such as giving and so forth, are the method because when they are thoroughly dedicated to omniscience, they become causes of complete enlightenment. Moreover, [the *Condensed Perfection of Wisdom Sūtra*] says:
>
> > Thoroughly dedicate to enlightenment
> > Giving, ethics, patience, effort, concentration, and wisdom.
> > Do not hold enlightenment to be supreme adhering
> > To it as a mass.[47] It is taught that way to beginners.

The meaning of these statements [by Jñānapāda]: If one lacks the vast method, no matter how much one familiarizes with selflessness, one does not attain Buddhahood which serves as the nurture of all migrators; therefore, one must strive at method, and this state helping the entirety of sentient beings is also the imprint [result] only of familiarizing with vast method because the imprint of familiarizing with selflessness is an abandonment—only an extinguishment of defilements.

This does not teach that through meditation on emptiness, without the vast method, one can extinguish all defilements but cannot bring about the welfare of all sentient beings. Nor does it teach that through cultivating only the vast method without meditation on emptiness one can attain a Form Body that brings about the welfare of all sentient beings, but cannot attain a Truth Body—which is an extinguishment of all defilements. For, with respect to the Truth Body and Form Bodies, it is impossible to have attained the one without having attained the other because since Truth and Form Bodies have the definite relation of relying on one causal collection, they are never separated.

Moreover, since the wisdom realizing emptiness that is impelled by the precious mind of enlightenment [that is, impelled by the aspiration to enlightenment for the sake of all sentient beings] purifies all the defilements conceiving self, it is the uncommon cause of a Truth Body endowed with the two purities [natural purity and purity from adventitious stains], but it is also a cooperative condition of Form Bodies. Similarly, although the vast methods are the uncommon causes of Form Bodies, they are also cooperative conditions of a Truth Body because if one does not strive at vast methods, no matter how much one familiarizes with the suchness of things, it is possible only to leave cyclic existence but one cannot arrive at a Truth Body which is an extinguishment of all defilements and because if one does not strive at the wisdom realizing emptiness, no matter how much one strives at vast methods, one cannot arrive at Form Bodies.

Nevertheless, the extinguishment of all defilements upon becoming a Buddha must be taken as an imprint of having meditated on emptiness, whereas becoming the sustenance of all migrators must be taken as the imprint of vast methods. For example, it is like the fact that although since all three conditions must be present to produce an eye consciousness apprehending blue, the eye consciousness is indeed an effect of all three, nevertheless its apprehension of a visible form and not other objects, such as sounds, is an imprint of the eye sense; its being generated as an experiential entity is the imprint of the immediately preceding condition [a former moment of consciousness]; and its being generated in the image of blue is the imprint of the observed-object-condition [the blue object].

The passage from Maitreya's *Ornament for the Great Vehicle Sūtras,* cited above:

> Because of profundity and because of vastness
> These two [wisdom and method] are taught for the two,
> Nonconceptuality and full maturation,
> Therefore, they are the unsurpassed method.

is a source showing that if both factors, method and wisdom, are complete, they are the unsurpassed means for achieving the fruit. The passage from the *Condensed Perfection of Wisdom Sūtra,* cited above:

> Thoroughly dedicate to enlightenment
> Giving, ethics, patience, effort, concentration, and wisdom.
> Do not hold enlightenment to be supreme adhering
> To it as a mass.[48] It is taught that way to beginners.

is a source showing that if the methods for achieving Buddhahood—giving and so forth—are dedicated to enlightenment and conjoined with the wisdom of nonapprehension [of inherent existence], they become [actual] methods [capable of causing attainment of Buddhahood].

After that, Jñānapāda sets forth the special method of the Mantra Vehicle:[49] "That is not so in fact because aside from cultivating different causes there is no meditation that accords with actualized complete enlightenment." The meaning of this is:

> The giving and so forth described as the method, which are explained to be method that is unsurpassed, or with respect to which there is none higher, are not that way because they lack meditation that accords in aspect with an actualized Buddha Body, because [in the Perfection Vehicle] one cultivates only paths completely different in aspect from the fruit [of a Form Body].

Establishing that if [a system] has no cultivation of a path that accords in aspect with a Form Body, it is not an unsurpassed method for achieving Buddhahood [Jñānapāda] says in that text:[50]

> The fruits that by their own entity have a nature of profundity and vastness are achieved from their own nature.

Concerning this, in general "the fruits" to be attained are a Truth Body with "a nature of profundity" and [a Form Body] adorned with the marks and beauties with a nature of "vastness." Moreover, that even both

- exalted mind entered in equipoise as one taste with the suchness of phenomena and never rising from it and
- at that very time exalted body, adorned with the flaming marks and beauties, abiding without ever showing change

are undifferentiable in one entity is the meaning of "by their own entity." Thus, the method and wisdom that achieve such also must accord with them; for example, just as when [practicing to] achieve the exalted mind of a Victor—a Truth Body—yogis place their mind now in the meaning of the suchness of phenomena and meditatively cultivate a path that accords in aspect with the exalted mind of a Victor, so also when [practicing to] achieve a Form Body, yogis must meditatively cultivate a path that accords in aspect with an exalted Body in that their own body appears having the aspects of the marks and beauties, because a Truth Body and a Form Body are thoroughly similar in the sense that if the one path of similar aspect is practiced, the other should be practiced, and if the one is omitted, the other should be omitted. In consideration of this, Jñānapāda's *Self-Achievement* says:[51]

> Therefore, as in the case with selflessness one should meditate on the nature of vastness in the manner of nondifference.

The vastness of this system is to be taken as deity yoga; I will explain later [in the section on Highest Yoga Tantra] how it is vast. He speaks of achieving through such a way as "achieved from their own nature."

Just as on the occasion of the fruit the two:

(1) the support, a body adorned with the marks and beauties, and
(2) the mind of nonapprehension [of inherent existence] which depends on it

abide at one time as an undifferentiable entity, so on the occasion of the path also the two:

(1) the method that is the yogi's body appearing to the yogi's own mind in the aspect of a One-Gone-Thus's body, and
(2) the wisdom that is the yogi's own mind at that time apprehending the suchness of phenomena, the absence of inherent existence,

must be taken as undifferentiable method and wisdom, a simultaneous composite, undifferentiable in the entity of one consciousness. This is because through familiarizing with the yoga of joining these two at the same time, in the end the state in which nondualistic pristine wisdom itself appears as Form Bodies to trainees is attained.

If even the supreme of methods, which is the appearance as a deity in this way, is devoid of the wisdom that is unmistaken realization of the nature of one's own mind, is thus bereft of wisdom, one cannot progress to Buddhahood; therefore, it is necessary to have a composite of the two. [To indicate this] Jñānapāda's *Self-Achievement*[52] says:

> Since a Subduer endowed with immeasurable effulgence of light serves as a foundation of limitless marvels for oneself and others, even if this having the character of being the supreme right method were manifestly cultivated but bereft due to being devoid of wisdom, it would not be a means of achieving all marvels; therefore, the nature of that [divine body] should be known without mistake.

That very wisdom realizing the absence of inherent existence and whose apprehended-aspect (*gzung rnam*) appears in the aspect of a deity is one entity with the mind of deity yoga, which is the vast, but the positing of method and wisdom as different is by force of the convention of different isolates relative to the fact that their opposites are different as follows:

- Wisdom is posited from the viewpoint of being the opposite of a mind that mistakenly apprehends the meaning of suchness because knowledge of the ultimate [emptiness] —the finality of objects of knowledge—is the supreme knowledge.
- Method is posited from the viewpoint of being the opposite of that which does not have the capacity of achieving its fruit, Buddhahood, because the methods of Buddhahood are capable of achieving Buddhahood.

In this way also Jñānapāda's *Self-Achievement*[53] says:

> Even if those [wisdom and method] also are one character with the unmistaken vast mind, the convention of

> difference causes the understanding that they are different. It is thus: Wisdom is known by way of an entity opposite from a mind mistaken about suchness, and the opposite from not capable with respect to its fruit is indicated to be method.

Even though here Jñānapāda is describing the procedure of establishing method and wisdom in a general way, at this point the bases [he uses] for positing method and wisdom are the special method and wisdom of Mantra.

In this way, nondualistically joining method and wisdom which are such that

- through the appearance of the apprehended-factor (*gzung cha*) [of the wisdom apprehending emptiness] as a divine maṇḍala circle a Form Body is achieved,
- and through the realization of [its] nature, emptiness, a Truth Body is achieved

should be known as the meaning of the method and wisdom and of the chief yogas set forth in Mantra.

Method in the Four Tantras

How [the Reason for Dividing the Great Vehicle into a Perfection Vehicle and a Vajra Vehicle] Is Explained by Other Masters of Highest Yoga

Ratnākarashāntipāda's *Commentary on (Dīpaṅkarabhadra's) "Four Hundred and Fifty"* (*guhyasamājamaṇḍalavidhiṭīkā*)[54] says:

> If one meditatively cultivates only [a path] having the nature of a deity, one will not become fully enlightened merely through this because the fulfillment of [yogic] activities is not complete. Or, if one meditates on the suchness of deities and not on deities, one will attain Buddhahood in many countless eons but not quickly. Hence, through meditating on both, one will attain the highest perfect complete enlightenment supremely quickly because to do so is very appropriate and has special empowering blessings.

Thus, Ratnākarashāntipāda says that if one cultivates only deity yoga, one simply cannot become fully enlightened, and if one does not meditate on a deity, through meditation on emptiness accompanied by other methods one will become fully enlightened over many countless eons, and if one meditates both on a deity and on emptiness, the path is faster. Therefore, this master also asserts that since the view of emptiness is common to both Great Vehicles, without deity yoga the path is extended like the Perfection Vehicle, but through joining deity yoga with the view of emptiness the path is quick. Ratnākarashānti is following the explanation above [in the *Vajrapañjara* and the *Self-Achievement*].

Also, in the eighteenth cluster of *Clusters of Quintessential Instructions* (*āmnāyamañjari*)[55] Abhayākara explains the method in accordance with Ratnākarashānti and quotes as a source the fourteenth chapter of the *Vajrapañjara:*[56]

> To overcome pride of ordinariness
> This meditation is known to be perfect.

And:[57]

> However, for the sake of purifying the unclean body one should meditate on a Buddha Body.

Also, Durjayachandra in his commentary on the first chapter of the *Hevajra Tantra*[58] quotes the first and fourteenth chapters of the *Vajrapañjara* and explains that causes cannot achieve an effect that is not concordant with them. Shrīdhara, in his *Innate Illumination, Commentary on the Difficult Points of the Yamāri Tantra* (*yamāritantrapañjikāsahajāloka*),[59] says:

> It should not be said that [Form Bodies] will arise through methods, such as giving and so forth, and by the power of prayer petitions. How could one who hesitates about those having the nature of complete enjoyment [an Enjoyment Body] and emanation [an Emanation Body] which are not being meditated become firm in mind [about them]?
>
> One might think, "Still, these will arise by the power of prayer-petitions." Then, since without having meditated on selflessness, [a Truth Body] could become manifest, what would be the use of the hardship of meditating on selflessness?
>
> One might think, "[A Truth Body] arises through meditation." Then what is wrong with a Complete

> Enjoyment Body and an Emanation Body? Why not meditate on them? Even those abiding in the Perfection Vehicle assert a Buddhahood having an essence of Three Bodies. Through meditation on them they will manifest.

The parallel is drawn that if one meditates on selflessness which has the aspect of a Truth Body, one must also do so on a deity which has the aspect of a Form Body, and if one does not, it is the same as asserting that without meditating on selflessness, a Truth Body can be actualized.

As sources for this Shrīdhara[60] also quotes the teaching:

> The cause of achieving Buddhahood
> Is Buddha yoga. Is it not seen
> Thoroughly that cause and effect
> Are thoroughly similar?

and furthermore the *All Secret* (*sarvarahasya,* a Yoga Tantra):[61]

> In brief even Buddhahood definitely
> Arises from stabilization and pristine wisdom.
> Without including Buddha yoga
> A yogi does not attain Buddhahood.

Samayavajra explains it similarly in his *Commentary on the Kṛṣhṇayamāri Tantra* (*kṛṣṇayamāritantrarājaṭīkā*),[62] as does Jinadatta in his *Commentary on the Difficult Points of the Guhyasamāja Tantra* (*guhyasamājatantrapañjikā*).[63]

Vinayadatta also explains the method at length in his *Rite of the Great Illusion Maṇḍala* (*mahāmāyāmaṇḍalopāyika*):[64] This meaning was spoken by the holy guru himself:

> Meditating that one is a Form Body and Truth Body,
> O, enlightenment is definitely attained.

> If through a Victor's concentration a Truth Body is gained,
> Why is a Form Body not meditated upon?
>
> Though a Form Body is attained through a collection of merit,
> That takes long and is thus lower than the other.
> From the features of causes having the features of the effects
> The Three Bodies simultaneously appear.

Though there are many other sources in treatises, I have cited them because they are clear.

How [the Reason for Dividing the Great Vehicle into a Perfection Vehicle and a Vajra Vehicle] Is Explained in the Texts of the Lower Tantras

In his *Self-Achievement* [a Highest Yoga text] Jñānapāda says that the vast deity yoga constitutes the difference in method between the Perfection and Mantra Vehicles; he proves this by citing a passage on deity generation by way of the [five] manifest enlightenments in [the Yoga Tantra] *Compendium of Principles* (*tattvasaṃgraha*), and he also clearly explains how the deities of the vajra element [a topic distinctive to Yoga Tantra] are all contained in this yoga.[65] Therefore, he asserts that deity yoga is a feature of the method not only of Highest Yoga but also of Yoga Tantra. Similarly, other masters' explanations [of deity yoga] indeed occur on occasions of explaining Highest Yoga, but it is the same in all tantra sets in which one generates oneself in the aspect of a deity because the reasons for needing to meditate this way are similar. However, deity yoga is also frequently mentioned in Yoga Tantras; the first section of the *Compendium of Principles*[66] says:

> If one meditates on a Buddha Body
> With one's own fine particles

Of body, speech, and mind as vajras,
One will become a complete Buddha.

In commentary on this, Shākyamitra's *Ornament of Kosala* (*kosalālaṃkāratattvasaṃgrahaṭīkā*) says:

> [This means:] If one meditates in four sessions each day on a Buddha Body by way of the disciplinary yoga of mental application through meditating on one's finest particles as vajras and so forth. What feat will be attained through meditating [on oneself] as having a Buddha body? It says, "One will become a complete Buddha." This means that one will attain a Buddha body adorned with the marks and beauties.

Ānandagarbha's commentary on the first part of the *Compendium of Principles Tantra* called *Illumination of the Principles* (*tattvāloka*)[67] also states:

> [This is said] in order to realize that those practicing the approach of Secret Mantra also should cultivate recollection of a Buddha; they should recollect a Form Body and the final nature of a One-Gone-Thus.

and:

> One should maintain an abiding in the center of all Ones-Gone-Thus; one should meditate [on oneself] in the manner of a Truth Body and a Form Body conjoined with [a Buddha], not of different nature but undifferentiable, until one has vividly seen oneself [as a Buddha].

Since it is very clear that a Truth Body is achieved by the wisdom realizing emptiness, I will not cite sources.

The way that deity yoga is also put forth in the texts of Action and Performance Tantras is as follows. Buddhaguhya's

Condensation of the Vairochanābhisaṃbodhi (*vairocanābhisaṃbodhitantrapiṇḍārtha*) says:

> In accordance with the order of the two [yogas] with and without signs, the entities of divine bodies are taught as two aspects from the viewpoint of thoroughly impure and thoroughly pure bodies. Moreover, about this the thoroughly pure is the entity of the signless meditative stabilization on a Truth Body having the nature of aspectless pristine wisdom. The thoroughly impure are posited as entities of imputed forms, having the character of the Buddhas' Bodies of Complete Enjoyment and Emanation and with color and shape through the force of appearing to beings who are trainees.

Thus, two yogas—meditations in accordance with the aspects of the Two Bodies—are taught; this is similar in both Action and Performance Tantras.

Though the two Great Vehicles do not differ in superiority or inferiority with respect to view, that they are divided by way of the vast—deity yoga—is also clearly stated in Ratnākarashānti's *Presentation of the Three Vehicles* (*triyānavyavasthāna*):[68]

> A second ultimate truth superior to the ultimate truth presented by the Supramundane Victor, Nāgārjuna, and so forth does not exist. Through mere conventionalities how could it become more vast?
>
> Because of a very pure object,
> The power of aids, and also deeds,
> The vehicle of the intelligent
> Is renowned as the greatest of the great.

He explains that:

1. one realizes oneself as having the nature of a very pure deity
2. empowering blessings are generated through keeping the pledges of the Victors
3. acting in accordance with the deeds of the Victors and their children, one brings about the welfare of sentient beings and acts to purify lands

whereby the objects of observation, aids, and concordant deeds are more extensive, due to which the Mantra Vehicle is superior to the Middle Way School of the Perfection Vehicle. And because he explains that the vehicle having these three attributes has the divisions of Action, Performance, Yoga, and Highest Yoga tantra sets, he asserts that these three attributes are general features of Mantra.

In brief, that the two—(1) the view ascertaining the absence of inherent existence, which is that phenomena are empty of establishment by way of their own nature, and (2) the deity yoga of generating oneself as a deity—conjointly achieve the fruit, the Two Bodies, is treated as the sole path of passage of all the chief trainees for whom the Vajra Vehicle was set forth. Within this context, you should hold as crucial the knowledge that, among the many paths explained in the individual tantra sets other than these two, some are methods for heightening realization of emptiness and some are branches of deity yoga.

Dispelling Objections

Someone says: It is not reasonable to posit inferiority and superiority using the reason that the Perfection Vehicle does not have a cause similar to a Form Body whereas the Mantra Vehicle does because it is not at all certain that an effect is always achieved through a cause that is similar to the effect, because if in order to achieve the effect that is a body adorned with the marks and beauties, it were necessary for its cause also to be meditative cultivation of a path that has the aspects of the marks and beauties, then it would entail very absurd consequences:

- it would be necessary also to meditatively cultivate a path that has the aspects of the marks and beauties as a cause for achieving a body adorned with the auspicious marks of, for instance, a Universal Monarch,[69]
- and similarly also on all occasions of accumulating the causes for acquiring a body of a happy migration or of a bad migration one would have to achieve causes having the aspect of those two types of migrators.

However, if it is not necessary to have a cause that accords in aspect with these effects, you must put forth a correct reason why the need for such must be applied to Buddhahood, but that also is not to be found. Therefore, "That a Form Body is achieved by means of a path having the aspect of a Form Body is a distinctive feature of the Mantra Vehicle," is reduced to being merely an object of faith!

Response to this: According to those of the Perfection Vehicle, through the force of having accumulated over many lives the causes of the entity of a Form Body, which are the supreme collections of merit, and the causes of a Form Body's features, the marks and beauties and so forth, which are to provide welcoming and parting escort for a guru and so on, Bodhisattvas—when they have arrived at a high ground—attain a body adorned with similitudes of the marks and beauties. These also become more and more sublime, and finally during the Bodhisattva's last lifetime the consummate marks and beauties of a learner are attained. When, at that time, on this foundation they actualize a Truth Body, this similar type of the physical marks and beauties becomes an Enjoyment Body. [Thus, the Perfection Vehicle] does not assert that without the existence of marks and beauties while on the path, these newly arise immediately upon attaining the fruit. Similarly, those of the Vajra Vehicle also do not assert that when Buddhahood is achieved in one lifetime, the consummate marks and beauties adventitiously arise without the existence, when on the path, of marks and beauties that accord with the marks and beauties of a nonlearner. Thus, it is the system of both Great Vehicles that if on the path of learning the marks and beauties are absent, a Form Body cannot be achieved.

In Mantra it is not said that beginners engaging in Mantra who will become fully enlightened in the present life must have been adorned with the marks and beauties on their body right from birth; also, such does not exist. Therefore, marks and beauties of their own body cannot be posited as acting as causes of marks and beauties of a Form Body; hence, through meditation they must newly achieve in this life a cause that is similar in type to the marks and beauties, and this moreover is not feasible other than through deity yoga.

In that case,

1. with respect to achieving a body of a happy or bad migration, the accumulation of causes that have such aspects at the time of the causes is not needed,
2. and prior to the achievement of a Buddha's Form Body causes that accord in aspect with it are needed.

How could these two be similar! We do not assert that one must cultivate a path that has the aspect of a Form Body for a *cause of maturation* (*rnam smin gyi rgyu*) in the sense of taking birth as a Form Body; rather, we assert that prior to achieving a Buddha's marks and beauties one needs *causes of similar type* (*rigs mthun gyi rgyu*) that accord with those. Therefore, this is not a source of dispute.

Question: Well then, how are:

- meditative cultivation of deity yoga in the three lower tantra sets
- and meditative cultivation of deity yoga even in Highest Yoga Tantra in situations when Buddhahood is achieved not in this lifetime but must be over a continuum of lives

concordant causes of a Form Body?

Answer: Even in these cases, familiarization in this way in this lifetime serves as a cause of similar type (*rigs mthun gyi rgyu*) when finally in another birth they achieve a Form Body in that lifetime, but it is not a cause of maturation (*rnam smin gyi rgyu*) in the sense of being born with a Form Body.

Having thus eliminated well the qualms as set forth, you must gain conviction that cultivation of deity yoga is indispensable; the first chapter of the *Vajraḍāka Tantra* (*vajraḍāka*, a Highest Yoga Tantra) says:

> Oneself is all Buddhas
> And all the Heroes themselves.
> Through union with one's own deity
> Its nature is thoroughly achieved.
>
> Through this all Buddhas,
> And all the Heroes themselves,
> And all Vajradharas
> Are achieved in this very life.
>
> Vajraḍākas, Vajrasattvas,
> One-Gone-Thuses, and glorious
> Supramundane Victors having supreme bliss
> In union with all Sky Goers say this.

and:

> Through this application of a Seal
> They eat all the three grounds [of form].
> Otherwise, the application is not complete,
> And they pass away like a flame.

and Bhavabhadra's *Commentary on the Vajraḍāka* (*vajraḍākavivṛti*)[70] explains:

> "Through this" [means] through this Seal of emptiness [a divine body qualified by emptiness] mentioned just before. This language is used for one who applies in an equal manner [the wisdom of emptiness and the method of deity yoga through] a conventional Seal with hands, face, and so forth. What do these yogis do? "They eat all the three grounds." This means that they overcome ordinary forms such as a body and so forth. In order to indicate that through mere concentration on emptiness enlightenment will not be achieved, the text says, "If otherwise, the application cannot be complete, and they pass away like a flame." "Otherwise" means "through only emptiness." "The application is not be complete" means that they have passed beyond appearance. "Pass away" means that they pass away from sorrow without even [fulfilling] their own welfare. How? Like a flame. A flame shines and burns into the sky by way of a continuum of oil, but when the oil is consumed, it too is extinguished and ends; hence, if the flame does not then even illumine itself, what need is there to mention anything about its illumining others! One should similarly view meditative stabilization only on emptiness.

Therefore, it is the excellent thought of the tantra sets that if the path of Mantra does not have meditative cultivation of deity yoga, no matter how much familiarization with emptiness and so forth there is, then on the occasion of the fruit, falling to an extreme of [solitary] peace cannot be prevented. If conviction is not gained well in these points, you should know that having forsaken deity yoga, you will train in only a portion of the Mantra path, due to which you will have utterly not found the body of the path.

One Goal

Though the Paths Differ, Their Fruits Do Not Differ as to Superiority and Inferiority

This has two parts: explaining the actual meaning and explaining the difference between the Perfection and Mantra paths.

Explaining the Actual Meaning of the Different Paths' Not Having Different Fruits

Someone says: If the paths of the two vehicles differ in superiority and inferiority, then the Buddhahoods that are their objects of attainment must also differ in superiority and inferiority because if the causes differ, it would be contradictory if the effects did not, because otherwise, the difference in causes would be senseless. Therefore, the eleventh ground of complete light is lower than the rank of Vajradhara because the fourth chapter of the first division of the *Saṃpuṭa Tantra*[71] explains that the two—Buddhahood, which is attained over ten million or countless eons, and Vajradharahood—are different:

> In brief the Buddhahood
> Attained over countless
> Or ten million eons
> You will attain in this birth
> Through the most excellent bliss,
> Or Vajradharahood.

and it also says:[72]

> In this birth you will attain Buddhahood or Vajrasattvahood. Those who have not attained the inconceivable state are Ones-Gone-to-Bliss, Buddhas. To illustrate what is to be illustrated [that is, the one who attains the inconceivable state] they are called [Vajra]sattva.

Response: This [explanation] is not feasible because that passage does not teach that through the path of Highest Yoga one achieves in a single life either the ground of complete light which is described in the Perfection Vehicle or the ground of Vajradhara which is described in Mantra and because not even those of the Perfection Vehicle assert that there is no difference between the two—[the tenth Bodhisattva ground called] "Buddha" which is attained over countless eons and the eleventh ground of complete light. For, about the two types of Buddhas attained over countless eons, Maitreya's *Ornament for the Clear Realizations* (I.70) speaks about a tenth ground Bodhisattva called a "Buddha":

> Having passed beyond the nine grounds, the pristine wisdom
> Through which one abides on the Buddha ground
> Is to be known as the tenth
> Ground of a Bodhisattva.[73]

whereas the Vajradhara ground [actual Buddhahood] is the eleventh ground. Though there are explanations in Mantra of twelfth, thirteenth, and fourteenth grounds, Indian scholars have described them as classifications of the grounds set forth in the Perfection Vehicle. I will explain this later on the occasion of the fruit [at the end of the section on Highest Yoga Tantra, not translated here].

Therefore, you should know that the eleventh ground of complete light and Vajradhara are treated as equivalent, that the sets of sūtras say it can be achieved over three countless eons, and in the tantra sets in one lifetime. You should not hold that because it is called Vajradhara it is not a fruit of the Perfection Vehicle; this should be taken in accordance with the statement by the glorious Shāntarakṣhita that Vajradharahood is the object of attainment by both paths in his *Work on the Establishment of the Principles* (*tattvasiddhināmaprakaraṇa*):[74]

> The glorious great bliss, Vajrasattva—the object of realization by other paths over many countless eons—is achieved without difficultly in this lifetime itself by those who possess the method of the Vajra Vehicle.

Also, Abhayākara's commentary on the passage from the *Saṃpuṭa Tantra* [p. 139] in his *Clusters of Quintessential Instructions* says:

> "Buddhahood" is a sovereign of the tenth ground. "High Buddhahood" is the attainment of a special path. "Vajradharahood" is a sovereign of the eleventh ground."

Also, Tripiṭakamāla's *Lamp for the Three Modes*[75] says:[76]

> Though the object is the same, [maṇḍala treatises
> Are superior because of being for the nonobscured,
> Having many skillful methods, no difficulties, and
> Being contrived for those with sharp faculties.]

Even [the objector] himself asserts that this means that the object of attainment of the Mantra and Perfection Vehicles is the same.

Furthermore, the Perfection Vehicle says that one who has gained the ground of complete light has abandoned all of the two obstructions along with their latent predispositions and has attained all Buddha qualities such as the powers, fearlessnesses, unshared qualities, and so forth; hence, if there were something exceeding the Buddhahood described in the Perfection Vehicle, one would have to assert that although the two obstructions were removed along with their latent predispositions, there would still be defects not yet removed and that although the hundred and forty-four uncontaminated qualities, such as the ten powers and so on, had been attained, one would still not have completely attained auspicious qualities. Therefore, it is indeed reasonable to analyze—as also many Indian scholars have—whether, without relying on the Mantra path, one can or cannot proceed to such a state through only the paths explained in the Perfection Vehicle; however, it is not seen to be logically feasible to assert that one can progress to the ground of complete light by the Perfection path alone but despite this [to hold] that still one has to progress higher.

Although the modes of progress on the two paths [of the Perfection and Mantra Vehicles] differ as to inferiority and superiority in the sense that on the former one cannot and on the latter one can become fully enlightened without relying on countless eons [of practice], this does not become a cause making the effects differ in quality. Nevertheless, this does not prove that the difference in causes is purposeless because even though the effects do not differ in quality, the effects differ greatly in terms of how distant or close they are.

Difference Between the Perfection and Mantra Paths

This has two parts: the difference according to our own system and the explanations by other masters.

Difference Between the Perfection and Mantra Paths According to Our Own System

The difference in speed between the three lower tantras and the Perfection Vehicle is that [in the paths of the three lower tantras] the practices of enlightenment are completed through many common achievements depending on the powers of deity yoga and repetition, and through many skillful means such as being directly sustained and empowered by Buddhas and great Bodhisattvas. The difference in speed in Highest Yoga Tantra is that even the stage of generation has many profound essentials that the lower tantra sets do not have, and the stage of completion has supreme profound essentials, which will be explained later.

A difference in speed that is the development of full enlightenment without relying on the passage of countless eons is a distinguishing feature of Highest Yoga; hence, such attainment by trainees of the lower tantra sets relies on their entering into the two stages of Highest Yoga; their own paths alone are not sufficient. Consequently, it should not be held that all differences of speed in Mantra are only due to the development of full enlightenment in one life in this age of conflict or to the development of full enlightenment without relying on countless eons [of practice].

Difference Between the Perfection and Mantra Paths According to [Faulty] Explanations by Other Masters

This has two parts: the difference according to Ratnarakṣhita's *Commentary on the Difficult Points of the Saṃvarodaya Tantra* (*saṃvarodayapañjikā*) and Tripiṭakamāla's *Lamp for the Three Modes.*

Difference Between the Perfection and Mantra Paths according to Ratnarakṣhita's "Commentary on the Saṃvarodaya Tantra"

Ratnarakṣhita explains[77] that meditation on freedom from proliferations [of inherent existence, conventionalities, and duality] on the occasion of the stage of completion is similar in both [the Mantra and the Perfection Vehicles]. He also points out that the *Meeting of Father and Son Sūtra* (*pitāputrasamāgama*) says that for Bodhisattvas who have attained the meditative stabilization of bliss pervading all phenomena, only a feeling of pleasure arises with respect to all objects of observation; pain and neutrality do not occur, and even though [pieces from their body] the size of a small coin (*kārṣāpaṇa*) are cut or even though their body is crushed by elephants, only a discrimination of bliss is maintained. Ratnarakṣhita says that this bliss [which is a quality of the Perfection Vehicle] does not conflict with the Mantra Vehicle [mistakenly assuming that this bliss is the same as great bliss in Mantra] and that this sūtra even sets forth its method. He [correctly] says that the main cause of all mundane and supramundane marvels is said to be the mind of enlightenment in the Perfection Vehicle and that the same is taught in Mantra; quoting the *Appearances Shining as Vajras* and so forth as sources, he "proves" that even great bliss is common [to both the Mantra and Perfection paths. Ratnarakṣhita correctly points out that] Maitreya's *Ornament for the Clear Realizations* (IV.48b) says, "Skill in means regarding making use of desire,"[78] and that the *Kāshyapa Chapter Sūtra* (*kāśyapaparivarta*) says through the example of a farmer that the manure of the afflictions is important for growing Buddha qualities;[79] thereby [he correctly shows that] making use of objects of the desire realm is common to both vehicles. Also, [though he correctly explains that] the ground of the fruit and so forth are similar in both vehicles, he [mistakenly] explains that the stage of generation is the distinguishing feature of Mantra; Ratnarakṣhita says in commentary on the thirteenth chapter of the *Saṃvarodaya Tantra*,[80] "Therefore if one does not cultivate the stage of generation, it just does not differ from the mode of Mantra." He [mistakenly] thinks that all cultivations of deity yoga are included in the stage of generation [whereas deity yoga occurs not only in both stages of Highest Yoga Tantra, generation and completion, but also in the three lower tantras], that the yogas of the channels, winds, and drops[81] are yogas for generating bliss [whereas these also generate the innate bliss realizing emptiness], and that bliss is similar [in both vehicles, whereas there are great differences].

Difference Between the Perfection and Mantra Paths according to Tripiṭakamāla's "Lamp for the Three Modes"

Tripiṭakamāla's *Lamp for the Three Modes*[82] says:

> Though the object is the same, mantra treatises
> Are superior because of being for the nonobscured,
> Having many skillful methods, no difficulties and
> Being contrived for those with sharp faculties.

He says that the fruit—described as omniscience—indeed does not differ in the two, the Mantra and the Perfection Vehicles, but that the four tantra sets surpass the Perfection Vehicle by way of four features.

Tripiṭakamāla's Faulty Explanation

> *Mantra's feature of being for the nonobscured:* When those of the Perfection Vehicle engage in giving and so forth, they do so without apprehending [the inherent existence of] the three spheres [of agent, action, and object]; therefore, they are not very obscured. However, since they engage in external giving such as giving away one's head and so forth, they do not have very sharp faculties; hence, they achieve enlightenment over a long period.
>
> Those who train in the Mantra approach do not have this obscuration. For, a perfection is the ability to fulfill a want of all sentient beings simultaneously, and since giving away one's head and so forth cannot nurture limitless sentient beings, Mantra practitioners see that a perfection is a fruit of meditative stabilization, and looking down on ordinary [giving and so forth], they seek a supreme method, this being to cultivate the meditative stabilization of nonduality of method and

wisdom continuously and without excluding any direction, whereby the welfare of limitless sentient beings can be fulfilled, through which the perfection of giving is completed, and at that time the remaining perfections are also completed. Because the ordinary giving of a body and so forth does not have this, it is not posited as a perfection.

Mantra's feature of having many methods: The asceticisms, vows, disciplines, and so forth that are set forth in the Perfection Vehicle as methods for high status [within cyclic existence] and liberation [from cyclic existence] accord with training in very peaceful activities; therefore, these cannot take care of all sentient beings. Mantra presents four tantra sets for the sake of bringing about the welfare of all sentient beings. Concerning this, one first realizes what type of affliction is predominant in oneself, and then, as in the case of desire, one generates oneself as Amitābha and enters a mind maṇḍala of [mentally] repeating a mantra, a speech maṇḍala of generating the vowels and consonants as deities, and a body maṇḍala of meditating on an immeasurable palace together with its base. Thus, three different approaches are set forth [regarding one affliction].

Mantra's feature of having no difficulties: Whether or not there is difficulty depends on the mind and not necessarily on any particular phenomenon, because what is difficult for some is easy for others. Hence, that which leads persons in accordance with their desires brings about the attainment of bliss through bliss; thus, difficult deeds are not taught in Mantra.

[In Mantra, practices are set forth in accordance with trainees' faculties as follows:] About that, the best among those with the best faculties—who are not involved in the faults of desire and so forth, have little conceptuality, are great in compassion, and are making effort at nondual suchness—are taught the Great Seal, the entity of the wisdom of selflessness of one taste with great compassion, also called "method and wisdom."[83]

Although the middling[84] [among those with the best] faculties have turned away from enjoying ordinary objects, they have not forsaken conceptions of desire and so forth. They are not able to enter the ocean of ultimate wisdom, and for them meditation on a Wisdom Seal [a meditated consort] is set forth. Jñānakīrti's *Abridged Explanation of All the Word*[85] explains that they meditate on the five lineages of Ones-Gone-Thus and their Knowledge Women,[86] the goddesses Lochanā and so forth. With regard to the way that suchness is entered through meditating on deities, when the mind itself is fixed firmly on a deity's body, it appears as the deity, and there is no external object, whereby one comes to understand the teaching not to adhere to the three spheres of an object of meditation, meditating, and meditator. One then abides as an exalted [divine] body free from conceptions of external objects and of apprehended-object and apprehending-subject. Also, one understands through a guru's quintessential instructions that these bodies do not inherently exist because of being one or many. Then, one understands that all phenomena likewise do not inherently exist. In consideration of this [process of meditation], limitless deity meditations are set forth.

Although the least among those with supreme faculties like nondual wisdom, they have not abandoned the desires of the desire realm; from approaching a desirable object their minds are distracted and do not enter into meditative stabilization. They are allowed Pledge Seals [actual consorts] that possess the attributes of Knowledge Women explained elsewhere [in tantras, such as qualities of form, beauty, age, lineage, excellent training in mantras and tantras, and maintenance of the tantric pledges].[87]

Action Seals [actual consorts not necessarily endowed with all attributes][88] are taught for those whose desire is very great, whose knowledge of suchness is not great, and whose minds cannot attain equipoise through other methods. Here also they practice by acting in accordance [with divinity by contemplating the consort as having a mantra body of a deity and a nature of wisdom and by contemplating themselves in the form of an omniscient Buddha wrought from great compassion].

With respect to this [last group], Tripiṭakamāla's *Lamp for the Three Modes* does not explain the type of faculty or what Action Seals are but Jñānakīrti[89] explains that the least among those with superior faculties have either Pledge or Action Seals. [With regard to the difference between these two] Jñānakīrti probably is referring to whether or not these actually engage in the act or whether or not the Knowledge Women are fully qualified.

Thus, among trainees engaging in Mantra who have the best faculties, those who do not desire the desire realm attributes of a Knowledge Woman [either meditated or actual] are taught meditation on the Great Seal [indivisibility of method and wisdom not involving a consort of any type]. Among those who desire the desire realm attributes of a Knowledge Woman, it is asserted that those who do not desire an external Knowledge Woman [an actual consort] are permitted meditation on a Wisdom Seal [a meditated consort], and those who desire an external Knowledge Woman are permitted both Pledge Seals and Action Seals [fully qualified and not fully qualified actual consorts]. Therefore, it would be contradictory to assert this system of this master [Tripiṭakamāla] as one's own and to assert [as is right] that the chief trainees of Highest Yoga must have great desire for the desire realm attributes of an external Knowledge Woman.

Mantra's feature of being contrived for those with sharp faculties: The master Tripiṭakamāla explains that because yogis of the four truths do not know suchness, they are of dull faculties, and that because yogis of the perfections are mistaken with respect to method, they have middling faculties. Because those engaging in the Mantra approach are not obscured with respect to anything, they have sharp faculties since with skill in means they use what would cause others to go to bad migrations and through it they attain a very pure state.

Jñānakīrti's *Abridged Explanation of All the Word*[90] says:

> Those who dislike meditation
> On a Wisdom Seal and so forth
> Have little force of wisdom, hence
> They do not meditate on the Great Seal.
>
> To help them the omniscient one
> Teaches the very forms themselves
> Of Vajrasattva and so forth
> With the name of the Great Seal.

He explains that for those who cannot meditate on the Great Seal due to little strength of wisdom and who dislike meditating on the other three Seals [Wisdom, Pledge, and Action], a body of a deity is taught upon having designated it with the name of the Great Seal, this being the meditation of the Yoga Tantras. Through this one should also understand Action and Performance Tantras.

Refutation of These Positions

Even those of the Perfection Vehicle assert that the two, the method—great compassion—and wisdom realizing suchness, the selflessness of phenomena, are the life of the path, and they say that if a perfection of giving involved fulfilling the wants of sentient beings through giving away material things such as one's head and the like, the perfection of giving could never be completed. Refuting such, the Perfection Vehicle says that increasing the attitude of generosity to its highest limit upon having purified the stains of (1) miserliness toward all property for oneself and (2) selfish grasping is the perfection of giving. Shāntideva's *Engaging in the Bodhisattva Deeds* (*bodhisattvacaryāvatāra,* V.9–10 says:

If through eliminating the poverty of beings,
A perfection of giving occurred,
Then since there are still poor beings,
How did the former Protectors achieve a perfection?

Through an attitude of giving to all beings
All one's possessions with their fruits
A perfection of giving is said to occur,
Thus it is just the mind.

Therefore, Tripiṭakamāla's explanation of Mantra's feature of nonobscuration also appears to be in trouble. The feature of being for those with sharp faculties also appears to be in trouble because if it is taken as meaning [its trainees are] not obscured with respect to method, it would be a repetition of the feature of nonobscuration, and if it is asserted as using desire for the attributes of the desire realm in the path, then since [according to Tripiṭakamāla's wrong explanation] the highest trainees of Mantra do not have such desire, this feature would be absent in the chief trainees of Mantra.

Also, it is [correctly] explained in many places that the very best trainees engaging in Mantra are led completely through the first stage [of generation], then are led on the second stage [of completion], and when the stage of completion becomes firm, engage in behavior in dependence on a Knowledge Woman whereby they become fully enlightened in that lifetime. Therefore, this assertion [by Tripiṭakamāla] that meditation on a Wisdom Seal and the granting of a Pledge Seal and so forth are for those of middling and low faculties appears to be hard to posit. Hence, the discriminative should analyze these and the like.

The explanations by Tibetan lamas of "many methods" as many collections of activities of pacification and so forth, and "no difficulties" as using the attributes of the desire realm in the path do not appear in the works of either this master [Tripiṭakamāla] or Jñānakīrti.

Identifying the Four Tantras

Detailed Explanation of the Forms of Entry to the Vajra Vehicle

This has three parts: number of doors of entry to Mantra, identifying the features positing the different doors of entry, and modes of advancing on the paths possessing these features.

Number of Doors of Entry to Mantra

The thirteenth chapter of the *Vajrapañjara*[91] says:

> Action tantras are for the lower.
> Yoga without actions is for those above them.
> The supreme Yoga is for supreme beings.
> The Highest Yoga is for those above them.

Accordingly, for the trainees of the Vajra Vehicle, four sets of tantras are set forth for the lower, the middling who are above them, the supreme, and the very supreme who are above them. Hence, there are four doors of entry from the approach of four sets of tantras.

Shraddhākaravarma's *Introduction to the Meaning of the Highest Yoga Tantras*[92] also explains:

> The approaches for engaging in the Secret Mantra, Effect, Vajra Vehicle are fourfold—generally renowned as Action Tantras, Performance Tantras, Yoga Tantras, and Highest Yoga Tantras.

Identifying the Features Positing the Different Doors of Entry to the Vajra Vehicle

This has two parts: a question and an answer.

Question about the Features Positing the Different Doors of Entry to the Vajra Vehicle

These doors of entry to Mantra, which are different levels in the tantra sets from the viewpoint of lower and higher trainees, are not by way of lower and higher objects of intent or objects of attainment because even all those who enter the Vajra Vehicle do not differ as to their having generated the Great Vehicle aspiration, seeking highest enlightenment [as their attainment] for the sake of all sentient beings [their objects of intent]. Also, [the differences between the doors of entry to Mantra] are not by way of having differences in their general paths that serve as the main causes of the Two Bodies, the objects of attainment, because [the four tantra sets] are similar in that a Truth Body is achieved through the wisdom realizing the absence of inherent existence, and they are also similar with regard to the generality that a Form Body is achieved through cultivating deity yoga.

Hence, even all are only the one vehicle called the "Vajra Vehicle"; if individual vehicles or doors of entry that are different levels in the tantra sets were posited merely through the presence of many different path attributes such as various deity yogas, then there would have to be many different vehicles even in each Highest Yoga Tantra, and there would be many doors of entry that would be different tantra sets even in one Highest Yoga Tantra such as *Guhyasamāja* because the *Compendium of Wisdom Vajras* (*jñānavajrasamuccaya*, an explanation of the *Guhyasamāja Tantra*) says that there are five types of persons, lower and higher—lotus, sandalwood, [white lotus, utpala, and jewel]. Therefore, you should explain the reason why four doors of entry to Mantra are presented as different tantra sets from the viewpoint of higher and lower trainees.

Answer about the Features Positing the Different Doors of Entry to the Vajra Vehicle

This has two parts: indicating the incorrectness of others' answers and giving our own answer.

Indicating the Incorrectness of Others' Answers [Regarding the Features Positing the Different Doors of Entry to the Vajra Vehicle]

Some Tibetan lamas[93] say that the four tantra sets were taught for the sake of accommodating four lineages among [non-Buddhist] Forders (*tīrthika*). Since there are the four—the desirous who are followers of Īshvara, the hateful who are followers of Viṣhṇu, the ignorant who are followers of Brahmā, and the indefinite who hold the tenets of whichever of these they encounter, these are respectively taught Highest Yoga Tantras, Performance Tantras, Action Tantras, and Yoga Tantras. Moreover, it is said that Ānandagarbha, Ashvaghoṣha,[94] and so forth assert this following the *Compendium of Principles*.

Response: Even if this is taken as that it happens that those persons are tamed by way of those respective tantras, such cannot identify the different features of those who engage in Mantra through the four tantra sets because it happens that persons of all four types are tamed by each of these tantras.

To assert that such persons are needed as the chief trainees of these tantra sets would be most unreasonable because since the main trainees of the Mantra Vehicle are the supreme among trainees engaging in the Victor's teaching, they do not need to assume a wrong view before engaging in Mantra and because there would also be the fault that those who initially engage in correct tenets instead of engaging in wrong tenets would not be chief trainees of these tantras.

Moreover, this is not the assertion of the master Ānandagarbha; the first chapter of his *Commentary on the Guhyasamāja Tantra* (*guhyasamājaṭīkā*) says:

> Because the Supramundane Victor abides there, "vagina" indicates the place. Moreover, the four goddesses called Lochanā, Māmakī, Pāndaravāsinī, and Tārā are here the consorts; they are taught in the seventeenth chapter of this text. Why does he abide in their secret place? This is for the sake of generating a liking for the abandonment of desire through desire in those who delight in the tantras of Viṣhṇu and so forth, and who have not completely abandoned the objects [of desire]. It is this way: They wish to achieve Viṣhṇu and the others through using women, excrement, urine, and so forth. Those engaged in seeking feats taught by Viṣhṇu will enter into a consort's secret.
>
> The blessed vagina is Viṣhṇu
> Abiding in the female genitals.
> Because it gives men pleasure,
> It is called Narayana.

and so forth. Thus, through such passages Ānandagarbha states at length that those who like the *Viṣhṇu Tantra* are taught the deeds of desire of Highest Yoga [and, therefore, the explanation given above that followers of Viṣhṇu are just hateful could not be by Ānandagarbha]. There is no way that this presentation that Highest Yoga was taught for these trainees could come from the *Compendium of Principles;* it appears that this was only put together upon drawing [unjustified] conclusions from [the teaching] that the four divisions of the *Compendium of Principles* were taught for those who have the afflictions of desire, anger, and so forth. Hence, a valid source [for the view that the four tantras were taught for four lineages of Forders] is not to be seen.

Also, some Tibetan lamas[95] explain that following the *Wisdom Vajra Compendium* [an explanatory Highest Yoga Tantra, in the *Guhyasamāja* cycle], the Superior [Nāgārjuna] and his spiritual sons and Jñānapāda as well as his followers assert that the four tantra sets were presented from the viewpoint of four different rites of deity generation in conformity with the four Buddhist schools of tenets. It appears that since these masters are followers of the *Guhyasamāja Tantra,* this is being [wrongly] inferred from the mere explanation in its explanatory tantra, the *Wisdom Vajra Compendium,* that on the occasion of Action Tantras there is no pride in oneself as a deity and no bliss of a wisdom-being. Therefore, no source is seen for a comparison with the four schools of tenets.

Even if one [mistakenly] associated Solitary Realizers with generation rites in Yoga Tantra, Solitary Realizers are not a division of the four schools of tenets [which are Great Exposition School, Sūtra School, Mind-Only School, and Middle Way School], and I will also explain later [in the section on Action Tantra][96] that the passage in the *Wisdom Vajra Compendium* means not that there is no generation of oneself as a deity in Action Tantras [but that *some* types of Action Tantra trainees are frightened and terrified by one-pointed cultivation of deity yoga]; therefore, this is not feasible.

Moreover, Alaṃkakalasha asserts [in his *Commentary on the Vajra Garland Tantra* (*vajramālāṭīkā*)[97]] that Brahmins are taught Action Tantra and those of the royal caste (*kṣatriya*) are taught Yoga Tantra. Those in the merchant caste (*vaiśya*) whose desire and hatred are slight but whose ignorance is extremely great and who believe in Viṣhṇu are taught Performance Tantra; those in the merchant caste whose desire and hatred are great but whose ignorance is slight are taught Yoga Tantras such as the *Guhyasamāja* [which is actually a Highest Yoga Tantra] and so forth. Those who are related to the servant caste (*śūdra*) whose desire and hatred are the great of the great and whose ignorance is the slight of the slight are taught mother tantras such as the *Little Saṃvara Tantra* (*laghusaṃvara*) and so forth. If Alaṃkakalasha propounds this thinking that there is partial similarity between the trainees of the four tantras and the four castes, such does not encompass the different features of those who engage in Mantra through the four tantra sets. If it is asserted that the four castes are needed for the trainees of the four tantra sets, this is not seen to be correct because such is never definite and is not even predominantly so. Though the deities of, for instance, the vajra element [taught in the *Compendium of Principles*] are described as having features that accord with kings and their retinue, it cannot be proven through this reason that its trainees are members of the royal caste.

In general, the chief trainees of the Great Vehicle must have predominant compassion. In particular, the chief trainees of Highest Yoga wish to attain Buddhahood extremely quickly in order to accomplish the welfare of others due to being highly moved by great compassion. Therefore, it is nonsense to propound that they must have very great hatred.

Our Own Answer [Regarding the Features Positing the Different Doors of Entry to the Vajra Vehicle]

The presentation of four different doors of entry to Mantra by way of tantra sets is not that these are different vehicles and is not also merely due to there being different features of path such as of deity yoga and so forth. Rather, because the main trainees in the Vajra Vehicle are of four very different types, the doors of entry are posited as fourfold. The different features of trainees occur in two ways: through the force of there being four different ways of using desire for the attributes of the desire realm in the path and through the force of there being four levels of capacity through which the emptiness and deity yogas that use desire in the path are generated in the mental continuum. With respect to these, the first[98] is set forth in the third chapter of the sixth division of the *Saṃpuṭa Tantra*:[99]

> The four aspects of laughing, gazing,
> Holding hands and the two embracing,
> Reside as the four tantras
> In the manner of insects.

The *Hevajra Tantra* also makes a presentation similar in meaning to this. Although Abhayākara's *Clusters of Quintessential Instructions* explains this passage in the *Saṃpuṭa Tantra* in terms of path tantras but not as tantra texts, his *Clusters,* commenting on the first chapter of the seventh division, explains it also in terms of tantra texts while Vīryavajra also explains it in terms of the four tantra sets in his *Commentary on the Saṃpuṭa Tantra* (*saṃpuṭaṭīkā*). The eleventh chapter of the *Ornament of the Vajra Essence Tantra* (*vajrahṛdayālaṃkāra*) after setting forth many types of desire tantras within method tantras, also says:

> This shows the tantra divisions
> Through the embrace of the two.
> Similarly know them through
> Holding hands, laughing, and gazing.

Through speaking in terms of tantras as communicators [texts], the passage indicates the divisions of the four tantra sets. Thus, the names of the tantra sets are also the four—tantras of gazing [Action], tantras of laughing [Performance], tantras of holding hands or embracing [Yoga], and tantras of union of the two [Highest Yoga].

As was explained earlier, that the uncommon cause of a Form Body is described as deity yoga is [from the viewpoint of] the main method. That factors of method act as heighteners of the wisdom realizing emptiness is the system of both Great Vehicles; it is as Shāntideva's *Engaging in the Bodhisattva Deeds* (IX.I) says:

> The Subduer said that all these
> Branches are for the sake of wisdom.

The way that the path of wisdom is heightened through deity yoga is this: The special method and wisdom is deity yoga, that is, the appearance of one's chosen deity in the aspect of father and mother union. Though Highest Yoga has many distinctive features in its path, it is designated with the name "tantra of union of the two" from this point of view, and in these [Highest Yoga] tantras themselves there are a great many descriptions of deities in the aspect of union of the two. From this approach desire is used in the path, whereby in dependence upon the essential of the meeting and staying together of the two minds of enlightenment[100] the realization of emptiness is heightened.

Because the lower tantras lack such a special method of using desire in the path, among the seven branches[101] the one of union is not set forth in the three lower tantras. Still, because the usage of joy arising from laughing, gazing, and holding hands or embracing in the path exists in the lower tantras, in general the mere using of desire for the attributes of the desire realm in the path exists [in the three lower tantras]. Moreover, the twenty-fifth cluster of Abhayākara's *Clusters*[102] says:

> The four tantras of Action, Performance, Yoga, and Highest Yoga are characterized by way of laughing, gazing, embracing or holding hands, and union of the two. Thus, in some Action Tantras and so forth the means by which the desire of the god and goddess—Method and Wisdom—is manifested is gazing; in some [Performance Tantras], laughing; in some [Yoga Tantras], holding hands; in some [Yoga Tantras], embracing; in some [Highest Yoga Tantras], uniting the two.

and the third chapter of the continuation of the *Hevajra Tantra* says:

> Through laughing, gazing,
> Embracing, and uniting
> The tantras also are in four aspects.

It is as Ratnākarashānti's *Commentary on the Difficult Points of the Hevajra Tantra* (*hevajrapañjikā*)[103] on this says:

> "Four" means Action, Performance, Yoga, and Highest Yoga Tantras which are characterized by laughing, gazing, embracing, and union of the two. Thus, in some Action Tantras and so forth there is laughing that indicates the desire of the god and goddess, Method and Wisdom; in some, after that there is gazing; in some, embracing; and in some, union of the two.

When he says, "The gods gaze," this means that, as in the case of laughing and so forth, the gazers are the gods. What is the function of gazing and so forth? It is said that these are the means by which the desires of [the god and the goddess called] Method and Wisdom are shown; the god and the goddess show desire for each other [in these ways]. Furthermore, because the deities—Vairochana, Lochanā, and so forth—never have desire, here one must apply this to practitioners who take on the pride of being these particular deities because the meaning at this point is that the trainees of the tantra sets must use desire, as in gazing and so forth, in the path and because if the statements in Action, Performance, and so forth of male and female deities' gazing at each other and so forth are not applied to the trainees, the differences of the trainees could not be identified from this viewpoint.

Furthermore, not only are laughing and so forth set out in Highest Yoga [as a way of identifying the four tantras], but so are individual instances set forth in the lower tantra sets; the *Detailed Rite of Amoghapasha* (*amoghapāśakalparāja*) [an Action Tantra] says,[104] "The Supramundane Victor faces Bhṛkuti," and:

> He aims his eye to the right at the goddess Tārā, bashful and with bent body, [displaying] the seal[105] of bestowing the supreme. On the left, Sundari of the lotus lineage, bashful, according with the ways of Secret Mantra, gazes at Amoghapasha.

and the *Vairochanābhisaṃbodhi* (*vairochanābhisaṃbodhi*) [a Performance Tantra] says:[106]

> On the right the goddess called
> Buddhalochanā, with
> Slightly smiling face.
> Having a circle of light a full fathom,
> Her unequalled body is most clear,
> She is the consort of Shākyamuni.

and:[107]

> Draw an Avalokiteshvara,
> Like a conch, a jasmine, a moon,
> Hero, sitting on a white lotus seat.
> On his head sits Amitābha,
> His face is slightly smiling.
> On his right is the goddess
> Widely renowned as Tārā,
> Virtuous and removing fright.

and the *Vajrashekhara* [a Yoga Tantra] says:[108]

> One's own goddess embraced in the center,
> The goddess Vajrakilikilā,
> Turns her head toward the side.
> Smiling and gazing everywhere
> She holds the Supramundane Victor's hands.

and the *Shrīparamādya* (*śrīparamādya*) [a Yoga Tantra] says:[109]

> To her side is Mahāvajra
> Intent on brandishing an arrow.
> His proud embracing arm raises
> A banner of victory
> [Adorned] with monsters of the sea.

These are only illustrations [in these tantra sets that mention gazing and so forth]; having generated themselves as the appropriate deity, practitioners use in the path the joyous bliss arising from their mutual desire by way of gazing back and forth at each other, and so forth. Moreover, in the lower tantra sets this is not done while observing an external Seal [an actual consort], and even in the higher tantra set [Highest Yoga] it is not said that such is done [in the lower tantras]; therefore, these should be taken as goddesses, such as Lochanā and the like, that one imagines in meditation.

With regard to the statement that "In consideration that trainees of little power cannot use great desire in the path, desire is used in the path in stages beginning with the small," it is clear, as will be explained, that when deity yoga [meditation on oneself as a deity] has become steady and meditative stabilization on emptiness has been attained, one takes cognizance of a goddess, such as Lochanā, who is of one's own lineage, and thereupon uses [desire in the path by way of gazing and so forth]; it is as Vīryavajra's *Commentary on the Saṃpuṭa Tantra* explains:

> The text says, "Laughing, gazing,[110] holding hands." This means that within the sound of laughter nonconceptual bliss is generated; or nonconceptual bliss is generated from gazing at the body, or from the touch of holding hands, or the embrace of the two, or from the touch [of union]. "In the manner of insects" indicates uncontaminated great bliss and emptiness; just as an insect

> is generated from wood and then eats the wood itself, so meditative stabilization that is generated from bliss [in dependence on desire] is meditatively cultivated as [realizing] emptiness [whereupon desire is consumed].

The twenty-third of Abhayākara's *Clusters*[111] says:

> A tantra of laughing is, for instance, like [the bliss] of those of the [godly realm called] "Liking Emanation."

Such statements merely cite gods as examples; they do not teach that those are the chief trainees of the tantra sets.

Though uncertain in terms of *all* who are intent upon the Vajra Vehicle and those who cultivate *some* aspects of its paths, the *chief trainees* initially engaging in the Vajra Vehicle are of the desire realm, and in general they are intent upon seeking enlightenment through only using in the path desire for the desire realm attributes of a Knowledge Woman. About this moreover, Highest Yoga speaks of using the desire of laughing and so forth in the path in cognizance of both actual and meditated Knowledge Women, but in the three lower tantras the joy observing the desire realm attributes of only meditated Wisdom Knowledge Women is used in the path. Since in Yoga Tantras even mere meditation on the union of the two organs is inappropriate, joy taking cognizance of another touch—that of holding hands or embracing—is used in the path in Yoga Tantras. Joy that arises in dependence on observing laughing and gazing—which are other than touching—is used in the path in Action and Performance Tantras.

The above was an explanation of the meaning of the names designated to the four tantra sets in Highest Yoga [as tantras of gazing, laughing, holding hands or embracing, and union of the two] together with an indication of distinctions in their trainees and paths. Now, I will explain the meaning of the names designated to the four tantra sets as they are renowned in common in the higher and lower tantra sets [as Action, Performance, Yoga, and Highest

Yoga Tantras] and will thereby describe distinctions in their trainees. The means of using such attributes of the desire realm in the path are the emptiness and deity yogas; those who rely on a great many external activities in order to actualize these two yogas are trainees of Action Tantras. Those who balance external activities and internal meditative stabilization without relying on very many activities are trainees of Performance Tantras. Those from between the two, external activities and internal meditative stabilization, mainly rely on meditative stabilization and rely on only few external activities are trainees of Yoga Tantras. Those who do not rely on external activities and are able to generate the yoga of which there is none higher are trainees of Highest Yoga Tantras.

[This explanation of the trainees] is done in accordance with the meaning of the names [of the four tantra sets] since Action Tantras are so called because *activities* are predominant; Performance Tantras are so called because activities and meditative stabilization are *performed equally;* Yoga Tantras are so called because *internal yoga* is very central; and Highest Yoga Tantras are so called because there is *no higher yoga*. These are explained in terms of their respective main trainees' entry to the path, but there is no certainty [that all trainees will conform] because Ānandagarbha's *Illumination of the "Compendium of Principles"*[112] explains that the Continuation of the Continuation of the *Compendium of Principles* was set forth for those who are frightened and scared by cultivation [of deity yoga].[113] Also, though trainees in general have indeed more, or less, interest in external activities and in internal meditative cultivation of yoga, there are instances of interest in a path that does not fit a person's faculties; hence, the main trainees of the four tantra sets are not identified through interest. Therefore, it should be realized that explanations of their main trainees as relying or not relying on many or few external activities and so forth are feasible. Tripiṭakamāla's *Lamp for the Three Modes*[114] explains:

> Due to predispositions from conditioning in other births, they do not attain mental equipoise without a

> home in the forest away from people, and without activities such as bathing, drawing maṇḍalas, worshipping, burnt offerings, asceticism, repetition [of mantra], and so forth; hence, Action Tantras were taught for them. Even those manifestly adhering to suchness have reliance on activities since through the power of faith they also attain pristine wisdom by means of activities set forth by the One-Gone-to-Bliss; for them Fundamental Tantras that do not have too many branches of activities were set forth.

"Fundamental Tantras" are equivalent to those renowned as Performance Tantras.

That those that predominantly teach external activities even though they contain internal meditative stabilization are assigned as Action Tantras is set forth in Buddhaguhya's *Word Commentary on the Vairochanābhisaṃbodhi* (*vairocanābhisaṃbodhitantrabhāṣya*):[115]

> Even Action Tantras are indeed mainly concerned with external practices, but internal practices are not absent.

and Vajragarbha's *Commentary on the Condensation of the Hevajra Tantra* (*hevajrapiṇḍārthaṭīkā*) also explains that [tantras spoken for] those who have little capacity for meditation on suchness[116] but are mainly involved in external activities are Action Tantras.

That those that teach internal meditative stabilization and external activities equally are assigned as Performance Tantras is as Buddhaguhya's *Word Commentary on the Vairochanābhisaṃbodhi*[117] says:

> Although this tantra also is indeed a tantra that mainly involves method and wisdom, it also teaches practice of activities in order to accommodate migrators who are trainees inclined toward activities, due to which it

> is designated and renowned as an Action Tantra or a Both Tantra [Performance Tantra].

Therefore, the *Ornament of the Vajra Essence Tantra* also speaks of "Both Tantra," saying, "Action, Both, and Yoga Tantras."

Tripiṭakamāla's *Lamp for the Three Modes*[118] explains:

> For the sake of others who are interested solely in meditation on nondual suchness and consider groups of many activities to be distracting, Performance Tantras that mainly employ yoga and secondarily teach only a few branches of activities were set forth.

Here, "Performance Tantras" are Yoga Tantras.

Preparation for Mantra

Modes of Advancing on the Paths Possessing These Features

This has two parts: common stages of the path in the two Great Vehicles and uncommon stages of the path in the Vajra Vehicle. [Only the first part is translated here.]

Common Stages of the Path in the Two Great Vehicles

The *Vajrapāṇi Initiation Tantra* (*vajrapāṇyabhiṣeka*) says:

> "This very vast, very profound maṇḍala of the great retention mantras[119] of the great Bodhisattvas, difficult to penetrate, more greatly secret than the secret, which is not fit to be shown to sinful sentient beings, has been mentioned very rarely by you, O Vajrapāṇi. How can it be explained to sentient beings if they have not heard about it before?"
>
> Vajrapāṇi said, "Mañjushrī, those Bodhisattvas who practice the Bodhisattva deeds through the approach of Secret Mantra, when they have engaged in meditative cultivation of the altruistic mind of enlightenment and achieved the altruistic mind of enlightenment, may enter the maṇḍala of retention mantras where the initiation for great pristine wisdom is bestowed. Those who have not completely achieved the altruistic mind of enlightenment are not to enter; they should not even

> be allowed to see a maṇḍala; they should not be shown seals [that is, hand gestures] and secret mantras.

Thus, it is said that prior to bestowing initiation the altruistic mind of enlightenment must be completed; therefore, first you should train in the aspirational and practical minds of enlightenment and then enter a maṇḍala.

The stages of training in the aspirational and practical minds of enlightenment are these: Initially you should rely in the proper way on a qualified spiritual guide of the Great Vehicle through thought and deed. When, having been taught the ways in which leisure [a life endowed with the inner and outer circumstances for practice] is meaningful and difficult to find, you have trained your mind such that a great wish to extract the essence of this life-support of leisure is generated, the supreme means to extract the essence is just entry into the Great Vehicle, and the door of entry to the Great Vehicle is just the altruistic mind of enlightenment because if a real altruistic mind of enlightenment exists in your mental continuum, your being of the Great Vehicle also is not artificial, whereas if it is only verbal, your being of the Great Vehicle is also only verbal. Thus, the wise should gradually remove whatever is discordant with that altruistic attitude and generate it with all its characteristics.

For that also, if you do not initially turn your mind away from this life, it will be an obstacle to the paths of either the Lesser or Great Vehicle; therefore, you should be mindful of death in the sense of being aware that you will not stay long in this life, and you should think how after death you may wander to bad migrations, and thereby turn your mind away from this life. Then, an attitude of attachment to the good things of a future life should also be overcome through thinking well about the faults of all of cyclic existence, whereby your mind will be inclined toward liberation.

After that, to overcome the attitude of seeking the bliss of peace for yourself, you should train for a long time in love, compassion, and the altruistic mind of enlightenment—which has love and compassion as its root—and practice a nonartificial mind of enlightenment. Then, you should come to know the Bodhisattva deeds and generate a wish to train in them. If you can take on the burden of the deeds of Victor Children, you should take the Bodhisattva vows and practice its precepts. Then, if you can take on the burden of the pledges and vows of the Vajra Vehicle, you should listen to Ashvaghoṣha's *Fifty Stanzas on the Guru* (*gurupañcāśikā*) and having enacted the pure modes of reliance on a guru, enter into Mantra. The *Fifty Stanzas on the Guru* says:

> To students with pure thought
> Who have gone for refuge to the Three Jewels
> This [text on] following a guru
> Should be given for recitation.
> Then through giving them mantra[120] and so forth
> They are made vessels of excellent doctrine.

It says that the *Fifty Stanzas on the Guru* is to be explained to those who have trained in "pure thought"—the altruistic mind of enlightenment—and who have taken the uncommon refuge, and it says that after the master gives the *Fifty Stanzas on the Guru,* they are made into vessels [of Mantra] through initiation.

Rāhulashrīmitra's *Clarification of Union* (*yuganaddhaprakāśa*)[121] also says that prior to initiation one should take [a vow of] individual emancipation, generate an altruistic mind of enlightenment and take its vow, and then petition the guru for the bestowal of initiation:

> The stages are these: at a time of virtue
> By the date, constellations, and so forth,
> Students with pressed palms and bending down
> Should disclose all ill-deeds
> And take the three refuges.
> They should relyingly resort well
> To the altruistic mind of enlightenment

And take the lay and also Bodhisattva vows
And then also purification and renewal.
In concordant stages they also should rely
In excellent ways on a Vajra master,
But fearing here to take too long
I will write no more about it.
Having done such, they should ask the guru,
"Please bestow initiation on me."

The lay vow and its purification [of infractions against vows previously taken] and renewal [restoring sullied vows to purity] are in terms of householders; renunciants who are entering Mantra should maintain purely the vows of a novice and so forth.

The first chapter of Āryadeva's *Lamp Compendium of Practice,*[122] after proving that one should train in stages and not in everything at once, says that after one has previously trained in the Buddha Vehicle, one should train in a new vehicle, Mantra:

> The stages are these: At the beginning, one trains in the thought of the Buddha Vehicle. When one has trained in the thought of the Buddha Vehicle, one trains in a new vehicle, the meditative stabilization of single mindfulness.

Therefore, the thought of the Buddha Vehicle is the aspirational and practical minds of enlightenment. Hence, the necessity in that way to generate the aspirational and practical minds of enlightenment and thereupon to be endowed with the deeds of the six perfections is not carried over here from the Perfection Vehicle; rather, the Mantra texts themselves say again and again that one should train in these paths; therefore, these are shared [paths] arising in the Vajra Vehicle itself. Since I have explained these extensively in the *Stages of the Path Common to the Vehicles,* I will not elaborate on them here.

To say in conclusion:

Not discriminating with stainless reasoning
The difference between good and bad explanations
In our own and others' textual systems, and
Without correctly discriminating the main features
Common and uncommon in the Lesser Vehicle, Great Vehicle,
Mantra and Perfection, it is only an act of faith
Even to propound that the general Buddhist teaching,
The Great Vehicle, and especially the Vajra Vehicle
Are the supreme doors of entry for the fortunate.
Hence, O, O, you with intelligence and aspiration,
Train the eye of understanding with pure reasoning
And seek firm conviction in the teaching's essentials
Until you are immovable by opposite influences.

The first section of *The Stages of the Path to a Great Vajradhara: Revealing All Secret Essentials,* called "General Teaching of the Doors of Different Stages for Entry to the Teaching," is concluded.

III

Supplement

Jeffrey Hopkins

Rehearsing the Differences between the Vehicles

Because people are of different capacities, dispositions, and interests, Shākyamuni Buddha taught many different paths. He set forth Sūtra and Mantra, and within Sūtra he taught four different schools of tenets (Great Exposition School, Sūtra School, Mind-Only School, and Middle Way School) and within Mantra, he set out four different tantra sets—Action, Performance, Yoga, and Highest Yoga (literally "Unsurpassed Yoga").[1]

In each of the four schools of the Sūtra system he described three varieties of paths—for Hearers, Solitary Realizers, and Bodhisattvas. Each of the four schools also has internal subdivisions, and the four divisions of Mantra also contain many different types of processes and procedures of meditation. The result is that there are many different levels of commitment—ranging from the assumption of tantric vows down to the assumption of only the refuge vow—many different paths and many different styles.

To appreciate the special distinctiveness of Mantra, it is necessary to determine the difference between the Sūtra and Mantra vehicles, and to do that, first it is necessary to settle the difference between the vehicles in Sūtra—the Hearer Vehicle, Solitary Realizer Vehicle, and Bodhisattva Vehicle or Great Vehicle—and then consider the further division of the latter into its Sūtra and Mantra forms.

Difference between the Sūtra Vehicles

"Vehicle" (Tib. *theg pa,* Sans. *yāna*) has two meanings:

1. Since in Sanskrit *yā* means "to go," and *na* indicates the "means" of going, a vehicle comprises those practices carrying one to a higher state—those practices that when actualized in the mental continuum cause manifestation of a higher type of mind.
2. Somewhat unusually, "vehicle" can also refer to the destination—the place or state at which one is aiming. This is because just as a vehicle can bear or carry a certain load, so the state of Buddhahood, which is the goal of the Bodhisattva Vehicle, can bear or carry the welfare of all sentient beings, whereas the state of a Lesser Vehicle Foe Destroyer can bear much less.

Since "vehicle" has these two meanings, the distinction between the two Buddhist Vehicles—Hearer and Solitary Realizer (Lesser Vehicle) and Bodhisattva (or Great Vehicle)—must occur either within the sense of vehicle as the means by which one progresses or within the sense of vehicle as the destination, or state, to which one is progressing, or in both meanings.

In the exposition of the Lesser Vehicle and the Great Vehicle according to the Middle Way Consequence School, considered to be the acme of philosophical systems by most Tibetan schools, there is a tremendous difference between the two in the sense of vehicle as that to which one is progressing. In the Lesser Vehicle, practice culminates as a Foe Destroyer, one who has overcome the foe of ignorance but is not omniscient and thus is not a Buddha. Unlike a Buddha, a Foe Destroyer does not have the ability spontaneously to manifest in myriad forms in order to help beings. Since the states of being a Buddha and a Foe Destroyer are very different, there is a significant difference between the Great and Lesser vehicles in the sense of vehicle as that to which one is progressing—the respective goals of Buddhahood and Foe Destroyerhood.

With this difference in goal, there must also be a difference in the two vehicles in the sense of the practices by which one progresses to these goals. The difference between the Lesser and Great vehicles in terms of the means of progress can occur in only two places—method and wisdom, these two comprising the entire path, in that method mainly produces the Form Body of a Buddha and wisdom mainly produces the Truth Body, also called the Body of Attributes. In the Consequence School's explanation, the Lesser and Great vehicles do not differ with respect to wisdom in that both require realization of the subtle emptiness of inherent existence of *all* phenomena such as body, mind, head, eye, wall, consciousness, and so forth. The Lesser and Great vehicles differ in terms of *how* wisdom is cultivated—Bodhisattvas using myriad reasonings for getting at the subtle emptiness and Hearers and Solitary Realizers using only a few reasonings to realize the same emptiness; however, in terms of the object of the mind of wisdom, the emptiness of inherent existence, there is no difference between the emptiness a Lesser Vehicle practitioner realizes and the emptiness a Great Vehicle practitioner realizes. In this sense there is no difference in wisdom. Tsongkhapa discusses this point in some detail in his commentary on Chandrakīrti's *Supplement to (Nāgārjuna's) "Treatise on the Middle"*[2] and also indicates a nuanced way that there is a difference in approach:

> To establish that even a single phenomenon does not truly exist, Great Vehicle practitioners use limitless, different reasonings as set forth in Nāgārjuna's *Treatise on the Middle,* due to which their minds become greatly broadened with respect to suchness. Lesser Vehicle practitioners use only brief reasoning to establish suchness by valid cognition, and since they do not establish emptiness the way Great Vehicle practitioners do, they do not have a mind broadened with respect to suchness.... This difference arises because Hearers and Solitary Realizers strive to abandon only the afflictive emotions [the obstructions to liberation], and realization of a mere abbreviation of the meaning of suchness is sufficient for that. Great Vehicle practitioners are intent

> on abandoning the obstructions to omniscience, and for this it is necessary to have a very broadened mind of wisdom opened to suchness.

Bodhisattvas' more extensive use of reasoning helps in achieving their greater aim of overcoming the obstructions to omniscience.

Since wisdom in the Lesser and Great vehicles does not differ in terms of the type of emptiness being realized, the difference between the two vehicles must lie in method. "Method" here specifically means motivation and the deeds that it impels. No matter how much compassion Lesser Vehicle practitioners have, their primary motivation is to release themselves from cyclic existence. However, in the Great Vehicle the primary motivation is the *altruistic* aspiration to highest enlightenment induced by great love and compassion in which one takes on the burden of the welfare of all beings. Thus, there is a significant difference between the Lesser and Great vehicles in terms of method, even though not in wisdom.

Hence, the Lesser and Great vehicles differ in both senses of vehicle, as the means by which one progresses as well as that to which one progresses.

Difference between the Perfection Vehicle and the Mantra Vehicle

In the Great Vehicle itself, there are two vehicles—the Perfection Vehicle and the Mantra (or Tantra) Vehicle. The Perfection Vehicle is the Sūtra Great Vehicle, and the Mantra Vehicle is the Mantra (or Tantra) Great Vehicle.

Do the Sūtra Great Vehicle and the Mantra Great Vehicle differ in the sense of vehicle as that to which one is progressing? The goal of the Sūtra Great Vehicle is Buddhahood, but the Mantra Great Vehicle cannot have another goal separate from Buddhahood as there is no attainment higher than the Buddhahood described in Sūtra as attainment of the Truth Body (Body of Attributes) and Form Bodies. Sūtra describes a Buddha as having removed all obstructions and attained all auspicious attributes, having no movement of coarse winds, or inner energies;[3] thus such Buddhahood has to include the attainments of even Highest Yoga Mantra, the primary aim of which is to stop the movement of all coarse winds and manifest the most subtle consciousness—the mind of clear light—while simultaneously appearing in totally pure form.[4] Hence, the Vajradharahood often mentioned as the goal of Mantra and the Buddhahood described in Sūtra are the same.

There being no difference between the Perfection Vehicle and the Mantra Vehicle in terms of the goal—the destination—they must differ in the sense of vehicle as the means by which one progresses. Therefore, they must differ either in terms of method or wisdom or both. If the difference lay in wisdom, there would be many problems because the Perfection Vehicle contains Nāgārjuna's Middle Way teachings on emptiness, and there would have to be some other more subtle emptiness than that which Nāgārjuna establishes with many different reasonings in the twenty-seven chapters of his *Treatise on the Middle,* whereas there is none. Thus there is no difference between Sūtra and Mantra in the view, which here refers to the objective view, that is, the object that is viewed[5]—emptiness or ultimate truth—and does not refer to the realizing consciousness, since Sūtra Great Vehicle and Highest Yoga Mantra do differ with respect to the subtlety of the consciousness realizing emptiness. Specifically, in Highest Yoga Tantras such as the *Guhyasamāja Tantra* or the *Kālachakra Tantra,* more subtle, enhanced consciousnesses are generated to realize the same emptiness of inherent existence. Still, because the object realized is the same whether the consciousness is more subtle or not, the "objective view" is the same.

In this way, between the Sūtra and Mantra Great Vehicles there cannot be any difference in the factor of wisdom in terms of the object understood by wisdom. Hence, the difference again has to lie in method. Nevertheless, in both the Sūtra and the Mantra Great Vehicles, the foundation of method is the altruistic intention to become enlightened for the sake of all sentient beings, and thus the motivational basis of the deeds of the path is the same. The other main factor of method has to do with the deeds induced by that motivation. In the Sūtra Great Vehicle these are the practices induced by that altruistic aspiration—the perfections of giving, ethics, and patience, and since these are also practiced in Mantra, the difference cannot be found there either. Furthermore, Mantra has an even greater emphasis than Sūtra on the deeds of the perfections in that a tantric practitioner is committed to engage in them at least six times during each day.

Moreover, the distinction could not be made on the basis of speed of progress on the path because within the four tantra sets—Action, Performance, Yoga, and Highest Yoga Mantra—there are great differences in speed, such as the possibility of achieving Buddhahood in one lifetime in Highest Yoga Mantra but taking at least two periods of countless eons in the other three, according to Tsongkhapa. Also, in the Sūtra Great Vehicle there are five different modes of progress, slow to fast, which are compared to an ox chariot, elephant chariot, sun and moon, magical creation of a Hearer, and magical creation of a One-Gone-Thus. In addition, the difference must not lie in some small or insignificant feature, but in an important one.

Tsongkhapa's intricate comparison of the Perfection and the Mantra vehicles has shown how similar these two vehicles are in their basic structure in terms of goal, wisdom of emptiness, and altruistic motivation, thereby literally setting the stage for appreciating the central difference. He finds the profound distinction in the fact that in Mantra there is meditation in which one meditates on one's body as similar in aspect to a Buddha's Form Body, whereas in the Sūtra Great Vehicle there is no such meditation. This is deity yoga,[6] which all four tantra sets have but Sūtra systems do not. Deity yoga means to imagine oneself as now having the Form Body of a Buddha; one meditates on oneself in the aspect of a Buddha's Form Body, imagining oneself as presently an ideal, altruistically active being. This is the central distinctive feature of

Tantra in that it occurs in all four sets, even though it does not occur in all tantras, due to which it is not a definition of tantra.

In the Perfection Vehicle there is meditation similar in aspect to a Buddha's Truth Body/Body of Attributes—a Buddha's mind of wisdom. A Bodhisattva enters into meditative equipoise directly realizing emptiness with nothing appearing to the mind except the final nature of phenomena, the emptiness of inherent existence; the mind of wisdom and emptiness are like water poured into water, undifferentiable. Even though, unlike their tantric counterparts, Sūtra Bodhisattvas do not specifically imagine that the state of meditative equipoise *is* a Buddha's Truth Body/Body of Attributes,[7] meditation similar in aspect to a Buddha's Body of Attributes does occur in the Sūtra system in the sense that the state of meditative equipoise on emptiness mimics a Buddha's pristine mind of wisdom in its aspect of perceiving the ultimate. However, the Sūtra Perfection Vehicle does not involve meditation similar in aspect to a Buddha's Form Body. There is meditation on Buddhas and so forth as objects of offering and so forth, but there is no meditation on oneself in the physical body of a Buddha.

Such meditative cultivation of a divine body is included within the factor of method because it is mainly aimed at achieving a Buddha's Form Body. In the Sūtra system the sole means for achieving a Buddha's Form Body is, on the basis of the altruistic intention to become enlightened, to engage in the first three perfections—giving, ethics, and patience—in "limitless" ways over a "limitless" period of time, specifically three periods of "countless" great eons ("countless" being said to be a figure with fifty-nine zeros). Though the Mantra Vehicle also involves practice of the perfections of giving, ethics, and patience, it is not in "limitless" ways over "limitless" periods of time. Despite emphasis on the perfections in the Mantra Vehicle, practice in "limitless" ways over "limitless" time is unnecessary because one is engaging in the additional technique of meditation on oneself in a body similar in aspect to a Buddha's Form Body.[8] In other words, in the tantric systems, in order to become a Buddha more quickly, one meditates on oneself as similar in aspect to a Buddha in terms of both body and mind. This practice is significantly distinctive and thus those systems that involve it constitute a separate vehicle, the Mantra Great Vehicle.

In deity yoga one first meditates on emptiness and then uses this consciousness realizing emptiness—or at least an imitation of it—as the basis of emanation of a Buddha. The mind of wisdom itself appears as the physical form of a Buddha. This one consciousness thus has two parts—a factor of wisdom and a factor of method, or factors of (1) ascertainment of emptiness and (2) appearance as an ideal being—and hence, through the practice of deity yoga, one *simultaneously* accumulates the collections of merit and wisdom, making their amassing much faster.

The systems that have this practice are called the *Vajra* Vehicle because the appearance of a deity is the display of a consciousness which is a *fusion* of wisdom understanding emptiness and compassion seeking the welfare of others—an inseparable union symbolized by a vajra, a diamond, the foremost of stones as it is "unbreakable." Since the two elements of the fusion, compassionate method and penetrating wisdom, are the very core of the Perfection Vehicle, one can understand that Sūtra and Mantra, despite being different, are integrated systems. One can understand that compassion is not superseded in Mantra but is essential to Mantra and that the wisdom of the Perfection Vehicle is not forsaken for a deeper understanding of reality in the Mantra Vehicle.

Summary

To encapsulate the points made in Tsongkhapa's argument up to here: The difference between the vehicles as explained in the Consequence School must lie in the sense of vehicle as that by which one progresses or that to which one progresses. The Lesser Vehicle differs from the Great Vehicle in both. The destination of the lower vehicle is the state of a Hearer or Solitary Realizer Foe Destroyer and of the higher vehicle, Buddhahood. Concerning "vehicle" in the sense of means by which one progresses, although there is no difference in the wisdom realizing the subtlest nature of phenomena, there is a difference in method—Lesser Vehicle not having and Great Vehicle having the altruistic intention to become enlightened and its attendant deeds.

Sūtra Great Vehicle and Mantra Great Vehicle do not differ in terms of the goal, the state being sought, since both seek the highest enlightenment of a Buddha, but there is a difference in the means of progress, again not in wisdom but in method. Within method they differ not in the basis, or motivation, of the deeds, this being the altruistic intention to become enlightened, nor in having the perfections as deeds, but in the additional technique of deity yoga. A deity is a supramundane being who is a manifestation of compassion and wisdom. Thus, in the special practice of deity yoga one joins one's own body, speech, mind, and activities with the exalted body, speech, mind, and activities of a supramundane being, manifesting on the path a similitude of the state of the effect.

Reason as the Arbiter

The basic appeal throughout Tsongkhapa's presentation of the difference between the vehicles is to a rational investigation of path structure, but it is not that he does not cite supportive Indian sources. For instance, in establishing that according to the Middle Way Consequence School even those who are of the Lesser Vehicle by path must realize the most subtle emptiness, he presents an abridged version of his own extensive argument on this in his commentary to Chandrakīrti's *Supplement to (Nāgārjuna's) "Treatise on the Middle,"*[9] citing Chandrakīrti's *Supplement* and Nāgārjuna's *Precious Garland, Treatise on the Middle,* and *Praise of the Nonconceptual,* as well as two Perfection of Wisdom Sūtras, and a Lesser Vehicle Sūtra. (That the Middle Way Consequence School's view on the emptiness of inherent existence is needed in order to become a Foe Destroyer is controversial, as it means that no follower of the Great Exposition School, the Sūtra School, the

Mind-Only School, or even the Autonomy School can complete the Lesser Vehicle path and become a Foe Destroyer by means of any of those paths alone.)

Considering counterarguments, Tsongkhapa makes reference to presentations in both Lesser Vehicle and Great Vehicle texts that propound the opposite, that is, that to get out of cyclic existence it is sufficient to have the fully developed wisdom understanding that the person is not substantially existent, which is a coarser type of selflessness. Again, the conflict is settled by reasoning through differentiating what is definitive and what requires interpretation. This not being a main subject of the *Great Exposition of Secret Mantra,* he leaves the matter with a brief admonition to learn how to make such distinctions—implicitly indicating the benefit of studying his *The Essence of Eloquence*[10] where the dominant argument is that scriptural reference is not sufficient since a supporting scripture would require another which, in turn, would require another *ad infinitum,* and thus reasoning is necessary. The working principles revolve around showing that the conception of inherent existence is the root of cyclic existence and that some trainees are temporarily incapable of receiving teaching on such a subtle topic. Adjudication of the opposing scriptures is made:

1. on the basis of the ontological fact, determined by reasoning, that the emptiness of inherent existence is the final mode of abiding of phenomena
2. in the context of the existential situation of the epistemological needs of the trainees to whom the doctrines were taught
3. in the face of reasoned refutation of opposing scriptures

Tsongkhapa resolves other seeming contradictions by taking into account the frame of reference of a remark. For instance, Kalkī Puṇḍarīka's commentary on the *Kālachakra Tantra,* called the *Stainless Light,* explains the term "vajra" in "Vajra Vehicle" in the context of the *Kālachakra Tantra,* a Highest Yoga Tantra, in such a way that the meaning applies only to that class of tantra and not to all four classes. Tsongkhapa explains that since the three lower tantra sets do not have the paths necessary for the generation of a fusion of totally supreme emptiness (here referring to a form empty, or devoid, of material particles) and supreme immutable bliss ("immutable" here referring to nonemission), this explanation—in the Kālachakra mode—of "Vajra Vehicle" is too narrow. He adds that explaining "Vehicles of Cause and Effect" in this way is also too narrow for a general presentation. Rather, the general meaning of "Vajra Vehicle" must apply to all four classes of tantra, not just Highest Yoga. Tsongkhapa is making the point that the type of union of method and wisdom described in those texts applies only to Highest Yoga Mantra and that a meaning of "Vajrayāna" applicable to all four tantra sets must be found elsewhere. As explained above, he indicates that this is deity yoga, an indivisible union of method and wisdom.

Regarding scriptural authority for the distinction between the Sūtra and Mantra Great Vehicles, Tsongkhapa quotes a passage from the *Lady Sky-Traveler Vajra Tent Tantra,* rejects the commentaries of Kṛṣhṇapāda and Indrabodhi, and critically uses the commentary of Devakulamahāmati, accepting some parts and rejecting others. Having established that deity yoga is the dividing line between the two Great Vehicles, he reinforces this with citations from or references to works on Highest Yoga Mantra by Jñānapāda, Ratnākarashānti, Abhayākara, Durjayachandra, Shrīdhara, Samayavajra, Jinadatta, and Vinayadatta. The general drift is illustrated by a passage from Ratnākarashānti's *Commentary on (Dīpaṅkarabhadra's) "Four Hundred and Fifty"* as Tsongkhapa cites the title, or *Commentary on (Dīpaṅkarabhadra's) "Rite of the Guhyasamāja Maṇḍala"* as it is listed in the *Tibetan Tripitaka*:[11]

> If one cultivates only [a path] having the nature of a deity, one cannot become fully enlightened through that because the fulfillment of [yogic] activities is not complete. Or, if one meditates on the suchness of a deity

> and not on that deity, one will attain Buddhahood in many countless eons but not quickly. Through meditating on both, one will attain the highest perfect complete enlightenment very quickly because to do so is very appropriate and has special empowering blessings.

Since a Buddha has both a Truth Body/Body of Attributes and a Form Body it is *very appropriate* that on the path one cultivate both emptiness yoga and deity yoga, the former having as its main result the Body of Attributes and the latter, Form Bodies. In short, the path to speedy attainment of enlightenment must involve both deity yoga and emptiness yoga; one without the other is not sufficient. Furthermore, as Tsongkhapa points out, these two exist in one consciousness; thus, his assertion of the difference between the Sūtra and Mantra Great Vehicles is made on the basis of the simultaneous union in one consciousness of the factors of method and wisdom, specifically the appearance of the divine form and ascertainment of its emptiness.

Having cited such passages in Highest Yoga Tantras and commentaries to show the distinctive presence of deity yoga, he makes brief citations for Yoga, Performance, and Action Tantras by referring to Shākyamitra, Ānandagarbha, and Buddhaguhya, skirting for the time being the considerable controversy over whether Action Tantra and Performance Tantra have deity yoga, since he tackles that problem at the beginning of the section on Action Tantra.

Despite Tsongkhapa's many citations of tantras and Indian commentaries, it is clear that they are used only as evidence for his argument. Tradition is only supportive, not the final authority. The arbiter is reason, specifically in the sense of determining coherence and consistency within a path structure. Tsongkhapa refutes Ratnarakṣhita and Tripiṭakamāla, for instance, not because they differ from the aforementioned sources but because their presentations fail in terms of consistency with the path structure. By doing so, he moves the basis of the argument from scriptural citation to reasoned analysis of a meditative structure.

Refutation of Ratnarakṣhita

Tsongkhapa analyzes and refutes Ratnarakṣhita's and Tripiṭakamāla's presentations on the difference between the Perfection and Mantra vehicles (the first is not included in Butön's presentation and the second is). In his *Commentary on the Difficult Points of the Saṃvarodaya Tantra*, Ratnarakṣhita explains that the generation stage, which he takes to be deity yoga, is the distinctive feature of Mantra. Ratnarakṣhita rejects meditation on emptiness as a distinctive feature because it occurs also in the Perfection Vehicle, and he rejects bliss because Bodhisattvas of the Perfection Vehicle are able to maintain a feeling of pleasure or bliss even in the midst of extreme torture.

In a typically laconic way, Tsongkhapa leaves many points unsaid or only hints at them. He merely says:

> [Ratnarakṣhita] says this, thinking that all cultivations of deity yoga are included in the generation stage, that the yogas of channels, winds, and drops are for generating bliss, and that bliss is similar [in the Sūtra and Mantra Great Vehicles].

Tsongkhapa is making several points important to his own system:

1. Although all four tantra sets involve deity yoga, only Highest Yoga Mantra has a generation stage; Action, Performance, and Yoga Tantra do not. The reason is that the deity yoga of the generation stage in Highest Yoga Mantra must be modeled after the processes of death, intermediate state, and rebirth, whereas the three lower tantras, while using deity yoga, do not present deity yoga this way. Specifically, the meditation on emptiness that is at the beginning of deity yoga must, in

Highest Yoga Mantra, include a mimicking of the eight signs of death:

four appearances
(1) like a mirage
(2) like smoke
(3) like fireflies within smoke, and
(4) like the flame of a butter lamp

the dawning of three subtler consciousnesses
(5) the mind of vivid white appearance
(6) the mind of vivid red or orange increase, and
(7) the mind of vivid black near attainment

and the dawning of the most subtle consciousness
(8) the mind of clear light

This is called "bringing death to the path as the Truth Body/Body of Attributes." The yoga must also mimic the process of assuming an intermediate state through appearance as a seed syllable and then the process of rebirth through appearance in divine physical form. These latter two are called "bringing the intermediate state and birth to the path as the Complete Enjoyment Body and Emanation Body" respectively. Since the deity yogas of the three lower tantras—Action, Performance, and Yoga—do not involve such a patterning on the stages of being born in cyclic existence, they cannot fulfill the characteristics of a generation stage. Since the generation stage does not occur in three out of the four tantra sets, it cannot differentiate the Sūtra and Mantra Great Vehicles, and thus Ratnarakṣhita is wrong to hold that the generation stage is the distinctive feature of Mantra in general.

2. Just as meditation on emptiness occurs in Highest Yoga Mantra in both the generation stage and the completion stage, deity yoga also occurs in both stages. (The distinctive feature of the completion stage is that the three subtler minds and the

fourth subtlest one are actually manifested through causing the winds to enter, dissolve, and remain in the central channel.) Therefore, Ratnarakṣhita is wrong in holding that all cultivations of deity yoga are included in the generation stage.

3. The blissful minds generated in the completion stage in Highest Yoga Mantra are more subtle consciousnesses than any generated through Sūtra practice, and once generated, they are used to realize the emptiness of inherent existence. Hence, Ratnarakṣhita is wrong in holding that bliss is similar in the Sūtra and Mantra Great Vehicles.

According to Tsongkhapa, when these points are not differentiated, the distinctive features of Highest Yoga Mantra are blurred. It can be seen that one of his aims in finely and critically delineating the difference between the Sūtra and Mantra Great Vehicles is so that the uncommon techniques of Highest Yoga Mantra can be appreciated. The doctrine of the most esoteric system affects the presentation of the less esoteric.

Refutation of Tripiṭakamāla

The second position that Tsongkhapa examines is that of Tripiṭakamāla as found in his *Lamp for the Three Modes*. Though Tsongkhapa earlier cited the *Lamp for the Three Modes* as a source for the division of vehicles into three types—Lesser Vehicle, Sūtra Great Vehicle, and Mantra Great Vehicle—from the viewpoint of trainees' interests (and abilities) and although he cites it later as a source for etymologies of the names of the four tantra sets, here he presents and refutes the *Lamp for the Three Modes* at length. Because Tripiṭakamāla's presentation is central to the expositions not only of Butön and Longchenpa (as well as other major scholars in Tibetan orders), Tsongkhapa's refutation of it is a radical and dramatic attempt to change the focus of tantric exposition. Let us consider the refutation in detail.

Tripiṭakamāla holds that the Mantra Vehicle is superior by way of four features: being for the nonobscured, having many methods, not being difficult, and being contrived for those of sharp faculties. Butön paraphrases Tripiṭakamāla's own explanation of these, and Tsongkhapa condenses it (both without, to my sight, any warpage), and I shall condense it even further.

1. ***Being for the nonobscured.*** Tripiṭakamāla explains that those following the Perfection Vehicle try to complete the perfection of giving, for instance, by physical acts of charity that include, in dire instances, even giving away one's own body. He says that followers of the Mantra Vehicle see that since "a perfection is the ability to fulfill a want of all sentient beings simultaneously" and since this cannot possibly be done by giving away one's body, head, or the like, Māntrikas engage in the superior technique of meditatively satisfying the wishes of all beings. This lack of obscuration, according to Tripiṭakamāla, characterizes the trainees of the Mantra Vehicle as superior.

Tsongkhapa disagrees with Tripiṭakamāla's basic notion of how the Perfection Vehicle describes fulfillment of a perfection. He cites Shāntideva's description of the perfection of giving in his *Engaging in the Bodhisattva Deeds,*[12] an unchallengeable treatise of Sūtra Great Vehicle:

> If through eliminating the poverty of beings
> A perfection of giving occurred,
> Then since there are still poor beings,
> How did the former Protectors achieve perfection?
> Through an attitude of giving to all beings
> All one's possessions with their fruits
> A perfection of giving is said to occur,
> Thus it is just the mind.

According to Shāntideva, the perfection of giving is a matter of bringing the *attitude* of generosity to full development, not of satisfying the wants of all sentient beings. Otherwise, a perfection of giving never could have previously occurred, since obviously there are still beggars in the world. In that case, Shākyamuni Buddha could not have become enlightened, since he would not have attained the perfection of giving. Tripiṭakamāla's description of this first feature of Mantra's being for the nonobscured is, as Tsong-khapa says, "in trouble."

2. ***Having many methods.*** Tripiṭakamāla explains that the techniques of the Sūtra system are all peaceful and thus "cannot take care of all sentient beings." It might seem that he is suggesting that the achievement of activities of pacification, increase, control, and ferocity in Mantra is unique to Mantra, but he does not even mention this line of argument and, instead, speaks of the mental, verbal, and physical aspects of maṇḍala meditation for the sake of undermining a single afflictive emotion, such as desire. Tsong-khapa does not address this explanation, only mentioning that Tibetan explanations of this feature as referring to the four types of activities are not based on Tripiṭakamāla's own words.

3. **and** 4. ***Not being difficult and being contrived for those of sharp faculties.*** Under these headings Tripiṭakamāla discusses four levels of capacity of Mantra trainees:

1. The supreme of the supreme meditate on the Great Seal—an indivisibility of wisdom and method—without using either a meditated consort or actual one.
2. The next beneath them use a meditated consort, called a Wisdom Seal.
3. The next use a fully qualified actual consort, called a pledge seal.
4. The next use an actual consort not necessarily endowed with all attributes.

If we add Jñānakīrti's explanation,[13] there is a fifth level, that of trainees of Yoga Tantra and below who meditate on the body of a deity that is given the name "Great Seal"—in other words, deity yoga without a consort.

The first four represent levels within Highest Yoga Mantra.

According to Tripiṭakamāla, the supreme of the supreme trainees of Highest Yoga Mantra do not use desire for attractive visible forms, sounds, odors, tastes, and touches in the path; they do not make use of even a meditated consort, never mind an actual one. Tripiṭakamāla holds that those just below the very top rank meditate on an imaginary consort, and he posits the usage of an actual consort only for the third and fourth levels of practitioners. It is clear that he does not hold Tsongkhapa's view that an actual consort is needed even by the very best of trainees in order to bring about a withdrawal of the grosser levels of consciousness as in the process of dying. It seems that he views the usage of a meditated or actual consort only as a technique for those distracted by desire. His thought is likely that by meditating on emptiness and so forth in the midst of ritualized sex, a practitioner could overcome the sense that sex is separate from the scope of emptiness and thereby could undermine sexual desire.

The psychological value of exposing oneself to one's own inner desires, fears, and so forth in the midst of a different, intentional background in meditating on emptiness is unquestionable. However, it seems that Tripiṭakamāla was not cognizant of the doctrine of the levels of consciousness manifested in orgasmic bliss and thus did not even conceive of utilizing them in the path. He had a completely different notion of the purpose of using desire in the path; for him desire is brought to the path only by those whose meditation is disturbed by lustful thoughts.

According to Tsongkhapa, just the opposite is the case. Through using an actual consort a person proficient in the meditations of Highest Yoga Mantra manifests the three subtler and the final, subtlest consciousness, thereby enabling completion of the path—from the path of accumulation[14] to the path of no-more-learning[15]—in one lifetime. Later in the *Great Exposition of Secret Mantra* Tsongkhapa explains this to be the system of the *Guhyasamāja Tantra,* and thus, from his point of view, it is totally mistaken to claim that the supreme of the supreme trainees of Highest Yoga Mantra do not use desire in the path; such a mistaken view misses what, for Tsongkhapa, is the most powerful feature of the Highest Yoga Mantra path. Also, it is self-contradictory (1) to claim that the Mantra Great Vehicle is superior to the Sūtra Great Vehicle due to not being difficult in the sense of using desire in the path and (2) then to hold that the supreme of the supreme trainees do not use desire in the path.

Again, Tsongkhapa is emphasizing the special features of Highest Yoga Mantra. As with his refutation of Ratnarakṣhita, this refutation of Tripiṭakamāla is primarily based on a difference of views on Highest Yoga Mantra; Tripiṭakamāla is indicted for being misinformed about the most profound form of the path. For Tsongkhapa, sense, coherence, and consistency are of utmost importance; thus, divergent views *must* be refuted; they cannot just be repeated.

The Nyingma master Longchenpa's exposition of Tripiṭakamāla's stanza is different in both style and content. He takes the "object" of the first line ("Though the object is the same")—which Butön explains as referring to the fact that nondual omniscience is similarly the goal of both the Sūtra and Mantra systems—as indicating not that the goal of Buddhahood is the same, but that the basis, the essence of clear light, is similarly described in both systems. He takes the line as meaning that the Sūtra and Mantra Great Vehicles similarly delineate this basis as well as the phenomena that depend upon it; thus, he incurs no self-contradiction when later he says that the goal of Mantra is higher than that of Sūtra. Longchenpa creatively comments on Tripiṭakamāla's stanza in a way that fits his own system, without even hinting that Tripiṭakamāla himself explains this stanza differently.[16]

From Longchenpa's explanation of the four distinctive features of Mantra, let us consider how Tsongkhapa and his followers might object to two of them—being for the nonobscured and not being difficult. Longchenpa says that those of the Perfection, or Definition, Vehicle are obscured with respect to the basis, paths, and fruits. He identifies the basis as the profound and the vast—the first being ultimate reality and the paths to it and the second being (1) the mode of procedure of the path of compassion and (2) the conventional phenomena in terms of which that procedure is carried out. He says:[17]

> The Definition [Vehicle] has no more than only a profundity that is concerned with a basis fabricated by the mind, an ultimate truth known by determinative inferential valid cognition breaking down [objects] through reasoning.

His assertion that in the Perfection Vehicle the ultimate truth is known only inferentially would not sit well with Tsongkhapa who holds that in the Perfection Vehicle inferential realization is a necessary prerequisite to direct realization of the ultimate. Indeed, if there were no direct realization of emptiness in the Perfection Vehicle, it would contradict the assertion of ten Bodhisattva grounds, which are levels centering around direct realization of emptiness in meditative equipoise. Longchenpa's view that the ultimate truth described in the Perfection Vehicle is a mere mental fabrication is diametrically opposite to Tsongkhapa's who holds that inference incontrovertibly knows the actual ultimate truth, albeit by the route of a generic image[18] and not directly. For Tsongkhapa, inferential realization leads to direct perception of the same emptiness. The change is epistemological, not ontological.

For Longchenpa, however, the ultimate truth as presented in Mantra or, more specifically, in Highest Yoga Mantra is actualized in the completion stage of the path of method in Highest Yoga Mantra through concentrating on special points in the body to induce the winds to enter the central channel so that the inner heat[19] can be generated, melting the drops at the top of the head and causing their descent within the channel structure and the subsequent generation of the four empties, or four subtle consciousnesses.[20] He says:[21]

> Mantra, however, delineates—as the ground—nonconceptual pristine wisdom unfabricated by the mind, the essence of the Body of Attributes, merely through concentrative emphasis on focal points of body, speech, channels, winds, drops of essential fluid, and so forth without depending on reasoning.

Here the procedure for getting at the ultimate truth is not reasoning but special techniques for inducing manifestation of pristine wisdom; a more profound means of perception realizes a more profound reality. When the mind of clear light is actualized and objects are seen as manifestations of it, one is beyond the need for discarding nonvirtues and adopting virtues as everything has become an appearance of this fundamental mind; everyone and everything of its own nature appears as divine. The style of the narrative itself is meant to yield glimpses of this hierophany in which everything, of its own accord, shines in self-established purity, divinity.

One can see how difficult it might be for those trained in Longchenpa's and Tsongkhapa's traditions to appreciate the other's approach. Neither could find in the other's teaching the particularly attractive taste that they find in their own—it would appear to be devoid of the most intriguing essence of their own path. Yet, for me, once this distinction of approach and of content is made, the two styles are more like two sides of a coin, without appreciation of which the whole picture might not be gained. I would suggest that to appreciate both styles, it is helpful to recognize the seeming contradictions and inconsistencies in each presentation when viewed from the other perspective.

With respect to Mantra's feature of not being for the difficult, Longchenpa concludes that "achievement arises through using the attributes of the Desire Realm and so forth." This specifically refers to making use of the pleasant visible forms, sounds, odors, tastes, and touches of a consort in the path. As we have seen, desire for these is used in or as the path[22] in the sense that desire leads to a blissful consciousness realizing emptiness. Specifically, in

Highest Yoga Mantra sexual union is used to manifest (in orgasm but without emission) the subtler levels of consciousness mentioned above.[23] However, their mere actualization is not sufficient; those bliss consciousnesses, according to Tsongkhapa, must take the emptiness of inherent existence as their object, thereby eradicating desire. Longchenpa does not explicitly say such, but he would seem to hold that, far from merely arising from being fed up with the rigors of a wearying path, the practice of using desire in the path serves as a technique for highly qualified persons to proceed on the path more quickly.

In the three lower tantras—Action, Performance, and Yoga—desire is also used in the path, though not to generate subtler consciousnesses. However, Tsongkhapa is unwilling to hold that the usage of desire in the path is a distinguishing feature of Mantra because Sūtra Bodhisattvas are well known for using the afflictive emotions of desire and so forth to aid sentient beings, thereby accumulating merit,[24] which contributes to their eventual full enlightenment. As a source he cites the *Kāshyapa Chapter Sūtra:*

> Just as the filth of city-dwellers
> Helps the field of a sugarcane grower,
> So the manure of a Bodhisattva's afflictions
> Assists in growing the qualities of a Buddha.

In his commentary, the Dalai Lama gives as an example a Sūtra Bodhisattva king's using desire in the path in order to father children so that they can be of service to the kingdom. The implication is that desire is necessary for erection and orgasm; thus, even though the causal motivation[25] for such copulation is compassion and thus is nonafflicted, the motivation at the time of the act[26] is mixed with the afflictive emotion of desire.

As an amusing aside, let me cite the comment by the late seventeenth- and early eighteenth-century Gelug scholar Jamyang Shaypa[27] that Bodhisattva Superiors,[28] those who have reached the path of seeing[29] and above, can have a "serviceable organ"[30] without an afflictive emotion being involved:[31]

> If [Bodhisattva Superiors] are able to display endless emanations in actuality [and not just in imagination], what need is there to mention that they could emanate an actual serviceable organ!

Since Bodhisattvas on the first ground and above could magically display an erection, they would have no need to use such an afflictive emotion to father a child. More seriously, this calls into question the assertion that the scope of Sūtra Bodhisattvas' usage of desire in the path would be limited to those on the paths of accumulation.

Hatred also is said to be used in the Sūtra Great Vehicle path, as in killing a highly injurious person who cannot be tamed in any other way. Again, the causal motivation is compassion (both for the evil person and for others oppressed by him/her), but does the act of killing have to involve hatred or does it just *look* like a hateful act? Among my Tibetan teachers, one lama said that hatred might be necessary to bring the act of stopping the other person's life to completion, whereas another said it would not.[32]

In any case, the Sūtra ways of using the afflictive emotions in the path in which negative emotions impel virtuous acts are not comparable to the tantric use of a bliss consciousness arising from desire *to realize emptiness*. Hence, there remains the question of whether the usage of desire in this particularly tantric way could be indeed a differentiator of the Sūtra and Mantra Great Vehicles. Tsongkhapa briefly addresses this more refined position:

> We must assert that the trainees of the four tantras each use pleasure in the path in dependence on the four types of desire for the attributes of the desire realm [gazing, laughing, holding hands, and union. The presence or

> absence of such an ability to use pleasure in the path] is suitable as a difference between persons who are initially entering the Mantra or Perfection Vehicles; however, such cannot distinguish the vehicles.

Is Tsongkhapa making the point that differences between practitioners of vehicles cannot determine differences in vehicles? This seems unlikely, since the difference in persons comes by way of an ability to practice a certain path, or vehicle. Or, is he saying that such a difference occurs with respect to trainees "initially" entering these vehicles but does not hold true throughout the practice of the vehicle and thus cannot distinguish the vehicles? If this is the case, then in Tsongkhapa's system deity yoga would absurdly have to be practiced at *every single* point in the Mantra Vehicle, something that he himself does not assert. Rather, he seems to be admitting that the difference in the trainees of the respective vehicles indeed indicates a difference in the paths but is not *sufficient* to distinguish the vehicles since it is not central. The Dalai Lama speaks directly to this point:

> Although it indicates an inequality in the capacities of the two types of persons, it is not the profound and complete distinction between the Perfection and Mantra vehicles.

This statement reinforces a focal point in Tsongkhapa's basic argument, namely, that the difference between the vehicles must be *significant* in terms of the general structure of the path, this being in terms of method and wisdom, which are the chief causes respectively of the two aspects of the goal of the path—a Buddha's Body of Attributes and Form Bodies. Deity yoga does indeed fulfill this criterion.

The special tantric way of using desire in the path can perhaps be subsumed under deity yoga, the special union of method and wisdom found only in Mantra, since it is performed within imagination of oneself and the consort as deities, whether the consort is an actual one or not. However, because the technique of using desire in the path is for the sake of enhancing the *mind of wisdom* realizing emptiness—not necessarily in the sense of generating a subtler consciousness realizing emptiness as is done in Highest Yoga Mantra but at least in the sense of generating a blissful consciousness realizing emptiness—it should be included within the factor of wisdom, in which case there would be a difference between the Sūtra and Mantra Great Vehicles in terms of how wisdom is enhanced, a difference not limited to Highest Yoga Mantra but also present in the three lower tantras. Still, for Tsongkhapa, this would not make the factor of wisdom the differentiator between the two vehicles since just as he recognizes the difference between the Lesser Vehicle and Great Vehicle modes of cultivating wisdom—the former by just a brief form of reasoning and the latter by "endless" reasonings—and yet he does not posit it as a sufficiently significant difference to be the central distinction between those vehicles, so here the difference in the usage of desire in the path in the two Great Vehicles is clearly for him not sufficiently significant. Rather, in Tsongkhapa's system, the centrally significant distinguishing feature of Mantra is deity yoga—meditation on oneself as having a body similar in aspect to a Buddha's Form Body.

Deity yoga involves an enactment in meditation of the pure condition of Buddhahood while still on the path. The abode, body, resources, and deeds of a Buddha are an Effect Vehicle[33] in the sense of being that to which one is progressing. Because in Mantra the cause vehicle—the means by which one progresses to that state—involves using an imitation of the state of the effect in the path, it is also called an Effect Vehicle. Thus, the term "Effect Vehicle" has two meanings: (1) the actual state of the effect that is the goal of the path and (2) the means of progress (cause vehicle) that is called an Effect Vehicle since it involves a meditative imitation of the state of the effect. "Vehicle" as the goal of the path—Buddhahood—"proceeds" most likely in the sense of being able to carry or bear the welfare of limitless sentient beings.

The imagination of oneself in the body of a Buddha in an inestimable mansion with divine companions and articles and emanating radiance that purifies lands and the persons therein is *mantra,* which is understood as "mind-protection." With *man* meaning "mind" and *tra* (taken to be *trā*[34] with the final long vowel *ā* being dropped in the compound) meaning "protection," *mantra* means to protect the mind from ordinary appearances and apprehension of oneself and one's surroundings as ordinary. Clear appearance of the divine figure and so forth protects the mind from ordinary appearances of a usual body, house, resources, and activities, for the mental consciousness is involved in divine appearances to the point where the factors necessary to generate an eye consciousness, for instance, deteriorate for the time being and the sense consciousnesses do not operate. With clear appearance of pure mind and body there is a sense of being the divine "I" designated in dependence upon them; this counters the conception of ordinariness,[35] that is to say, being an ordinary person with an ordinary impure body of flesh, blood, and bone and with an ordinary impure mind.

This practice is found in all four tantra sets and occupies a significant place in the path as an enhancement of method. Since it is not found in Sūtra systems, it can serve as the central differentiator between the two Great Vehicles, Sūtra and Mantra, or Perfection Vehicle and Mantra Vehicle.

Quintessential Points on the Difference between the Lesser Vehicle and Great Vehicle and the Two Great Vehicles*

1. The Dalai Lama teaches that one needs to combine learnedness, practical application, and a good mind. Therefore, mere learnedness about the difference between the vehicles is not sufficient.
2. Generation of a good mind is the essential purpose of differentiating the vehicles; the immediate purpose is to know the difference between the vehicles in order to facilitate practice.

Lesser Vehicle and Great Vehicle

3. One can distinguish the terms "Lesser Vehicle" and "Great Vehicle" from the viewpoint of schools of tenets and from the viewpoint of path.
4. One can be of the Great Vehicle by tenet and of the Lesser Vehicle by path, as in the case of the great Foe Destroyers of the past. Thus, there are some who are capable of assuming a Great Vehicle tenet system but who are temporarily incapable of generating a Great Vehicle path of the altruistic intention to become enlightened.
5. The two Lesser Vehicle tenet systems (Great Exposition School and Sūtra School) and the two Great Vehicle tenet systems (Mind-Only School and Middle Way School) each present a Lesser Vehicle path (Hearer and Solitary Realizer paths) and a Great Vehicle path (Bodhisattva path).

* Several points are drawn from the Dalai Lama's *The Buddhism of Tibet and The Key to the Middle Way*.

6. The reason for four schools of tenets is persons' differing capacities, including the pride of wanting the highest despite being incapable of it; thus, low, nonfinal systems are taught as if they were final.
7. The difference between Lesser Vehicle and Great Vehicle and between the two Great Vehicles must be found in the sense of vehicle as that to which one progresses (the fruit) and/or as that by which one progresses (method, wisdom, or both).
8. Valid foundation and the conditionable nature of the mind make limitless development of method and wisdom possible.
9. The difference between the Lesser Vehicle and the Great Vehicle lies in the sense of the vehicle as that to which one is progressing (Foe Destroyer and Buddha, which bear, like a vehicle, the welfare respectively of only oneself and of all sentient beings) and as those practices by which one progresses (specifically method, not wisdom).
10. From the viewpoint of the Middle Way Consequence School, the wisdom of both vehicles is the same because the root of cyclic existence is the conception of persons and other phenomena as inherently existent, and even Lesser Vehicle Foe Destroyers (those who have attained the fruit of Lesser Vehicle paths) are liberated from cyclic existence, having destroyed the root foe, afflictive ignorance.
11. Therefore, both Lesser Vehicle and Great Vehicle paths involve realization of the subtle emptiness, which is the lack of inherent existence in persons and other phenomena.
12. Therefore, the difference between the Lesser Vehicle and the Great Vehicle in the sense of vehicle as that by which one progresses lies not in wisdom but in method—motivation and its attendant deeds. The Lesser Vehicle motivation is mainly the wish to attain liberation from cyclic existence for oneself whereas the Great Vehicle motivation is mainly the wish to attain Buddhahood in order to help all sentient beings.

13. There are two kinds of obstructions: afflictive obstructions (preventing liberation from cyclic existence) and obstructions to omniscience (preventing simultaneous realization of the two truths—ultimate truths and conventional truths, or emptinesses and the objects qualified by emptiness).
14. The afflictive obstructions are (1) the ignorance conceiving the inherent existence of persons and other phenomena, (2) the other afflictions that this induces, and (3) their seeds.
15. Obstructions to omniscience are predispositions, which are established by the *conception* of inherent existence, but which produce the false *appearance* of inherent existence as well as the incapacity to realize the two truths directly and simultaneously.
16. If one's aim is merely to abandon the afflictive obstructions, it is sufficient to approach emptiness through merely a few forms of reasoning. If one's aim is to eradicate the obstructions to omniscience and thereby attain Buddhahood, it is necessary to approach emptiness through limitless forms of reasoning.
17. Thus, although there is no difference in the *type* of wisdom between Lesser Vehicle and Great Vehicle, there is a difference in the mode of cultivation and the eventual effect of the cultivation.

Perfection Vehicle and Mantra Vehicle

18. The two Great Vehicles, Perfection Vehicle and Mantra Vehicle, have the same fruit and the same wisdom; therefore, the difference lies in method, which is tantra's special feature of deity yoga.
19. A practitioner of tantra must have particularly intense compassion, being in great haste to become a Buddha in order to help others.
20. Method in the Perfection and the Mantra Vehicles is the same with respect to the basis of practice, which is the

altruistic mind of enlightenment, and the deeds of practice, which are the six perfections. Therefore, the Mantra Vehicle does not discard or transcend the conventional mind of enlightenment (the altruistic aspiration to Buddhahood for the sake of others and the Bodhisattva deeds) or the ultimate mind of enlightenment (direct realization of emptiness by a Bodhisattva). However, Mantra has the additional feature of deity yoga.

21. The difference in speed between the two Great Vehicles is due to a faster accumulation of merit in the Mantra Vehicle (if one is capable of practicing it), resulting from the cultivation of deity yoga. This involves meditation cultivating a similitude of a Buddha's Form Body, residence, resources, and activities.
22. Emptiness yoga is a general feature of Buddhist deity yoga, distinguishing it from non-Buddhist deity yoga.
23. In emptiness yoga one must confidently stabilize on the vacuity that is a negative of inherent existence found after searching for the concretely existent self that so palpably appears to us.
24. Deity yoga involves causing the mind realizing emptiness and fused with that emptiness to itself appear as a deity, out of compassion, in order to help others.
25. "Vajra" means an indivisible union of the wisdom realizing emptiness and compassion.
26. The Perfection Vehicle does not have deity yoga even though it has meditation cultivating a similitude of the Truth Body, the space-like meditative equipoise on emptiness.
27. All tantric practices are either deity yoga, emptiness yoga, or enhancers of these two.
28. The Perfection Vehicle *alone* is not sufficient for the attainment of Buddhahood, nor are the three lower tantras *alone*. Highest Yoga Tantra is required for overcoming the extremely subtle obstructions to omniscience.
29. For tantra in general, the difference in speed over the Per-

fection Vehicle is the passage from the beginning of the path of accumulation to the path of seeing faster than the one period of countless eons required in the Perfection Vehicle.

30. The attainment of Buddhahood in one lifetime is a distinctive feature of Highest Yoga Tantra. Thus, the greater speed of Mantra over the Perfection Vehicle is not necessarily the attainment of Buddhahood in one lifetime of the degenerate era.
31. Because the practices of the Perfection Vehicle are indispensable to and the very substance of the Mantra Vehicle, we should view even its ancillary practices, such as that of impermanence, which is conducive to realizing emptiness, as substantial contributors to the Mantra path.

Emptiness

Tsongkhapa says that only the Buddhist teaching is the entrance of those wishing liberation from cyclic existence and that within Buddhism it is only through understanding the Middle Way Consequence School's presentation of emptiness that the ability to eradicate suffering can be gained.[36] Emptiness as explained by the Consequence School is considered to be more subtle than that expounded by any other system. Other systems are helps and aids and, though a particular person might progress more now by assuming one of them rather than attempting to penetrate Consequence School, the subtle emptiness must eventually be understood. All practices lead to the center by creating the capacity to practice the one path that actually arrives at the center. The actual final arrival is on only one path.

Though a Lesser Vehicle path is not final, for those of the Lesser Vehicle it is a means to highest enlightenment, Buddhahood. In this context, "Lesser Vehicle" and "Great Vehicle" refer not to the four Buddhist schools of tenets, two Lesser Vehicle—Great Exposition School and Sūtra School—and two Great Vehicle—Mind-Only School and Middle Way School—but to the Lesser Vehicle and Great Vehicle *paths* that each of the four schools presents. (See chart 1.) Lesser Vehicle paths are for people bearing the lineage of Hearers and Solitary Realizers, and Great Vehicle paths are for those bearing the lineage of Bodhisattvas. Among the four presentations of Lesser Vehicle and Great Vehicle paths, Tsongkhapa here clarifies the presentation of the final system, the Middle Way Consequence School.

"Great Vehicle" sometimes refers to the Mind-Only and Middle Way schools of tenets and at other times refers to the Bodhisattva path, as presented by either Lesser Vehicle or Great Vehicle schools of tenets, for even the Lesser Vehicle schools propound a Bodhisattva path. Great Exposition School and Sūtra School—the Lesser Vehicle schools—accept the rendition of Buddha as a Bodhisattva in his *Birth Tales* (*jātaka*) and in the discipline (*vinaya*) division of the scriptures. According to the Lesser Vehicle schools Shākyamuni Buddha is the only one to complete the Bodhisattva path in our era.

According to the Great Exposition School and the Sūtra School, Hearer and Solitary Realizer Foe Destroyers (*arhan*) are lower than a Buddha. All three are equally liberated from cyclic existence and will all equally disappear upon death with the severance of their continuum of consciousness and form. However, while they are alive, a Bodhisattva at the effect stage is called a Buddha whereas the others are only called Foe Destroyers—those who have destroyed the foe of the afflictions, mainly desire, hatred, and ignorance—because a Buddha has special knowledge, more subtle clairvoyance, and a distinctive body. A Bodhisattva accumulates merit and wisdom for three countless eons, thus attaining the greater fruit of Buddhahood. For the Great Exposition School and the Sūtra School, a person treading the path of Buddhahood is very rare.

Both Lesser Vehicle tenet systems present three vehicles which they say are capable of bearing practitioners to their desired fruit. Both present an emptiness that must be understood in order to reach the goal, and in both systems this emptiness is the absence of substantial existence of persons. They prove that a person is not a self-sufficient entity and does not substantially exist as the controller of mind and body, like a lord over subjects. Through realizing and becoming accustomed to this insubstantiality, the afflictions and, thereby, all sufferings are said to be destroyed. According to the Lesser Vehicle tenet systems the path of wisdom is the same for those of the Lesser Vehicle—Hearers and Solitary Realizers—and for Bodhisattvas. The length of time that practitioners spend

Chart 1: Four Schools and Three Vehicles

	School		Vehicle	Effect
Mahayana	Madhyamika	Prasangika	Bodhisattva	Buddha
			Solitary Realizer	Foe Destroyer
			Hearer	Foe Destroyer
		Svatantrika	Bodhisattva	Buddha
			Solitary Realizer	Foe Destroyer
			Hearer	Foe Destroyer
	Chittamatra		Bodhisattva	Buddha
			Solitary Realizer	Foe Destroyer
			Hearer	Foe Destroyer
Hinayana	Sautrāntika		Bodhisattva	Buddha
			Solitary Realizer	Foe Destroyer
			Hearer	Foe Destroyer
	Vaibhāṣhika		Bodhisattva	Buddha
			Solitary Realizer	Foe Destroyer
			Hearer	Foe Destroyer

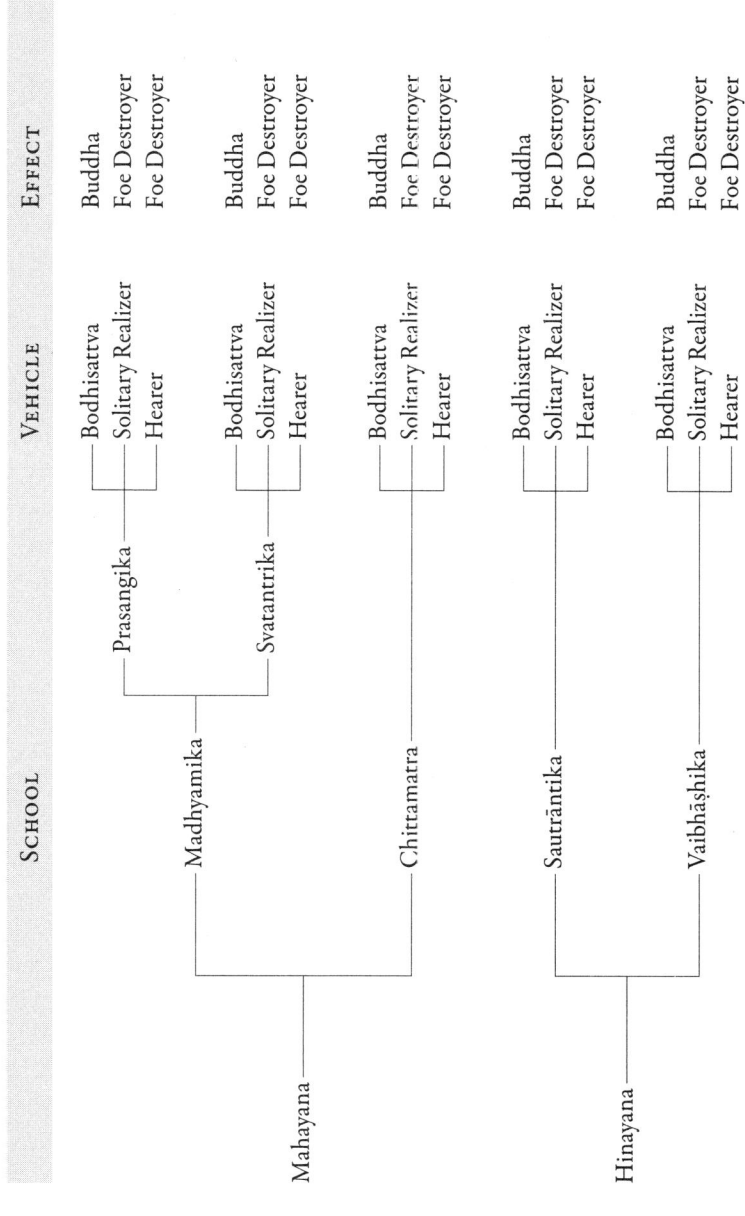

amassing meritorious power constitutes the essential difference between the vehicles.

The Great Vehicle systems—Mind-Only School and Middle Way School, the latter being further divided into an Autonomy School and a Consequence School—do not just describe or report the Great Exposition School and Sūtra School assertions on the Lesser Vehicle but present their own versions of Lesser Vehicle paths. For instance, according to the system of the Consequence School, one must understand the subtle emptiness—the absence of inherent existence—of persons and other phenomena in order to leave cyclic existence. Therefore, Hearers and Solitary Realizers must understand the subtle emptiness just as Bodhisattvas do. According to the Consequence School, the difference between the Lesser Vehicle path of Hearers and Solitary Realizers and the Great Vehicle path of Bodhisattvas is that those of the Great Vehicle have succeeded in generating an altruistic aspiration to highest enlightenment for the sake of all sentient beings, which is induced by love and compassion. When through long training this altruistic aspiration arises spontaneously—whether going, wandering, lying, or standing still just as strongly as it does in meditation—then one is a Bodhisattva and a Great Vehiclist by path, not just by tenet.

Consequentialists by tenet would certainly want to generate love, compassion, and the altruistic aspiration, but in the meantime they might have developed to the point of spontaneity merely the wish to leave cyclic existence. In that case, they would be Lesser Vehicle by path, though Great Vehicle by tenet. In other words, when they have practiced over a long time to the point where the thought definitely to leave cyclic existence arises spontaneously night and day—whether going, wandering, lying, or standing still, never for a moment admiring the prosperity of cyclic existence—then they achieve the bottom line of the Lesser Vehicle path, the path of accumulation. They have temporarily laid aside full development of altruism, seeking instead to relieve only their own pressed situation. As Consequentialists, they would concentrate on the emptiness of inherent existence rather than the coarser emptiness of substantial existence as presented in the Great Exposition School and Sūtra School. This Lesser Vehicle way is said to be a more protracted path to Buddhahood than immediately extending one's understanding of the plight of cyclic existence to others, developing love and compassion, and engaging in meditation on emptiness in order to achieve others' welfare by becoming a Buddha.

According to the Consequence School, the basis of a Bodhisattva's practice is generation of an altruistic aspiration to highest enlightenment for the sake of all sentient beings. Bodhisattvas engage in the six perfections—giving, ethics, patience, effort, concentration, and wisdom—in limitless varieties for at least three countless eons in order to empower the mind so that they may overcome the obstructions to omniscience. They attain liberation from cyclic existence at the beginning of the eighth of the ten Bodhisattva grounds after two countless eons of practice, spending this vast length of time amassing meritorious power in order to empower their mind to counteract the appearance of objects as if objects cover their own parts, or bases of designation.

The teaching that such a tremendous length of time is required to destroy these obstructions inspires yogis to develop a willingness for long-term practice; they imagine practically limitless future lives involving practice of the six perfections. Bodhisattvas become like a mother holding her sole sweet baby who kicks her, pulls her hair, and sticks a finger in her eye. She is patient, knowing how long her task will take. In the same way, Bodhisattvas are willing to spend an eon to achieve a slight improvement in one sentient being.

Though Bodhisattvas must practice for two countless eons before they attain liberation from cyclic existence whereas a Hearer can leave cyclic existence in as little as three lifetimes, Bodhisattvas have engaged in the meantime in a path that will make their eventual attainment of Buddhahood much faster. (See chart 2.) When Hearers devote time to their own welfare, they pollute the mind with self-cherishing such that it lengthens the path to Buddhahood. Still, Hearers and Solitary Realizers all eventually proceed to the Bodhisattva path. After sometimes spending eons in solitary

Chart 2: Paths

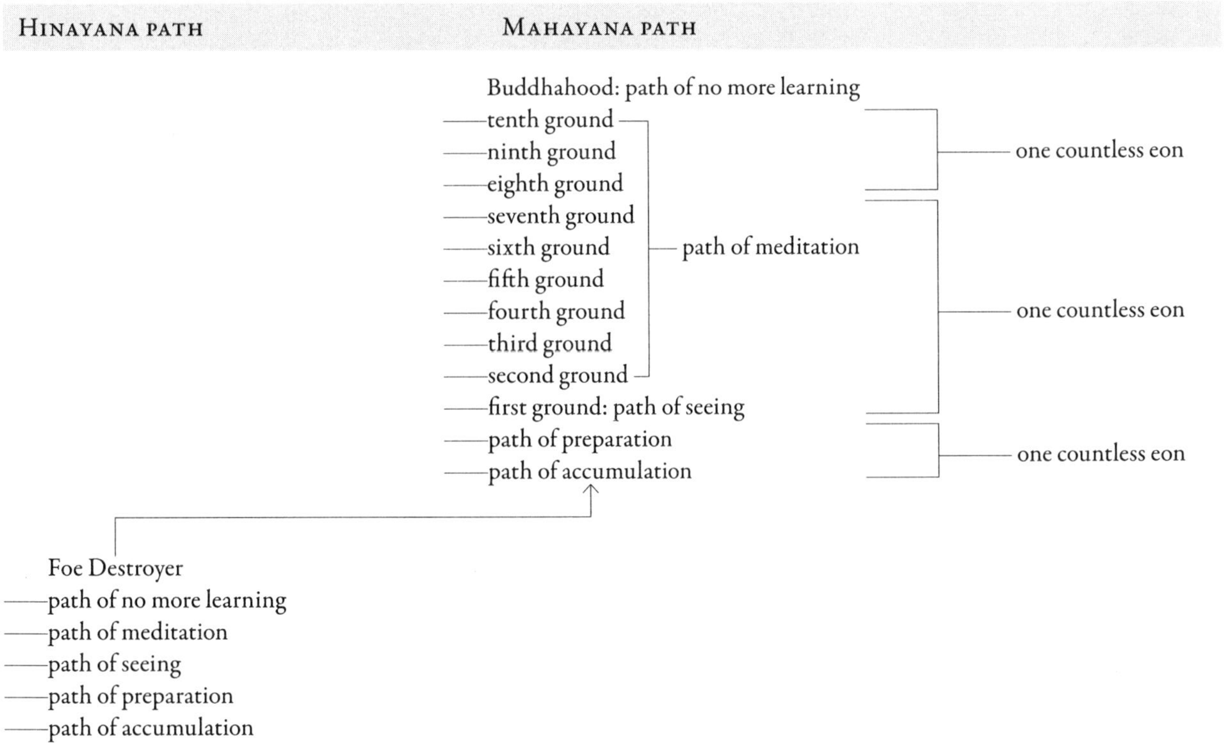

Hinayana path
Mahayana path
Buddhahood: path of no more learning
tenth ground
ninth ground
eighth ground
seventh ground
sixth ground
fifth ground
fourth ground
third ground
second ground
path of meditation
first ground: path of seeing
path of preparation
path of accumulation
one countless eon
one countless eon
one countless eon
Foe Destroyer
path of no more learning
path of meditation
path of seeing
path of preparation
path of accumulation

trance, they are aroused by Buddhas who make them aware that they have not fulfilled even their own welfare, not to mention the welfare of others, and they finally enter the Bodhisattva vehicle. Thus, though there are three vehicles, there is only one final vehicle.

According to the Consequentialist system, Hearers and Solitary Realizers have the most subtle wisdom, realizing the subtle selflessness of both persons and phenomena, whereas according to the Mind-Only and Autonomy systems, Hearers and Solitary Realizers do not realize the subtle selflessness of phenomena and thus do not have the most subtle wisdom. The Great Exposition School, Sūtra School, Mind-Only School, and Autonomy School all assert that Hearers and Solitary Realizers are liberated from cyclic existence through realizing and accustoming to merely the subtle selflessness of the person. Let us examine this.

Selflessness is divided into two types: of persons and of phenomena. The selflessness of persons is also divided into two: coarse and subtle. (See chart 3.) The Great Exposition School and Sūtra School do not assert a selflessness of phenomena because, for them, phenomena truly exist and are other entities from a perceiving consciousness.

With regard to the selflessness of persons, all systems present subtle and coarse forms. According to the non-Consequentialist systems the coarse is the emptiness of a permanent, unitary, independent person. The misconception of such a self is only artificial, not innate—it is based only on having taken up a non-Buddhist system. In other words, we do not naturally misconceive the person to have the three qualities of being permanent, unitary, and independent.

According to all systems except the Consequence School, the subtle personal selflessness is the emptiness of a substantially existent, self-sufficient person. Here a yogi realizes that a person does not substantially exist in the sense of existing as a self-sufficient entity as the controller of mind and body. The mind and body falsely seem to depend on the person whereas the person does not seem to depend on mind and body. The person seems like a master, and mind and body the subjects; this misconception is of two types, artificial and innate, the former being a conception of substantial existence reinforced by a system of thought and the latter being an habitual or untutored conception. Most religions, philosophies, and systems of psychology reinforce these innate misconceptions, thereby compounding the basic error with further superimposition.

The Mind-Only School asserts the subtle selflessness of persons in the same way as the Great Exposition School and the Sūtra School but they also assert a selflessness of phenomena that is more profound and subtle; it is an emptiness of a difference in entity between apprehended-object and apprehending-subject. Subject and object—apprehender and apprehended—appear to be distant and cut off but are not so in reality. A yogi attempts through reasoning and examples, such as similarity with dreams, to overcome assent to this false appearance and finally to remove the mistaken aspect in all appearance.

In the Middle Way School, the selflessness of phenomena is the emptiness of a mode of abiding not posited by the mind. Things seem to have their own independent existence—their own mode of existence without being posited through appearing to the mind—whereas they are actually posited only through appearing to the mind, much as a magician's illusion is posited to be real through appearing to the audience's spell-bound mind. The Consequence School subdivision of the Middle Way School further refines this selflessness as an emptiness of inherent existence, which, roughly speaking, means that objects are not even the collection of their parts and are only designated in dependence upon that collection. Though phenomena appear to exist concretely, when sought analytically they are unfindable. Yogis meditate in order to overcome assent to this false appearance of concreteness and eventually to empower the mind such that the mistaken element disappears entirely.

In the non-Consequentialist systems, Hearers and Solitary Realizers only realize the selflessness of persons. These systems say

Chart 3: Selflessness

School	Selflessness Asserted		Description
Prasangika	selflessness of phenomena	subtle:	lack of inherent existence of phenomena other than persons
	selflessness of persons	subtle:	lack of inherent existence of persons
		coarse:	lack of being a self-sufficient entity
Svatantrika	selflessness of phenomena	subtle:	lack of being an entity not posited through appearing to a non-defective consciousness
		coarse:	lack of difference in entity between subject and object*
	selflessness of persons	subtle:	lack of being a self-sufficient entity
		coarse:	lack of being a permanent, partless, independent self
Chittamatra	selflessness of phenomena	subtle:	lack of a difference in entity between subject and object and lack of naturally being a base of a name
	selflessness of persons	subtle:	lack of being a self-sufficient entity
		coarse:	lack of being a permanent, partless, independent self
Sautrāntika and Vaibhāṣhika	selflessness of persons	subtle:	lack of being a self-sufficient person
		coarse:	lack of being a permanent, partless, independent self

*asserted only by Yogachara-Svatantrika

that a person falsely seems to have a character different from the character of mind and body which they exemplify with a master and subjects, the former controlling the latter. However, the Consequentialists, as presented by Jamyang Shaypa, a late seventeenth and early eighteenth-century Gelugpa scholar, say that mind and body seem to be like salespersons and the person like a head salesperson. The difference is that a head salesperson is a salesperson, but a master is not a servant. In this more subtle version the person falsely seems to be the boss, seems to be in control of mind and body, but not necessarily as a separate entity. Thus, according to the Consequence School, there is no *innate* conception of a self of persons—coarse or subtle—in which the person is conceived to be a different entity from mind and body.

What the non-Consequentialist systems identify as the subtle selflessness of persons, the Consequentialists identify as the coarse selflessness of persons, and further what the non-Consequentialists describe as the innate subtle conception of a self of persons, the Consequentialists identify as artificial and coarse. This means that according to the Consequence School we conceive the person to have a different character or different entity from mind and body only based on mistaken philosophies. Therefore, according to this highest of systems, we cannot leave cyclic existence through realizing the selflessness of the person as described by the other systems. Not only that, but also the other systems have not accurately delineated what is refuted in the coarse personal selflessness.

According to the Mind-Only School and the Autonomy School, Bodhisattvas are more intelligent than Hearers and Solitary Realizers and thus perceive a deeper, more fundamental emptiness—the selflessness of phenomena—thereby eradicating a more basic problem. The Consequence School, on the other hand, considers what others describe as the subtle selflessness of persons as the coarse selflessness of persons; the others' subtle selflessness is then replaced by the emptiness of an inherently existent person. The Consequence School also substitutes inherent existence for difference of entity between apprehended-object and apprehending-subject. Thus, in this system, that which is negated in the view of emptiness is the same in both the selflessness of persons and the selflessness of phenomena—inherent existence in both cases. Here, there is no difference in depth or subtlety between the selflessness of persons and of phenomena.

The Proponents of Mind-Only assert that the lack of difference in entity between apprehended-object and apprehending-subject is the subtle selflessness of phenomena. The Autonomists say that the lack of existence not posited through the object's appearing to the mind is the subtle selflessness of phenomena, and in both the Mind-Only School and the Autonomy School the subtle selflessness of phenomena is subtler than the subtle selflessness of persons. One has to be brighter, sharper, to understand it, and Bodhisattvas are sharper. However, when Consequentialists assign the absence of inherent existence of persons as the subtle personal selflessness and the absence of inherent existence of other phenomena as the subtle selflessness of phenomena, there is no difference in subtlety between the two. Once the one has been realized, the other could be realized.

Consequently, according to the Consequence School—the final system in Tibet—it is impossible to be liberated from cyclic existence without understanding the emptiness both of persons and of other phenomena. In this system, both Hearers and Solitary Realizers realize a selflessness that is subtler than what other systems call subtle; the great Lesser Vehicle Foe Destroyers of the past realized this deepest of emptinesses, and Bodhisattvas do not realize another more profound reality even though they are brighter. They merely approach this same emptiness through more avenues of reasoning.

The Consequence School is the only Great Vehicle system to assert that one type of realization is common to all three vehicles. The two Lesser Vehicle systems, the Great Exposition School and the Sūtra School, assert that all three vehicles realize the same subtle selflessness but this is only the person's nonexistence as a substantially existent, self-sufficient entity. The Mind-Only School and the Autonomy School assert that Bodhisattvas realize a deeper emptiness, the selflessness of phenomena, than do Hearers and Solitary Realizers, who realize only the subtle selflessness of persons. Furthermore, among the two divisions of Autonomists, Yogic-Autonomists and Sūtra-Autonomists, the former asserts a coarse selflessness of phenomena which is the same as the Proponents of Mind-Only subtle selflessness of phenomena—the lack of a difference in entity between apprehended-object and apprehending-subject. As Proponents of the Middle Way, they also assert a subtle selflessness of phenomena that is an emptiness of true existence—existence not posited through the object's appearing to the mind. They say that Solitary Realizers meditate on the coarse selflessness of phenomena—absence of a difference in entity between apprehended-object and apprehending-subject; Bodhisattvas meditate on the subtle selflessness of phenomena—the absence of true existence of all phenomena; and Hearers meditate on the subtle selflessness of persons—the nonexistence of persons as a substantially existent, self-sufficient entity. Thus, in the Yogic-Autonomy School there are three types of realization.

The Autonomists say that each object has its own particular mode of abiding but not one that is not posited through the object's appearing to the mind. For example, when a magician creates an illusion of an attractive feast, it has a mode of abiding posited by the audience's mistaken mind. The power of a mantra has affected everyone's consciousness, including the magician's. The audience assumes a feast covers that spot in its own independent right, whereas even though it appears that way to the magician, he does not believe it. He knows its nature and does not posit to it an independent entity. In the same way, phenomena appear to the nonmistaken consciousnesses of sentient beings—eye, ear, nose, tongue, body and mental consciousnesses—and through appearing to the mind, their own particular mode of abiding is posited, the error being that objects are granted a mode of abiding independent of appearing to the mind. That which is negated in the view of selflessness is an independent entity of objects.

For the Consequentialists, if something has its own particular mode of abiding, it is not posited by the mind; the two are contradictory. The Consequentialists assert that everything—be it a person or any other phenomenon—is like a magician's illusion in that it appears to exist inherently but does not. They present a deeper and more subtle object of negation than the other systems, which are considered in Tibet to be ways of overcoming coarser misconceptions. The reason for Buddha's propounding the other nonfinal systems is said to be that people who would be discouraged by not being able to penetrate the deeper teaching are taught a selflessness that is not so deep but are told that it is the deepest.

The coarse sense of self is easier to identify. For instance, when we are told, "Your hair is very shiny today," there is a sense of an "I" that controls or owns the hair. Or, sometimes when we are accused or praised, there is something very tight and firm, undeniable, unmistakable, almost touchable, seeable, in the center of the chest—the "I" who has been offended, hurt, praised, or helped. Sometimes when we examine this "I" with a subtle noninterfering consciousness while it is operating, it even seems as if it is a different entity. Sometimes, it is more like a lord and subjects than a head salesperson and his or her salespersons. This is the artificial, coarse conception of a self of persons, and we might progress more from concentrating on it than proceeding to the innate coarse form.

It takes truly practical and humble devotees of any religion to decide that they cannot succeed at the most subtle teaching at present. To help avoid this problem, even nowadays teachers pretend that they are presenting the view of the absence of inherent existence. Thus, it is not difficult to imagine that Buddha would present another system and say that it is the final system.

This provisionality necessitates a division of the Buddhist scriptures into two classes, definitive and requiring interpretation. The distinction between these is based on whether the main object of discourse is emptiness. If it is, then the mode of existence of the phenomena discussed in that sūtra is definite as just what is said in the sūtra and does not require interpretation. Scriptures that do not explicitly present emptiness as the main object of discourse require interpretation to know the final mode of existence of the phenomena discussed in those sūtras. For instance, Buddha said that there are five aggregates: forms, feelings, discriminations, compositional factors, and consciousnesses. This teaching is literal, definite, and reliable because the existence of the aggregates is certified by valid cognition; however, the teaching requires interpretation to know the final mode of existence of the aggregates—their emptiness of inherent existence.

Within scriptures requiring interpretation, there are two types, literal—as in the example of the aggregates above—and nonliteral. Nonliteral teachings are not supported by valid cognition and must be interpreted in terms of a particular trainee's need for such a doctrine. For instance, Buddha taught that liberation can be achieved through realizing and accustoming to the four noble truths: true sufferings, true origins, true cessations, and true paths. There are sixteen attributes of the four truths, which in brief are:

true sufferings

1. impermanence
2. misery
3. emptiness
4. selflessness

true origins

1. cause
2. origin
3. strong production
4. condition

true cessations

1. cessation
2. pacification
3. auspiciousness
4. definite emergence

true paths
1. path
2. reasonableness
3. achieving
4. deliverance

All Buddhist systems, therefore, hold that true sufferings, the internal and external phenomena of cyclic existence, are impermanent, miserable, empty, and selfless.

Products are impermanent in that they require no further cause for their disintegration than their own production; products have a nature of disintegration. This does not imply chaos, for just as a flame can be steady in a breezeless room, so, if calm abiding (*śamatha*) is developed, the mind can remain steadily fixed on whatever object is chosen. The flame of one moment, however, is not the flame of the next moment.

True sufferings are miserable in that they are involved in actual physical and mental pain itself or if they are pleasurable, can easily turn into pain. They are empty in the sense that they are not a permanent, unitary, independent person or the objects of use of such a person. They are selfless in that they are not a substantially existent person or the objects of use of such a person. Dharmakīrti said that knowing emptiness and selflessness is the aim of the other aspects and that these two aspects are the paths of liberation from cyclic existence.

According to the Consequence School system, however, these are merely coarse paths, serving only to train the mind, not to liberate it. Such realizations cannot serve as antidotes to the innate conception that persons inherently exist or exist by way of their own character. They will lead to liberation but will not liberate.

Therefore, according to the Consequence School, Lesser Vehicle paths, as presented by the Autonomy School, Mind-Only School, Sūtra School, and Great Exposition School, are suited for the majority of Hearers and Solitary Realizers, who are for the present incapable of practicing a path of liberation and need aids to develop that ability. Because the subsidiary trainees of the Lesser Vehicle are greater in number than the special trainees, systems particularly suited for them are needed. When the progression of the systems is understood, the variety of approaches not only is not contradictory but is most appropriate, inducing conviction in Buddha's extraordinary ability to teach.

Psychological Transformation

Religion requires analysis but not partisanship. In order to penetrate reality, a yogi needs a sharp mind; it dulls the mind to claim that religions are one in all respects, suggesting that the differences in trainees and in practices are of no consequence. Claiming that all religions are one suggests that practice is ineffective.

Tsongkhapa's statement that only Buddha taught the final path of liberation draws us into analysis to determine whether or not this path is actually the only final way. A positive decision would indeed impel great effort; an issue of great importance, affecting not just this short lifetime but also the many lifetimes in the future, is at stake. Tsongkhapa issues a call to analysis to see if the Buddhist path is true.

The process of passing from a mistaken notion to clear apprehension of the truth is said to pass through seven steps (reading from bottom to top):[37]

7. direct perception
6. inferential cognition
5. correct assumption
4. doubt tending to the factual
3. equal doubt
2. doubt tending to the nonfactual
1. wrong view

We begin with a wrong view such as: Buddha, his teaching, and those properly training in his teaching are not the teacher of liberation, the path to liberation, and the friends on the journey to liberation; or, another example: I definitely inherently exist.

Through contact with Buddhist teaching, the wrong view may change into doubt tending to the nonfactual: Buddha, his teaching, and those properly training in his path are *probably* not the teacher, path, and friends on the journey to liberation; or: I *probably* inherently exist. Doubt has been raised; the firmness of the wrong view is gone. It is a time of inquiry, leading to equal doubt: Maybe Buddha is the teacher of liberation and maybe he is not; or: Maybe I inherently exist and maybe I do not.

On the basis of study, contact with spiritual guides, and personal experience, doubt tending to the factual is generated: Buddha probably is the teacher of liberation; or: I probably do not inherently exist. Through familiarization with the logical proofs for omniscience and the efficacy of the path as well as with scripture, correct assumption is generated: Buddha is the teacher of the path to liberation, his teaching is the path, and those properly training in it are the friends on the journey to liberation; or: I do not inherently exist.

Still, assumption is not incontrovertible; though a decision has been made, it has not been induced by incontrovertible conviction. Therefore, a correct assumption about the Three Jewels—Buddha, his Doctrine, and the Spiritual Community—is not sufficient; the unshakable knowledge of inference is needed.

Inference is incontrovertible understanding based on reasoning: Buddha, his teaching, and those properly training in his path have qualities such as omniscience, complete cessation of the afflictions, and ability to aid in the path that can be verified through reasoning. Similarly, it can be proved that the "I" does not inherently exist through realizing that whatever is a dependent-arising does not inherently exist and that the "I" is a dependent-arising. After repeated inquiry, unshakable conviction is generated; through familiarization this can be brought to the point of direct cognition, such as directly knowing the true cessation of a certain portion of the afflictions based on Buddha's path or directly knowing emptiness—the absence of inherent existence—of the "I."

The process of passing from wrong views to the incontrovertible knowledge of realization, be it inferential or direct, depends on study, analysis, meditation, and acquaintance with a spiritual guide. Inferential understanding is not a discursive mulling over of ideas and concepts; it is the conclusion of the process of analysis in a definite realization. In the case of emptiness, through the route of an image a mere vacuity appears to a mind that ascertains a negative of inherent existence. This realization is called inferential and conceptual only because a mere vacuity of inherent existence appears through the route of a conceptual image. The mind is stilled; it has understood that the "I" is a dependent-arising and that whatever is a dependent-arising does not inherently exist; now, it *knows* that the "I" does not inherently exist. The impact of even attaining a correct assumption about the emptiness of "I" which means its unfindability among its bases of designation—mind and body—is said to be like being struck by lightning. Thus, inferential realization, far from being a vague shuffling of concepts, is even more dramatic.

When the ascertainment of the absence of inherent existence lessens, yogis review the process of reasoning, but otherwise they remain in the *result* of reasoning—in terms of appearance, a mere vacuity of inherent existence and in terms of ascertainment, the definite knowledge of an absence of inherent existence. By stabilizing on this mere vacuity and occasionally heightening the realization by further analysis, yogis bring this conceptual understanding to the point of direct cognition. The sense of the object—emptiness—and the subject—the wisdom—gradually disappear, leaving a fusion of object and subject, like fresh water poured into fresh water.

The resultant realization is nondual but not nonspecific. As much as colors and shapes can be known definitely and directly by the eye consciousness, so the mental consciousness can know emptiness definitely and directly. The absence of inherent existence is known directly, based on earlier familiarization with a reasoning proving emptiness. Thus, far from turning against the process of reasoning, this practice is built on reasoning. However, those who are addicted to discursive thought cannot pass to the conclusion of reasoning, much like seeing smoke, reflecting that wherever there is smoke there is fire, and repeatedly going through this process without ever concluding that fire is present.

As much as one can incontrovertibly know of the presence of fire when billows of smoke are seen and can act on that knowledge, so much can one penetrate the nature of phenomena through a similar process of reasoning and live in accordance with it. Also, just as one can eventually go outside and see the fire directly, so by accustoming to the space-like meditative equipoise, one can perceive emptiness directly, without the medium of a conceptual image.

Although an emptiness is a mere negative of inherent existence, it is amenable to reflection and can eventually be perceived nonconceptually. The *Kāshyapa Chapter Sūtra* says:

> Kāshyapa, it is this way: For example, fire arises when the wind rubs two branches together. Once the fire has arisen, the two branches are burned. Just so, Kāshyapa, if you have the correct analytical intellect, a Superior's faculty of wisdom is generated. Through its generation, the correct analytical intellect is consumed.

Right thought overcomes wrong thought and leads to direct knowledge; thus, discrimination based on correct reasoning is the primary means, when coupled with a mind of calm abiding, for developing direct insight. Even nonconceptual sense consciousnesses have a factor of discrimination, which is a nonconfusion of the objects perceived; without it, everything would be a confused mass. This faculty must be developed, first conceptually and then nonconceptually, with respect to the nature of phenomena. Thought must be used to develop indirect knowledge of the nature of phenomena, and, through familiarization, this is gradually transformed into direct knowledge. Just as an eye consciousness can have definite and certainly not contentless knowledge of a color, so the mental consciousness can know impermanence, suffering, emptiness, others' minds, and so forth without the medium of concepts.

Objection: This progression suggests that there is something new to be known. Nāgārjuna said that there is not the slightest difference between cyclic existence (*saṃsāra*) and nirvāṇa.

Answer: The altruistic aspiration to highest enlightenment for the sake of all sentient beings is the basis of a Bodhisattva's practice in both the Perfection Vehicle and Vajra Vehicle. The altruistic aspiration is induced by love and compassion, which are the result of seeing the suffering of cyclic existence, generating a wish to leave it, and then applying this understanding to others. If one does not want to be free of cyclic existence, there is no way to wish for others to be free of it. This wish to leave cyclic existence is common to the Lesser Vehicle and the Great Vehicle and within the Great Vehicle is common to the Perfection and Vajra Vehicles.

The Sanskrit word *nirvāṇa* was translated into Tibetan as "passed beyond sorrow," with "sorrow" identified as the afflictions, the chief of which is the conception of inherent existence. Cyclic existence is an uncontrolled process of birth, aging, sickness, and death motivated by the afflictions. It is clear that when Nāgārjuna says that cyclic existence is nirvāṇa, he is not asserting that cyclic existence is the state of having passed beyond sorrow. Rather, in this context "cyclic existence," or *saṃsāra,* refers to conventional truths, all objects except emptinesses; the term "nirvāṇa" refers to a natural nirvāṇa, not the nirvāṇa that is the true cessation of all suffering. A natural nirvāṇa does not come into existence in dependence on the path but is merely the emptiness of inherent existence that each object naturally has.

An emptiness is not created by realizing it; a yogi realizes what always was. "Natural nirvāṇa" (*svabhāvanirvāṇa*) may also be translated as "inherent nirvāṇa" though, of course, "inherent" here does not mean "inherently existent." The commentarial tradition in Tibet makes the point that a natural nirvāṇa is not an actual nirvāṇa because an actual nirvāṇa is a true cessation of all afflictions.[38]

Thus, the statement that *saṃsāra* is not in the least different from *nirvāṇa* does not mean that the uncontrolled process of cyclic existence which forms the basis for suffering is the cessation of all suffering. Rather, it refers to the relationship between conventional truths and ultimate truths.

The meaning of Nāgārjuna's statement is that there is not the slightest difference in *entity* between a conventional truth, a *saṃsāra*, and its emptiness, a natural *nirvāṇa*. They are different within the context of being included in one entity.

Since conventional truths—all objects except emptiness—are not ultimate truths—emptinesses—the two truths are not merely two ways of looking at the same object, and thus it cannot be said that a conventional truth, such as a table or a body, and its emptiness, its lack of inherent existence, are one. They are also not synonyms; an ultimate truth is not a conventional truth and a conventional truth is not an ultimate truth. Further, the two truths are a dichotomy because if something exists and is not an ultimate truth, it must be a conventional truth, and if something exists and is not an ultimate truth, it must be a conventional truth; a dichotomy includes all existents, and nothing can be both.

If a phenomenon, such as a body, and its emptiness were exactly the same, then when we saw the body, we would see its emptiness, in which case we would be liberated. However, we are not liberated; we habitually conceive the opposite of emptiness and are thereby drawn into afflictions. Therefore, ultimate truths and conventional truths are not exactly the same, but they are also not different entities because when one understands the emptiness of the body, for instance, this helps to overcome this misconception of the inherent existence of the body. In other words, because an emptiness of inherent existence is the nature of the body, realizing it helps to overcome misconception of the body. If an emptiness were one entity and the body another, thorough realization of emptiness would not affect the misconception of phenomena as inherently existent. A conventional truth, such as a body, and an ultimate truth, its emptiness of objective or inherent existence, are compatible in one entity but are different.

Ultimate truths do not contradict conventional truths; the emptiness of the body does not contradict the conventionally and validly existent body; it contradicts its inherent existence. Therefore, "conventional" does not mean "usual," because all phenomena usually appear to nonconceptual sense consciousnesses as if they cover their parts, as if they exist in and of themselves whereas they do not. We know conventional truths such as houses, bodies, and minds, but we do not know conventional truths *as* conventional truths. To know this, we must know emptiness, the absence of inherent existence of objects; then, we can understand that objects only nominally exist.

Except for emptinesses, all objects are conventional truths, or "truths for an obscured mind." They seem to exist the way they appear only to a mind obscured with ignorance. Every object has a natural nirvāṇa that is its nonexistence in the way it appears, its emptiness of inherent existence. When this is thoroughly known, the afflictions are gradually overcome to the point where all afflictions whatsoever are removed forever. There is then a nirvāṇa, an emptiness of the mind in the continuum of one who has overcome all afflictions.

In order to effect this transformation yogis cultivate a mind that is a similitude of a Buddha's Truth Body. Using a reasoning analyzing the ultimate, they investigate whether mind, body, or "I" exist as they appear—exist right with their bases of designation, which for mind are moments of consciousness, for body are limbs and a trunk, and for "I" are mind and body. Intently searching to discover whether phenomena exist from their own side, yogis gradually discover that they do not; a vacuity that is a negative of inherent existence appears with which their mind is fused, remaining in this space-like meditative equipoise as long as possible. This is the path of wisdom of the Perfection Vehicle, a path of transformation through cultivating—prior to the effect stage—a similitude of the nondual meditative equipoise that a Buddha never leaves.

The Vajra Vehicle has the further feature of cultivating while still on the path a similitude of a Buddha's Form Body. These similitudes of Buddha Bodies are cultivated in order to transmute not only the mind but also the process of physical appearance. The goal is still the Buddhahood that serves as the basis for the welfare of all sentient beings, but the method for eradicating desire, hatred, and ignorance involves using these in the path within the context of emptiness and deity yogas. As the Sakya master Sönam Tsemo (*bsod nam rtse mo,* 1142–1182) says in his *General Presentation of the Tantra Sets*:[39]

> If one has method, [desirable] objects serve as aids to liberation, like poison [used as medicine], fire [used in moxabustion], and so forth. Therefore, objects are not inherently fetters; perverse thoughts based on them act as fetters. Through abandoning the entities of the fettering causes, one is liberated; thus, objects serve as secondary causes of liberation. The *Hevajra Tantra* says:
>
> > One is liberated from the fetters
> > Of cyclic existence through those that bind,
> > When they are accompanied by method.
>
> With respect to the phrase "accompanied by method," what is the method for abandoning the causes of being bound? ... Knowing whatever objects and subjects appear as just one's own deity, one enjoys them. The *Guhyasamāja Tantra* says:
>
> > Use as you wish
> > All desired resources,
> > With the yoga of your deity
> > Offer them to yourself and others.

The Nyingma master Longchen Rabjam (*klong chen rab 'byams / klong chen dri med 'od zer,* 1308–1363) says in his *Treasury of Tenets:*[40]

> *Question:* If the Mantra Vehicle partakes of a path purifying defilements, what does it mean that it takes the effect as the path? Since the Cause Vehicle is generated to purify defilements, it would be similar.
>
> *Answer:* Though the Definition [Perfection] Vehicle and the Mantra Vehicle are the same in simultaneously cleansing the defilements of the realm and achieving Buddhahood, there is a difference of temporal distance and proximity. Also, the mere warmth of the path for which the Definition Vehicle strives over a long time is taken as the path in one instant of Mantra. Furthermore, due to cultivating in meditation a similitude of the state in the maṇḍala of the expanse, even objects of abandonment shine as aids. In this way the effect is taken as the path; however, the exact final fruit is not actually taken as the path. Therefore, it is necessary to cultivate the profound and the vast in meditation.

Mere withdrawal of the mind from conceptions of inherent existence or even mere deity yoga without the wisdom of emptiness will not serve as an antidote to the afflictions. The supreme method is cultivation of deity yoga within the context of realizing the emptiness of inherent existence. The wisdom understanding emptiness and fused with emptiness appears as a deity, and within this state what formerly bound one in cyclic existence can be used as aids to liberation.

Deity yoga requires creative imagination; yogis recognize that their present perceptions are colored by predispositions established by former actions and in order to gain control over the process of appearance enter into the practice of making ideal substitutions. Through imaginatively causing everything that appears to be conjoined with emptiness and deity yoga, they cleanse innate predispositions for misperception and misconception. However, the distinction between imagination and fact is still made, and Buddhahood has not become a figment of imagination. Longchen Rabjam says:[41]

> When one has become a Buddha, freed of all defilements, the features of a land appear thoroughly adorned within the context of neither composition nor separation of body and wisdom [which are indivisibly fused]. Such is actualized [in Mantra] through the force of clearing away the defilements that exist in the expanse by meditating on a similitude of such a land. Therefore, it is called the Effect Vehicle. The *Padmashekara Tantra* says:
>
> > When the nature of the stainless expanse
> > Having the Three Bodies, wisdom, and land
> > Is purified, it manifestly appears
> > In self-illumination. This which takes
> > A similitude as the path is rightly
> > Called the Effect Vehicle.
>
> In Mantra, knowledge of the nature that abides primordially in the excellent inherent effect of the expanse is taken as the basis and practiced. Therefore, it is called the Effect Vehicle. Furthermore, in terms of clearing away defilements, generation and completion are cultivated, and through training in suchness the adventitious defilements are purified. The gods, maṇḍalas, and so forth which are mentally meditated are fabrications of one's own mind; thus, this is not meditation that takes the effect—the expanse with gods and maṇḍalas—as the actual path. However, because it is close to the meaning of the expanse, it should be viewed as a profound, undeceiving path. Though the Mantra

> Vehicle is similar to the Cause Vehicle in not being able to take the expanse as the actual path, there is a great difference in the closeness of the paths [to the fruit] due to the difference of having a similarity of feature [with the fruit].

Due to its similarity with the effect and its speed in generating the effect, the Vajra Vehicle is called the Effect Vehicle. The process of transforming body and mind is modeled on the features of the effect being sought. Whereas the Perfection Vehicle has cultivation of only a similitude of a Truth Body and relies on other causes to develop a Form Body, the Vajra Vehicle has cultivation of similitudes of both Bodies. This is its distinguishing and elevating feature, the very life of which is to identify wrong conceptions about the nature of phenomena and gradually discover the meaning of emptiness. For it is the consciousness realizing emptiness that itself appears as the body of a deity.

Purpose of the Four Tantras

Tantras are divided into four sets, Action, Performance, Yoga, and Highest Yoga, by way of trainees' varying abilities to use desire in the path. When desire arising from gazing, laughing, holding hands or embracing, and union is used in the path in conjunction with emptiness and deity yogas, desire itself is extinguished. The First Panchen Lama, Losang Chökyi Gyaltshan (*blo bzang chos kyi rgyal mtshan,* 1570–1662), says:[42]

> A wood-engendered insect is born from wood but consumes it completely. In the same way, a great bliss is generated in dependence on a causal motivation which is the desire of gazing, laughing, holding hands or embracing, or union of the two organs. The wisdom of undifferentiable bliss and emptiness, which is this great bliss generated undifferentiably with a mind realizing emptiness at that same time, consumes completely the afflictions—desire, ignorance, and so forth.

The four tantras are divided on the basis of their main trainees' ability to use in the path these four forms of desire, which correspond to the four types of satisfaction found in the various levels of the desire realm. The gods of the Land of the Thirty-Three and all beings below them, including humans, gain satisfaction through sexual union. The gods of the Land Without Combat gain satisfaction through embracing; those of the Joyous Land, through holding hands; those of the Land of Liking Emanation, through laughing; and those of the Land of Controlling Others' Emanations, through gazing. Abhayākara, in explaining the four tantras, uses these gods as *examples*, so Tsongkhapa emphasizes that Abhayākara does not mean that gods are the main trainees for whom the four tantras were spoken. Four tantra sets were expounded to accommodate the abilities of four types of persons to use desire in the path.

Alaṃkakalasha, however, taught that the four tantras were expounded to accommodate the four castes. He explains:[43]

> Action Tantras were taught in order to accommodate Brahmins since they like bathing and cleanliness, hold the view that one is liberated through asceticism, consider their caste to be important, and hold that one is liberated through repetition and burnt offerings. . . . Performance Tantras, teaching both the internal yoga of wisdom and method and external activities, were set forth in order to accommodate the merchant caste since they cannot engage in severe asceticism, will not become involved in low actions, and look down on external cleanliness and so forth. . . . Yoga Tantras [in which the gods and goddesses of the maṇḍalas correspond to a king and his retinue] were taught in order to accommodate those of the royal caste since they cannot engage in asceticism but enjoy the pleasures of the five attributes of the desire realm. . . . Highest Yoga Tantras, which teach the nonconceptual usage of the five fleshes and so forth, as well as low actions, were taught for those of the servant class who without any sense of cleanliness eat everything, engage in all actions, and have little conceptuality.

Tsongkhapa points out flaws in this explanation, which are further elaborated by the First Panchen Lama:[44]

> It is wrong to posit the four tantra sets from the viewpoint of the four castes. If this means that those of the four castes are the special trainees of the four tantras,

> then this entails the fault of being too broad [since not all members of the castes practice tantra]. If this means that members of the four castes are needed for the main trainees of the four tantras, then this entails the fault of being too narrow [because the main trainees of the four tantras come from any part of society, not from a specific caste]. If this means that there are cases of the four tantras taming members of the four castes, then this entails the fault of indefiniteness [since there are cases of all four tantras taming members of all four; therefore, this could not serve to distinguish the tantras].

Tsongkhapa emphasizes that it is not even predominantly the case that the trainees of particular tantras would come from a particular part of society. He ridicules the idea that just because Yoga Tantras use maṇḍalas modeled on the royal court, their chief trainees must be members of the royal caste.

It seems more likely that this teaching applying the four tantras to the four castes arose from the usage of caste members as examples. For instance, a master might exhort his or her initiates that in order to meditate on themselves as the main figure in a Yoga Tantra maṇḍala, they would have to consider themselves as kings; or, in order to practice the strict cleanliness that accompanies certain rituals of Action Tantra, they would have to be like Brahmins, who are known for bathing many times a day; or, in order to practice the nondifferentiation of thoughts of cleanliness and uncleanliness in Highest Yoga Tantra, they would have to be like members of the lowest class.

Another explanation of the four tantras, reported by both Sönam Tsemo and Butön Rinchendrub (*bu ston rin chen grub,* 1290–1364) is that four rites of deity generation were taught to accommodate persons following the four schools of tenets. The tradition is:[45]

1. Just as Vatsīputrīyas and Aparāntaka-Vaibhāṣhikas assert truly existent external objects and an inexpressible self, so the

> rite of deity generation in Action Tantras involves laying out a painting of a deity in front of oneself, arranging offerings, bathing, observing cleanliness, inviting a wisdom-being [an actual deity] in front of oneself—corresponding to an external object—placing the mantra in his heart, and engaging in repetition within the context of viewing the deity as like a master and oneself as a servant. Just as these schools assert an inexpressible self, so the wisdom-being is neither the painting nor oneself.

This explanation of Action Tantra is based on the teaching in the *Compendium of Wisdom Vajras,* a Highest Yoga Tantra, that in Action Tantras there is neither pride in oneself as a deity nor entry of a wisdom-being into oneself (imagining oneself as a deity and then causing the actual deity, the wisdom-being, to enter). However, Tsongkhapa explains in his exposition of Action Tantra that this passage refers only to the lowest trainees of Action Tantras, who are frightened by meditating on themselves as a deity, not the main trainees of Action Tantra who are fully capable of practicing deity yoga.

> 2. Performance Tantras involving generation of oneself as a symbolic being and generation of a deity in front as a wisdom-being were taught for Kashmiri Proponents of the Great Exposition and Proponents of Sūtra. Repetition is performed within the context of viewing the deity—the wisdom-being in front—and oneself—the symbolic being [imagined as a deity]—as companions. This is similar to these schools' assertion of ultimately existent apprehended-object and apprehending-subject.

This apparent similarity is unfounded because the Tantra Vehicle is part of Great Vehicle from the viewpoints both of tenet and of path. Since emptiness yoga is an integral part of deity generation, adherents to Lesser Vehicle tenets are not the main trainees of any tantra, nor does any tantric system propound the ultimate existence of apprehended-object and apprehending-subject, the opposite of emptiness.

> 3. Yoga Tantras involving generation of oneself as a symbolic being and then causing the wisdom-being to enter oneself were taught for Solitary Realizers. This rite of deity generation is similar to Solitary Realizers' assertion of conventionally existent object and subject.

This explanation in Yoga Tantra is based on the Yogic-Autonomists' assertion that Solitary Realizers realize the nontruth of objects—the absence of a difference in entity between apprehended-object and apprehending-subject. However, "Solitary Realizer" is not a school of tenets but a type of practitioner whose path is presented by all four schools of tenets, Great Exposition School, Sūtra School, Mind-Only School, and Middle Way School.

> 4. Highest Yoga Tantras were taught for the Great Vehicle Proponents of Mind-Only and Proponents of the Middle Way who assert that neither subject nor object ultimately exists but exist only conventionally. These tantras involve generation of oneself as a symbolic being and the entry of a wisdom-being—corresponding to asserting apprehended-object and apprehending-subject conventionally—but do not involve requesting the deity to leave—corresponding to not asserting either subject or object ultimately.

Again, the similarity is slight and suggests that in the past a master merely indicated differences in rites of deity generation through comparison with differences between schools of tenets, and this was wrongly taken to mean that the tantras were taught for people adhering to those schools of tenets.

Butön, after reporting this tradition, says, "Tibetan lamas have said this, but I have not seen a source for it." The Kagyu master Padma Karpo (*pad ma kar po,* 1527–1592) says:[46]

> Some Tibetan teachers have explained that [the tantras] are differentiated into four types based on accommodations to [four types of non-Buddhist] Forders or based on four schools of Buddhist tenets. Since the sources that they cite do not appear in any texts, these explanations are only their own thoughts.

The Sakya master Sönam Tsemo reports that this tradition *claimed* to be following Nāgārjuna, and as the Gelug master, the First Panchen Lama, says,[47] "It is not correct that such was asserted by Nāgārjuna and Jñānapāda because such a presentation was not set forth in any writings by these two."

Because tantra involves the usage of desire, hatred, and ignorance in the path in order to overcome the afflictions and because practices are geared for persons having one or the other predominant affliction, many have assumed that the four tantras were taught for four types of persons dominated by different afflictions. Though a certain affliction in a tantric practitioner may be predominant in the sense of being stronger than the other afflictions, tantrists are not dominated by afflictions; rather, they have come under the influence of great compassion and are seeking the quickest means of attaining a state where they can effectively help suffering sentient beings. In his *Explanation of the Rite of the Guhyasamāja Maṇḍala,* the Seventh Dalai Lama says with regard to trainees of Highest Yoga Tantra:[48]

> Some see that if one relies on the Perfection Vehicle and so forth, one must amass the collections [of merit and wisdom] for three countless great eons, and thus it would take a long time and involve great difficulty. They cannot bear such hardship and seek to attain Buddhahood in a short time and by a path with little difficulty. These people who claim that they, therefore, are engaging in the short path of the Secret Mantra Vehicle are outside the realm of Mantra trainees. For to be called

> a Great Vehiclist in general one cannot seek peace for oneself alone but from the viewpoint of holding others more dear than oneself must be able, for the sake of the welfare of others, to bear whatever type of hardship or suffering might arise. Since Secret Māntrikas are those of extremely sharp faculties within those of the Great Vehicle, persons who have turned their backs on others' welfare and want little difficulty for themselves are not even close to the quarter of Highest Secret Mantra. . . . One should engage in Highest Yoga Tantra, the secret short path, with the motivation of altruistic mind generation, unable to bear that sentient beings will be troubled for a long time by cyclic existence in general and by strong sufferings in particular and thinking, "How nice it would be if I could achieve right now a means to free them!"

As Jangkya Rölpay Dorjay (*lcang skya rol pa'i rdo rje,* 1717–1786) says in his *Presentation of Tenets*:[49]

> It is said in the precious tantras and in many commentaries that even those trainees of the Mantra Vehicle who have low faculties must have far greater compassion, sharper faculties, and a superior lot than the trainees of sharpest faculties in the Perfection Vehicle. Therefore, those who think and propound that the Mantra Vehicle was taught for persons discouraged about achieving enlightenment over a long time and with great difficulty make clear that they have no penetration of the meaning of Mantra. Furthermore, the statement that the Mantra Vehicle is quicker than the Perfection Vehicle is in relation to trainees who are suitable vessels, not in terms of just anyone. Therefore, it is not sufficient that the doctrine be the Mantra Vehicle; the person must be properly engaged in the Mantra Vehicle.

Far from being taught for those unable to proceed on the Perfection Vehicle, the four tantras were expounded for persons of particularly great compassion who possess abilities to use what usually are causes of cyclic existence as means to transcend it.

Unfounded traditions on tantra have been widely reported in and around the world whereas in Tibet the many traditions on the reasons for the four tantras were winnowed by scholar-yogis to derive their own final position. The First Panchen Lama says:[50]

> Our own system is that the reason for positing four different doors of entry [to the practice of Mantra] from the viewpoint of four tantras is that the main trainees for whom the Vajra Vehicle was intended are of four types. These four types are posited because there are four ways of using desire for the attributes of the desire realm in the path and four types of higher and lower capacities for enhancing the yoga that is a union of the wisdom realizing emptiness and deity yoga which utilize these four modes in the path.

The Panchen Lama mentions another misconception of tantra that is also widely renowned in the world:[51]

> Those of the Perfection Vehicle realize the nature of phenomena by way of examples and reasons whereas here [in the Mantra Vehicle] emptiness is realized directly...

Also:[52]

> Those of the Perfection Vehicle believe and think, "All phenomena are free of conceptual proliferations," but do not realize them in this way. Here [in the Mantra Vehicle] emptiness is realized directly through many methods..."

However, nondualistic wisdom is the life of both the sūtra and the tantra paths, and in both paths initial reliance on reasoning to uncover the nature of phenomena, hidden to our direct experience, is necessary. Through repeated cultivation, conceptual knowledge of suchness becomes nonconceptual wisdom. Those who do not view the great texts that set forth the path of reasoning of the Middle Way, such as Nāgārjuna's *Treatise on the Middle,* as instructions for practice mistakenly hold tantra to be merely a different technique for realizing emptiness. Having discarded the path for realizing emptiness, they—through misapprehending the meaning of tantra—also discard the special tantric method for developing the Form Body of a Buddha, deity yoga.

Appendix

An illustration in tabular form of the structure of Tsongkhapa's *Great Exposition of Secret Mantra*

- Only the Victor's Teaching Is the Entrance for Those Wishing Liberation (p. 67)
  - Divisions of the Vehicles in General (p. 73)
    - How the Vehicles Are Divided (p. 73)
    - Reasons for the Divisions (p. 74)
    - Nature of the Individual Divisions (p. 75)
      - Presentation of the Lesser Vehicle (p. 75)
      - Presentation of the Great Vehicle (p. 82)
    - Even All the Divisions in the End Are Branches of the Process of Fullest Enlightenment (p. 83)
      - Number of Divisions of the Great Vehicle (p. 87)
      - Meaning of the Individual Divisions of the Great Vehicle (p. 88)

- Statement of Points Generating Qualms in the Discriminative (p. 92)
- Response (p. 93)
  - Refutation of Positions Conjectured by Others (p. 94)
  - Presentation of the Well-Grounded Position (p. 96)
    - Actual Reason for Dividing the Great Vehicle into a Perfection Vehicle and a Mantra Vehicle (p. 96)
      - Indicating the Reason (p. 97)
      - Citing Sources (p. 101)
        - In Highest Yoga (p. 101)
          - In Highest Yoga Tantras (p. 101)
          - In Highest Yoga Commentaries (p. 107)
            - In the Master Jñānapāda's Texts (p. 107)
            - By Other Masters of Highest Yoga (p. 115)
        - In the Lower Tantras (p. 118)
      - Dispelling Objections (p. 121)

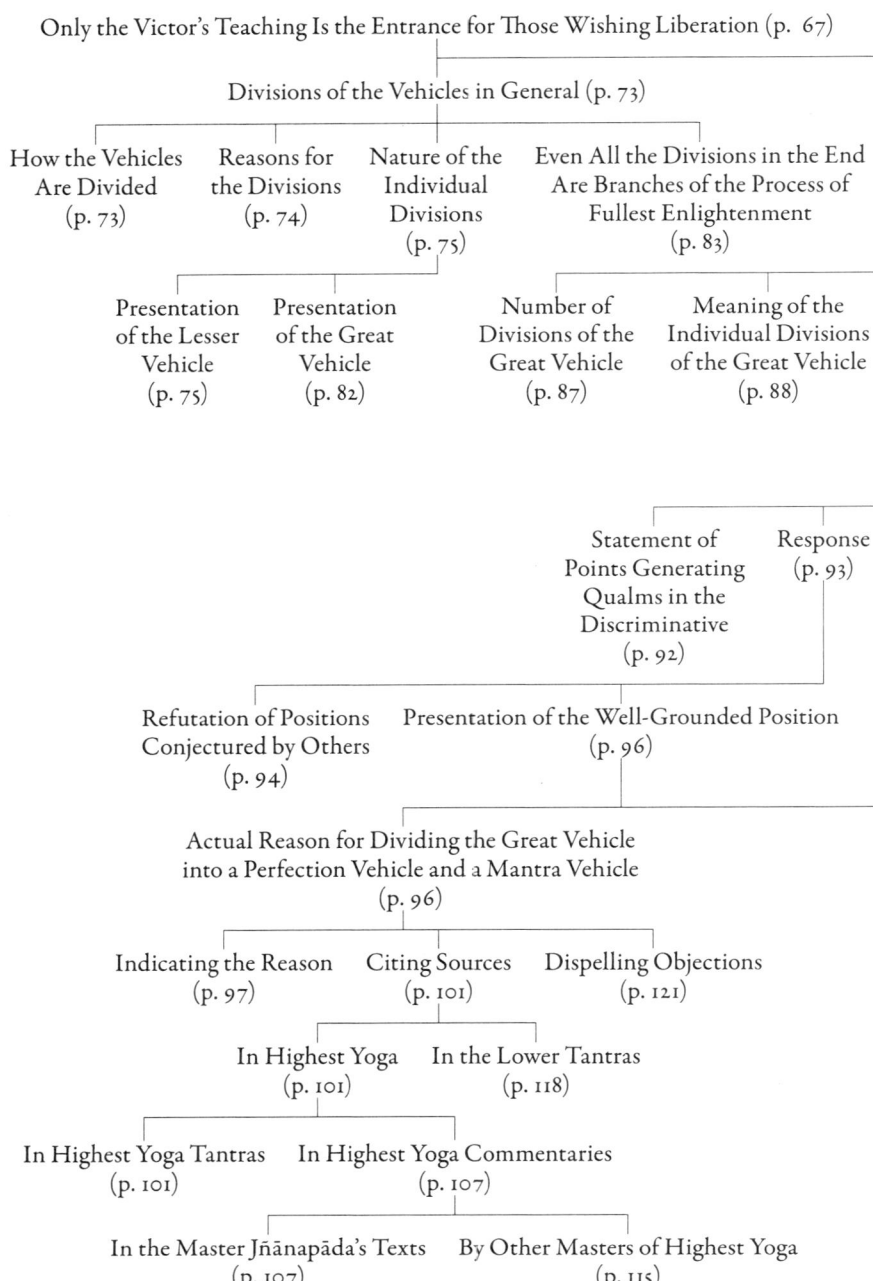

- Indicating the Doors of the Different Stages for Entry to the Teaching (p. 73)
  - Divisions of the Great Vehicle (p. 87)
    - Division of the Great Vehicle into Two (p. 87)
      - Reasons for Division of Great Vehicle into a Perfection Vehicle and a Vajra Vehicle (p. 92)
    - Detailed Explanation of the Forms of Entry to the Vajra Vehicle (p. 139)
      - Number of Doors of Entry to Mantra (p. 139)
      - Identifying the Features Positing the Different Doors of Entry to the Vajra Vehicle (p. 140)
        - Question (p. 140)
        - Answer (p. 141)
          - Incorrectness of Others' Answers (p. 141)
          - Our Own Answer (p. 144)
      - Modes of Advancing on the Paths Possessing These Features (p. 155)
        - Common Stages of the Path in the Two Great Vehicles (p. 155)
        - →*

- Though the Paths Differ, Their Fruits Do Not Differ as to Superiority and Inferiority (p. 127)
  - Actual Meaning (p. 127)
  - Difference Between the Perfection and Mantra Paths (p. 130)
    - According to Our Own System (p. 130)
    - According to [Faulty] Explanations of Other Masters (p. 131)
      - According to Ratnarakṣhita's "Commentary on the Saṃvarodaya Tantra" (p. 131)
      - According to Tripiṭakamāla's "Lamp for the Three Modes" (p. 133)

*The present translation ends at this point.

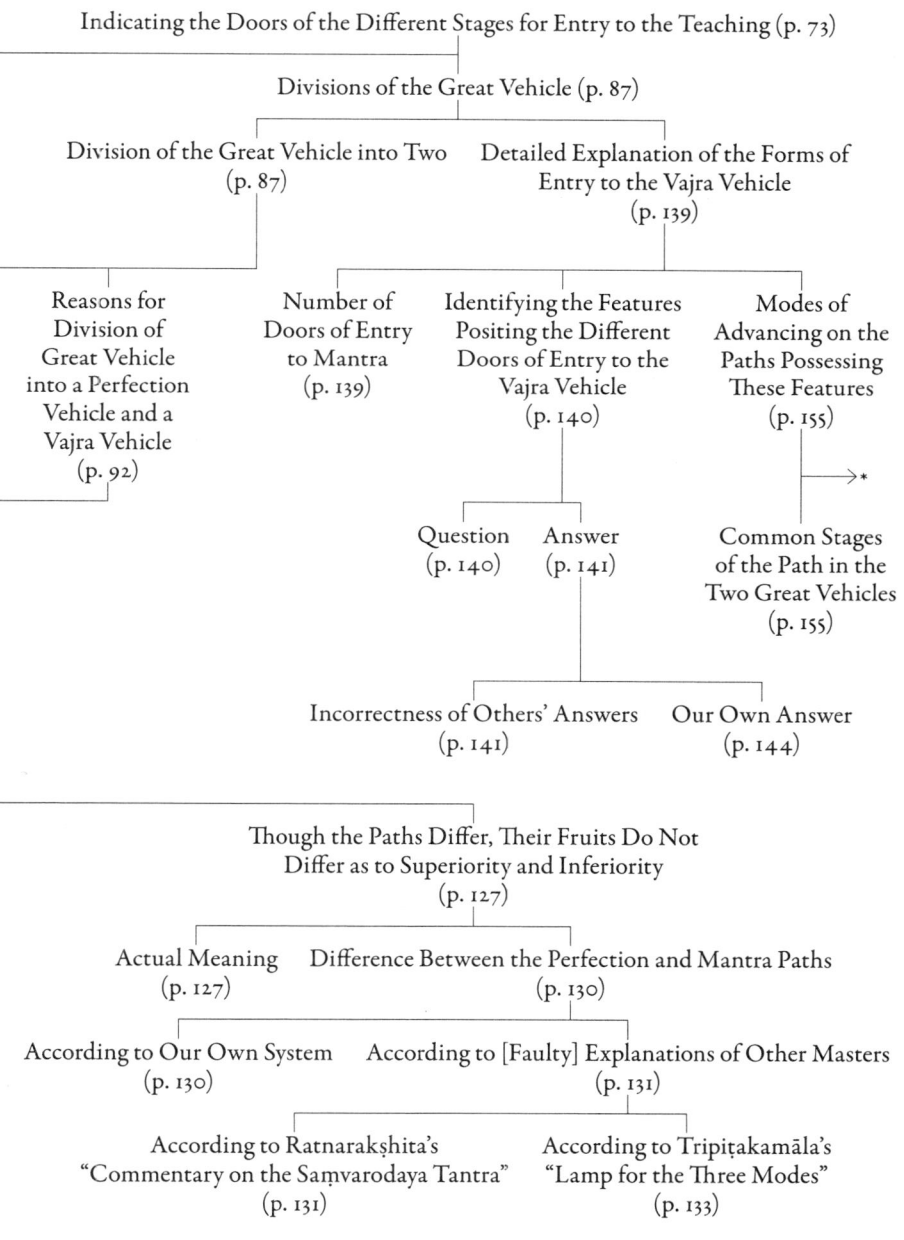

Notes

Preface

1. *bu ston rin chen grub.*
2. *rgyud sde spyi'i rnam par gzhag pa: rgyud sde rin po che'i mdzes rgyan,* Collected Works (New Delhi: International Academy of Indian Culture, 1969), vol. 15, 6.1–32.5. The very same presentation, with minor printing differences, is repeated in Butön's middle length version called the *Medium Length General Presentation of the Tantra Sets: Illuminating the Secrets of All Tantra Sets* (*rgyud sde spyi'i rnam par gzhag pa rgyud sde thams cad kyi gsang ba gsal bar byed pa*), vol. 15, 614.7–641.7. A considerably abbreviated version of the same is given in his *Condensed General Presentation of the Tantra Sets: Key Opening the Door to the Precious Treasury of Tantra Sets* (*rgyud sde spyi'i rnam par gzhag pa rgyud sde rin po che'i gter sgo 'byed pa'i lde mig*), vol. 14, 845.1–859.1. For a translation of the section in the extensive version on the multiple ways in which the Mantra Vehicle surpasses the Perfection Vehicle, see Jeffrey Hopkins, *Tantric Techniques* (Ithaca, NY: Snow Lion Publications, 2008), 205–242, followed by a translation of a similar section from Longchen Rabjam's *Precious Treasury of Tenets: Illuminating the Meaning of All Vehicles,* 243–261.
3. *phar phyin kyi theg pa, pāramitāyāna.*
4. *sngags kyi theg pa, mantrayāna.* The term "Tantrayāna" has great favor in much of current non-Tibetan scholarship but does not appear to have been popular in the Tibetan cultural region. There the favored term is "Mantrayāna" or "Guhyamantrayāna" (*gsang sngags kyi theg pa*).

II: The Great Exposition of Secret Mantra

1. Vajradhara. Knowledge mantras are mantras for the sake of abandoning ignorance and generating knowledge as well as for attaining clairvoyance and so forth.

2. Kyabchog Palsang (*skyabs mchog dpal bzang*) who also knew Sanskrit.
3. Sönam Sangpo (*bsod nams bzang po*).
4. P2004, vol. 47, 22.3.6.
5. Buddhas.
6. P2004, vol. 46, 22.3.6.
7. Chapter 1, stanza 217cd (Miyasaka's III.217cd, pp. 146–147): *pradhānārthāvisaṃvādād anumānaṃ paratra vā //*; the bracketed material is drawn from Khaydrub's commentary, 135b.6.
8. *bstan bcos bzhi brgya pa zhes bya ba'i tshig le'ur byas pa, catuḥśatakaśāstrakārikā;* P5246, vol. 95; stanza 280 which occurs in Chapter XII. Parenthetical additions are from Gyaltshab Darma Rinchen's commentary *Explanation of (Āryadeva's) "Four Hundred": Essence of Eloquence,* 90b.3–91a.3 (blockprint in the Dalai Lama's library); see *Yogic Deeds of Bodhisattvas: Gyel-tsap on Āryadeva's Four Hundred,* commentary by Geshe Sonam Rinchen, translated and edited by Ruth Sonam (Ithaca, NY: Snow Lion Publications, 1994), 241–242.
9. See pp. 17–19.
10. Tsongkhapa's *sde bdun la 'jug pa'i sgo don gnyer yid kyi mun sel* (Toh. 5416) has only a brief reference to the process, but his student Gyaltshab Darma Rinchen wrote extensively on the topic in his commentary to Dharmakīrti's *Ascertainment of Valid Cognition.*
11. See Bibliography and pp. 35–38.
12. P2668, vol. 61, 311.1.7–311.2.1.
13. P4530, vol. 81, 119.3.3.
14. P4532, vol. 81, 125.2.7ff.
15. See Jeffrey Hopkins, *Nāgārjuna's Precious Garland: Buddhist Advice for Living and Liberation* (Ithaca, NY: Snow Lion, 1998), 98.
16. About this line, the Dalai Lama says in *The Meaning of Life: Buddhist Perspectives on Cause and Effect* (Boston: Wisdom Publications, 2000), 86:

    > Contaminated actions and afflictive emotions are produced from wrong conceptuality, which itself is produced from the proliferations of the conception of inherent existence. Those conceptual proliferations are ceased *through* emptiness (*stong pa nyid kyis*), or, those proliferations are ceased *in* emptiness (*stong pa nyid du*)—the final line being taken in both of these ways. With the instrumental, it means that conceptual proliferations are ceased *through* cultivating the view realizing emptiness, but also since that into which they are ceased or that into which they are extinguished is the reality of emptiness itself, it is also taken

as that *into which* the fictive proliferations of the conception of inherent existence cease. That reality—the emptiness into which all of the afflictive emotions, ignorance and so forth, have been extinguished through the force of antidotal wisdom—is the true cessation that is liberation.

17. This and the next citation are quoted by Chandrakīrti in his *Clear Words*, commenting on XVIII.5.
18. "Kings of Doctrine" are Buddhas. "Endurance" means facility with realizing emptiness.
19. This is quoted by Chandrakīrti in his *Clear Words*, commenting on I.3. Louis de La Vallée Poussin identifies the passage as cited in the Saṃyuttanikāya III. 142 (22, 95, 15); Mervyn Sprung adds *Kindred Sayings*, vol. 3, 120–121.
20. Chandrakīrti's *Clear Words*, P5263, vol. 98, 43.5.7. "Exists" is taken as inherent existence; "does not exist" is taken as utter nonexistence.
21. See Bibliography pp. 272–273.
22. See Hopkins, *Nāgārjuna's Precious Garland*, 146 and 147.
23. P868, vol. 34, 281.1.3ff. (1) Ox chariot: someone who tries to cross the world systems in an ox chariot, advances one hundred yojanas over a long time, but is turned back by winds. These are Bodhisattvas who either take a liking to the Lesser Vehicle themselves or cause others to do so, thus dulling their wisdom. (2) Elephant chariot: one who advances two thousand yojanas in a hundred years and also takes a liking to Lesser Vehicle. The complete enlightenment of these two is indefinite; they will turn back from the path of highest wisdom. (3) Sun and moon: one who crosses the world systems over a long time in the manner of the sun and the moon. These are Bodhisattvas who devote themselves fully to Great Vehicle, not conjoining their wisdom with a lower motivation. (4) Magical creation of a Hearer: one who crosses the world systems in the manner of a Hearer's magical emanation, having even greater devotion to the Great Vehicle, its practitioners, and practices. (5) Magical creation of a One-Gone-Thus: one who wants to cross the world systems and petitions a One-Gone-Thus. This is a Bodhisattva who takes special care to set other sentient beings on the path. The complete enlightenment of these three is definite; they will not turn back from the path of highest wisdom.
24. This is quoted in Nāgārjuna's *Compendium of Sūtra*, P5330, vol. 102, 101.3.8ff.
25. P893, vol. 35, 124.5.4–124.5.7.

26. P893, vol. 35, 125.3.4–125.3.6.
27. P2, vol. 1, 121.3.3; cited in Butön's *Extensive General Presentation of the Tantra Sets,* 5.3, and in Ratnākarashānti's *Presentation of the Three Vehicles* (*co ne, rgyud, tsu,* 102b.7).
28. P4536, vol. 81, 154.5.7.
29. P4537, vol. 81, 159.3.4; cited in E. Obermiller, *History of Buddhism (Chos-ḥbyung) by Bu-ston* (Heidelberg: Heft, 1932; reprint, Tokyo: Suzuki Research Foundation, n.d.), 17.
30. XVIII. 69c–71b; P81, vol. 3, 200.4.2. *Man* is explained as *manana* (minding) and *trā* as *trāṇana* (protecting). "All vajras" refers to practitioners' body, speech, and mind.
31. P4536, vol. 81, 155.2.1.
32. The six-branched yoga as set forth in the *Kālachakra Tantra* are individual withdrawal (*pratyāhāra*), concentration (*dhyāna*), vitality and exertion / stopping-vitality (*prāṇāyāma*), retention (*dhāraṇā*), mindfulness (*anusmṛti*), and meditative stabilization (*samādhi*).
33. P4537, vol. 81, 159.3.7.
34. P4536, vol. 81, 155.2.3–155.2.7.
35. P81, vol. 3, 200.1.2–200.1.4.
36. See pp. 145–146, 128–129, and 224 for explanation of the stanza.
37. *rnal 'byor ma bzhi'i kha sbyor kyi rgyud, catur-yoginī-saṃpuṭatantra;* P24, vol. 2. Tsongkhapa cites only the first line and "and so forth."
38. The white and red minds of enlightenment are the vital essences of male and female.
39. For a concise commentary on Maitreya's complete text, see Jeffrey Hopkins and Jongbok Yi, *Ngag-wang-pal-dan's Explanation of the Treatise "Ornament for the Clear Realizations" From the Approach of the Meaning of the Words: The Sacred Word of Maitreyanātha* (Dyke, VA: UMA Institute for Tibetan Studies, 2014), downloadable at uma-tibet.org.
40. P11, vol. 1, 223.4.4–223.4.7.
41. P2326, vol. 54, 293.4.5–294.1.2.
42. P2326, vol. 54, 293.5.6.
43. P2325, vol. 54, 290.3.7–290.4.2.
44. P2324, vol. 54, 288.1.5–288.1.8. According to the Tohoku catalogue, his name is Indrabhūti.
45. P2326, vol. 54, 293.4.5–294.1.2.
46. P2723, vol. 65, 28.2.6–28.3.5.
47. This means "do not conceive enlightenment to exist concretely, or inherently."

48. This means "do not conceive enlightenment to exist concretely, or inherently."
49. P2723, vol. 65, 28.3.5.
50. P2723, vol. 65, 28.3.5.
51. P2723, vol. 65, 28.4.8.
52. P2723, vol. 65, 29.2.8–29.3.2.
53. P2723, vol. 65, 29.3.3.
54. P2734, vol. 65, 173.5.2–173.5.4.
55. P2328, vol. 55, 180.2.8–180.3.1.
56. P11, vol. 1, 235.2.8.
57. P11, vol. 1, 235.3.1.
58. P2315, vol. 53, 272.4.4.
59. P2781, vol. 66, 219.4.4–219.4.8.
60. P2781, vol. 66, 219.4.8.
61. P114, vol. 5, 57.1.5.
62. P2783, vol. 66, 274.3.1–264.3.7.
63. P2710, vol. 63, 237.1.1ff.
64. P2517, vol. 57, 316.5.5–316.5.6.
65. P2723, vol. 65, 29.5.1ff.
66. P112, vol. 4, 237.5.7.
67. P3333, vol. 71, 151.4.6–151.4.7.
68. *co ne, rgyud, tsu,* 100b.2.
69. A life as a Universal Monarch is attained through special virtuous acts (see Hopkins, *Nāgārjuna's Precious Garland,* stanzas 198–199), not through meditation imagining oneself as having the body and so forth of a Universal Monarch.
70. *co ne, rgyud, tsha,* 8a.6–8b.3.
71. Cited in Butön's *Extensive General Presentation of the Tantra Sets,* 21.5.
72. Cited also in Sönam Tsemo's *General Presentation of the Tantra Sets,* 10a.3.
73. Ngag-wang-pal-dan's commentary on this stanza is:

    That pristine wisdom, the support of the fourth initiation upon knowing and seeing [the eight grounds of the Lesser Vehicle] and abiding [on the ground of Bodhisattvas]—**the nine grounds**—and **through which** it is explained in sūtra **one abides on the Buddha ground, is to be known as the tenth ground of a Bodhisattva.** [The nine grounds are]:

    1. the **ground** of lineage, the paths of preparation of the three vehicles
    2. the **ground** of the eighth, the path of an Approacher to Stream-Enterer

3. the **ground** of seeing, the path of a Stream-Enterer
4. the **ground** of diminishment, the path of a mere Once-Returner
5. the **ground** of separation from desire, the path of a mere Never-Returner
6. the **ground** of realizing completion, the path of a Hearer Foe Destroyer
7. the **ground** of Hearers, the paths of the latter three gradualist Approachers [that is, Approachers to Once-Returner, Never-Returner, and Foe Destroyer]
8. the **ground** of Solitary Realizers, the Superior paths of a Solitary-Victor
9. the **ground** of Bodhisattvas, the nine Bodhisattva grounds described above.

Jeffrey Hopkins and Jongbok Yi, *Ngag-wang-pal-dan's Explanation of the Treatise "Ornament for the Clear Realizations" From the Approach of the Meaning of the Words: The Sacred Word of Maitreyanātha* (Dyke, VA: UMA Institute for Tibetan Studies, 2014), downloadable at uma-tibet.org.

74. *co ne, rgyud, tshu,* 26b.3.
75. P4530, vol. 81, 115.2.5–115.2.6; commentary until 118.2.6; cited in Butön's *Extensive General Presentation of the Tantra Sets,* 6.2.
76. Tsongkhapa cites only the first line *don gcig na yang ma rmongs dang;* the stanza has been filled out for context.
77. *co ne, rgyud, wa,* 46b.1 through 48a.1.
78. The context is the sixteen moments of forbearance and knowledge of the path of seeing in the Great Vehicle; Maitreya's *Ornament for the Clear Realizations* (IV.46–51) says:

{IV.46}
The sixteen moments of forbearance
And knowledge in the path of seeing
Are to be known as being Bodhisattvas'
Characteristics of irreversibility.

{IV.47}
Reversal from forms and so forth,
A firm mind, turning away from the Lesser Vehicle,
Thorough extinction of the branches
Of the concentrations and so forth,

{IV.48}
Lightness of body and mind,
Skill in means regarding making use of desire,
Clean behavior always,
Intensely pure livelihood;

{IV.49}
Individually stopping dwelling
In involvement and subsequent involvement
In the aggregates and so forth, interruptions,
Collections, engaging in the battle,

{IV.50}
Miserliness, and so forth;
The unobservability of merely a particle of doctrine,
Abiding in the three grounds
[Due to] certainty about one's own ground

{IV.51}
Giving up life for the sake of the doctrine—
Such sixteen moments
Are signs of irreversibility
Of dwelling on the path of seeing of the intelligent.

Translation from Jeffrey Hopkins and Jongbok Yi, *Ngag-wang-pal-dan's Explanation of the Treatise "Ornament for the Clear Realizations" From the Approach of the Meaning of the Words: The Sacred Word of Maitreyanātha* (Dyke, VA: UMA Institute for Tibetan Studies, 2014), downloadable at uma-tibet.org.

79. The *Kāshyapa Chapter Sūtra* says:

Just as the filth of city-dwellers
Helps the field of a sugarcane grower,
So the manure of a Bodhisattva's afflictive emotions
Assists in growing the qualities of a Buddha.

80. *co ne, rgyud, wa,* 47b.2.
81. The channels are passageways through which the drops—vital essences—course, impelled by the winds, or currents of energy.
82. P4530, vol. 81, 115.2.5–115.2.6; commentary until 118.2.6; cited in

Butön's *Extensive General Presentation of the Tantra Sets,* 6.2. Tsongkhapa condenses Tripiṭakamāla's own commentary, from which material has been added in brackets; cited in Butön's *Extensive General Presentation of the Tantra Sets,* 6.2.

83. Indivisible wisdom and method; P4530, vol. 81, 117.5.5.
84. See also Butön's *Extensive General Presentation of the Tantra Sets,* 10.5.
85. P4532, vol. 81, 133.2.1–133.4.7.
86. Knowledge Women (*vidyā*) are so called because of being women in dependence on whom an original innate bliss consciousness realizing suchness is generated. Wisdom Knowledge Women (*jñānavidyā*) are meditated or "emanated" partners who are imagined in meditation, whereas external Knowledge Women are actual physical partners. Knowledge Women are also called Seals (*mudrā*) because when in dependence on them a bliss consciousness realizing emptiness is generated, phenomena appear as the sport of this consciousness and are thus marked (or sealed) by it. Actual partners are called Pledge Seals (*samayamudrā*) if fully qualified through (a) possessing the appropriate lineage, age, and so forth, (b) having ripened their mental continuum by the practice of the common path, and (c) keeping the tantric pledges. If not fully qualified, actual partners are called Action Seals (*karmamudrā*), though Pledge Seals can also be called Action Seals from the viewpoint of actually engaging in the actions or deeds of desire. Meditated partners are called Wisdom Seals (*jñānamudrā*) due to being manifestations, within deity yoga, of a wisdom realizing emptiness. The Great Seal (*mahāmudrā*) to which Tripiṭakamāla referred on p. 134 is an indivisibility of wisdom and method and not either a meditated or actual woman. In his system, which is mistaken, inferior trainees rely on Action, Pledge, and Wisdom Seals in order to empower the mind in such a way that the Great Seal can be realized. Thus, according to him, the best of the superior trainees do not have desire for and do not use Action, Pledge, or Wisdom Seals.
87. See also Butön's *Extensive General Presentation of the Tantra Sets,* 10.6.
88. As Tsongkhapa says in the next paragraph, neither Tripiṭakamāla nor Jñanakīrti specify the difference between Pledge and Action Seals. The bracketed addition here comes from the Lati Rinpoche.
89. P4532, vol. 81, 125.4.2–125.4.3.
90. P4532, vol. 81, 134.2.6–134.2.7.
91. P11, vol. 1, 234.1.5–234.1.6; cited in Butön's *Extensive General Presentation of the Tantra Sets,* 39.6.
92. P4536, vol. 81, 155.1.6.

93. Butön in his *Condensed General Presentation of the Tantra Sets* (Collected Works, Part 14*pha,* (New Delhi: International Academy of Indian Culture, 1969), 895.2–895.7) explains this position and attributes it to Sönam Tsemo who, without endorsing this view, presents it in his *General Presentation of the Tantra Sets* (sGang-tog, 'Bras-ljongs-sa-ngor-chos-tshogs, 1969), 27a. 4–30b.4.
94. *rab 'byor bskyangs,* listed as one of the many names for Ashvaghoṣha in TBRC.
95. Sönam Tsemo is identified in the annotations to Butön's *Condensed General Presentation of the Tantra Sets* (896.1–896.6); however, it is clear that Sönam Tsemo is merely reporting this tradition without endorsing it in his *General Presentation of the Tantra Sets* (30b.4–31b.5).
96. In the second book in this series, *Deity Yoga,* see the chapter titled "Controversy about Deity Yoga in Action and Performance."
97. *co ne, rgyud, gi,* 3a.2–4a.3. This corresponds with Butön's explanation in his *Extensive General Presentation of the Tantra Sets*, Collected Works, Part 15 *ba,* (New Delhi: International Academy of Indian Culture, 1969), 35.7ff.
98. The explanation of the second begins on p. 150.
99. See pp. 128–129 and 224 for explanation; cited in Butön's *Extensive General Presentation of the Tantra Sets,* 32.7.
100. The red and white minds of enlightenment, or vital essences of female and male.
101. Complete enjoyment, union, great bliss, absence of inherent existence, compassion, uninterrupted continuity, and noncessation.
102. P2328, vol. 55, 207.4.8–207.5.2.
103. *co ne, rgyud, ga,* 291b.3–291b.5.
104. Cited in Butön's Extensive General Presentation of the Tantra Sets, 33.5.
105. In this context a seal is a hand sign, which is like a person's seal on a document in that it guarantees what it symbolizes, here guaranteeing Tārā's capacity to bestow Buddhahood.
106. Cited in Butön's *Extensive General Presentation of the Tantra Sets,* 33.7.
107. Cited in Butön's *Extensive General Presentation of the Tantra Sets,* 34.1.
108. Cited in Butön's *Extensive General Presentation of the Tantra Sets,* 34.3.
109. Cited in Butön's *Extensive General Presentation of the Tantra Sets,* 34.3.
110. It is interesting that the order of the first two is reversed here.
111. P2328, vol. 55, 201.5.2; cited in Butön's *Extensive General Presentation of the Tantra Sets,* 35.2.
112. P3333, vol. 71, 146.1.5.

113. In the third volume in this series, *Yoga Tantra,* the Dalai Lama says in his introductory section in the chapter titled "The Basics":

> Since the "Continuation of the Continuation" was spoken for those who cannot perform deity yoga but who achieve feats mainly in dependence on rites using external substances, repetition of mantra, and so forth, it might seem to contradict the explanation that Yoga Tantras were taught for trainees who mainly emphasize meditation. However, it is not contradictory because, although the chief trainees for whom the Yoga Tantras were spoken are those involved mainly in the yoga of the union of the profound and the manifest and capable of cultivating the entire spectrum of paths, there are also secondary trainees who need not be of this type.

114. P4530, vol. 81, 117.3.3–117.3.5; cited in Butön's *Extensive General Presentation of the Tantra Sets,* 41.5.
115. *co ne, rgyud, nyu,* 65b.4.
116. The yoga of nonduality of the profound (emptiness) and the manifest (appearance as a deity).
117. *co ne, rgyud, nyu,* 65b.5.
118. P4530, vol. 81, 117.3.5–117.3.6; cited in Butön's *Extensive General Presentation of the Tantra Sets,* 42.1. The Peking edition of Tripiṭakamāla's text does not use the term "Performance," reading *ston par mdzad pa'i rgyud* rather than *ston par mdzad pa'i* ***spyod pa'i*** *rgyud,* as in the Ngawang Gelek edition of Tsongkhapa's text, 79.3.
119. Retention mantras are mantras for the sake of retaining words and meanings without forgetting them as well as for keeping one from falling to bad migrations.
120. Tsongkhapa identifies "mantra" (see etymology of mantra on p. 106) here as primarily the bestowal of initiation which protects the mind from the suffering of bad migrations and so forth (P6187, vol. 160, 50.1.3).
121. *co ne, rgyud, ngi,* 233b.6–234a.2.
122. P2668, vol. 61, 295.1.4–295.1.5.

III: Supplement

1. *bya ba, kriyā; spyod pa, caryā; rnal 'byor, yoga; rnal 'byor bla med, anuttarayoga.*
2. *madhyamakāvatāra, dbu ma la 'jug pa.* The first five chapters of Tsongkhapa's commentary (*dgongs pa rab gsal*) are translated in Jeffrey Hop-

kins, *Compassion in Tibetan Buddhism* (London: Rider and Co., 1980; rpt. Ithaca, NY: Snow Lion Publications), 175–176. (For discussion of the translation of the title *Madhyamakāvatāra* as "*Supplement to the 'Treatise on the Middle,'*" see Hopkins, *Meditation on Emptiness,* 462–469 and 866–869.)

3. *rlung, prāṇa.* This is one among many points that Jam-yang-shay-pa (*'jam dbyangs bzhad pa,* 1648–1721) makes in defending the position that the Buddhahoods of Sūtra and Mantra are the same in his *Great Exposition of Tenets;* see Hopkins, *Maps of the Profound,* 637–645.
4. See Lati Rinbochay and Jeffrey Hopkins, *Death, Intermediate State and Rebirth in Tibetan Buddhism* (London: Rider and Co., 1979; rpt. Ithaca, NY: Snow Lion Publications, 1980), 69–73.
5. *yul gyi lta ba.*
6. *lha'i rnal 'byor,* **devatāyoga.*
7. The source here is the late Jampal Shanpan, abbot of the Tantric College of Lower Lhasa during the time of its relocation in South India and later the Throne-Holder of Gandan, head of the Gelugpa order.
8. See the Mongolian scholar Ngag-wang-pal-dan's (*ngag dbang dpal ldan*) statement of this in H.H. the Dalai Lama, Tsongkhapa, and Hopkins, *Deity Yoga,* 211–212.
9. Tsongkhapa's argument can be found in Hopkins, *Compassion in Tibetan Buddhism,* 150–181.
10. *drang ba dang nges pa'i don rnam par phye ba'i bstan bcos legs bshad snying po;* Peking 6142, vol. 153. My annotated translation of the General Explanation and the section on the Mind-Only School is in *Emptiness in the Mind-Only School of Buddhism* (Berkeley: University of California Press, 1999); for the point made here, see 69–71; see also Jeffrey Hopkins, *Reflections on Reality* (Berkeley: University of California Press, 2002), 96–99. For a translation of the complete text, see Robert A. F. Thurman, *Tsong Khapa's Speech of Gold in the Essence of True Eloquence* (Princeton, NJ: Princeton University Press, 1984). A Chinese translation was completed in Lhasa on the day commemorating Buddha's enlightenment in 1916 by Venerable Fa Zun, "Bian Liao Yi Bu Liao Yi Shuo Cang Lun," in *Xi Zang Fo Jiao Yi Lun Ji* (Taipei: Da Sheng Wen Hua Chu Ban She, 1979), vol. 2, 159–276.
11. *dpal gsang ba 'dus pa'i dkyil 'khor gyi cho ga'i 'grel pa, guhyasamājamaṇḍalavidhiṭīkā;* P2734, vol. 65.
12. V.9–10.
13. In his *de kho na nyid la 'jug pa shes bya ba bde bar gshegs pa'i bka' ma lus*

pa mdor bsdus te bshad pa'i rab tu byed pa, tattvāvatārākhyasakalasugata vacastātparyavyākhyāprakaraṇa; P4532, vol. 81.

14. *tshogs lam, saṃbhāramārga.*
15. *mi slob lam, aśaikṣamārga.*
16. For Dölpopa Shayrab Gyaltshan's explanation of this stanza, see Hopkins, *Mountain Doctrine,* 207, 447, and 456.
17. For a translation of Longchen Rabjam's (1308–1363) presentation of the difference between the Perfection Vehicle, also called the Definition Vehicle, and the Mantra Vehicle in his *Precious Treasury of Tenets: Illuminating the Meaning of All Vehicles* see Jeffrey Hopkins, *Tantric Techniques* (Ithaca, NY: Snow Lion Publications, 2008), 243–261; this citation is from 246.
18. *don spyi, arthasāmānya.*
19. *gtum mo.*
20. In Nyingma this is the general procedure of the path of method (*thabs lam*); the Great Completeness utilizes a more direct procedure in the path of release (*grol lam*). See, for instance, the second of Mipam Gyatsho's *Trilogy on Fundamental Mind* in Jeffrey Hopkins, *Mi-pam-gya-tsho's Primordial Enlightenment: The Nying-ma View of Luminosity and Emptiness, Analysis of Fundamental Mind, with oral commentary by Khetsun Sangpo* (UMA Institute for Tibetan Studies, uma-tibet.org, 2015).
21. Hopkins, *Tantric Techniques,* 246.
22. *chags pa lam du byed pa.*
23. In the Great Completeness manifestation of these subtle minds is not sufficient; a permanent fundamental mind must be realized. See, for instance, Mi-pam-gya-tso, *Fundamental Mind: The Nyingma View of the Great Completeness* with practical commentary by Khetsun Sangbo Rinbochay, trans. and ed. by Jeffrey Hopkins (Ithaca, NY: Snow Lion Publications, 2006).
24. *bsod nams, puṇya.*
25. *rgyu'i kun slong.*
26. *dus kyi kun slong.*
27. *'jam dbyangs bzhad pa ngag dbang brtson grus,* 1648–1722.
28. *'phags pa, ārya.*
29. *mthong lam, darśanamārga.*
30. *dbang po las rung.*
31. Jam-yang-shay-pa's *Great Exposition of the Concentrative and Formless Absorptions,* 149b.2.

32. This issue is crucial to determining how the afflictive emotion of hatred itself actually is used in the path in the Sūtra Great Vehicle and if it is, on what levels it is used, but a definitive answer is elusive.
33. *'bras bu'i theg pa, phalayāna.*
34. Or also as *trāya.*
35. *tha mal pa'i zhen pa.*
36. The general sources for the second and third topics of the supplement are Jamyang Shaypa's *Great Exposition of Tenets* and Könchog Jigmay Wangpo's condensation of it in his *Precious Garland of Tenets.* See Jeffrey Hopkins's *Meditation on Emptiness* (London: Wisdom Publications, 1983; rev. ed., Boston: Wisdom Publications, 1996) for extensive explanation and the sources in detail. Below, the source for a Lesser Vehicle rendition of the Bodhisattva path is Tagtshang's *Explanation of the Treatise "Freedom from Extremes through Understanding All Tenets": Ocean of Eloquence* (photographic reprint in the possession of Khetsun Sangpo, place and date of publication unknown), 28a.5.
37. This section particularly depends on the oral teachings of Kensur Lekden (1900–1971) as well as the two general sources mentioned in the previous note. In particular see Lati Rinbochay and Elizabeth Napper, *Mind in Tibetan Buddhism* (London: Rider, 1980; Ithaca, NY: Snow Lion, 1980; reprint, Ithaca, NY: Snow Lion, 1986).
38. Jamyang Shaypa, *Great Exposition of the Middle* (Buxaduor, India: Gomang, 1967), 192b.2.
39. 14a.4–14b.3.
40. Gangtok, Dodrup Chen Rinpoche: 1969 (?), 137a.5–137b.2.
41. Ibid., 136a.1–136a.6.
42. *Presentation of the General Teaching and the Four Tantra Sets,* Collected Works, vol. IV (New Delhi: Gurudeva, 1973), 17b.5–18a.1.
43. In his *Commentary on the Vajra Garland Tantra* (*vajramālāṭīkā*), *co ne, rgyud, gi,* 3a.2–4a.3. This corresponds with Butön's explanation in his *Extensive General Presentation of the Tantra Sets,* Collected Works, Part 15 *ba* (New Delhi: International Academy of Indian Culture, 1969), 35.7ff.
44. *Presentation of the General Teaching and the Four Tantra Sets,* 17a.2–17a.4.
45. The indented passages on this tradition are paraphrases of Sönam Tsemo's *General Presentation of the Tantra Sets* (30b.4–31b.5) and Butön's *Condensed General Presentation of the Tantra Sets* (89b.6ff.).
46. *General Presentation of the Tantra Sets, Captivating the Wise,* Collected Works, vol. 11 (Darjeeling: Kargyud Sungrab Nyamso Khang, 1974), 16a.5.

47. *Presentation of the General Teaching and the Four Tantra Sets,* 17b.1–17b.3.
48. *Explanation of the Rite of the Guhyasamāja Maṇḍala* (New Delhi: Tanzin Kunga, 1972), 17.2–18.2.
49. *Clear Exposition of the Presentations of Tenets, A Beautiful Ornament for the Meru of the Subduer's Teaching* (Varanasi: The Pleasure of Elegant Sayings Printing Press, 1970), 529.18–530.8.
50. *Presentation of the General Teaching and the Four Tantra Sets,* 17b.1–17b.3.
51. Ibid., 7b.2–7b.3.
52. Ibid., 8a.3.

Glossary

English	Sanskrit	Tibetan
Action Seal	karmamudrā	las kyi phyag rgya
Action Tantra	kriyātantra	bya rgyud
affirming negative	paryudāsapratiṣedha	ma yin dgag
affliction	kleśa	nyon mongs
artificial	parikalpita	kun btags
bliss	sukha	bde ba
calm abiding	śamatha	zhi gnas
Cause Vehicle	hetuyāna	rgyu'i theg pa
compassion	karuṇā	snying rje
Complete Enjoyment Body	saṃbhogakāya	longs spyod rdzogs pa'i sku
compounded	saṃskṛta	'dus byas
concentration	dhyāna	bsam gtan
conception of self	ātmagrāha	bdag tu 'dzin pa
continuum	saṃtāna	rgyud
conventional truth	saṃvṛtisatya	kun rdzob bden pa
cyclic existence	saṃsāra	'khor ba
definite goodness	niḥśreyasa	nges legs

English	Sanskrit	Tibetan
Definition Vehicle	lakṣaṇayāna	mtshan nyid kyi theg pa
definitive	nitārtha	nges don
deity yoga	devayoga	lha'i mal 'byor
dependent-arising	pratītyasamutpāda	rten 'byung
desire realm	kāmadhātu	'dod khams
direct perception	pratyakṣa	mngon sum
discipline	vinaya	'dul ba
Effect Vehicle	phalayāna	'bras bu 'i theg pa
effort	vīrya	brtson 'grus
element	dhātu	khams
Emanation Body	nirmāṇakāya	sprul pa'i sku
emptiness	śūnyatā	stong pa nyid
enlightenment	bodhi	byang chub
establishment by way of its own character	svalakṣaṇasiddhi	rang gi mtshan nyid kyis grub pa
ethics	śīla	tshul khrims
expanse	dhātu	dbyings
faculty	indriya	dbang po
five aggregates	pañcaskandha	phung po lnga
Foe Destroyer	arhan	sgra bcom pa
Forder	tīrthika	mu stegs pa

ENGLISH	SANSKRIT	TIBETAN
Form Body	rūpakāya	gzugs sku
form realm	rūpadhātu	gzugs khams
formless realm	ārūpyadhātu	gzugs med khams
fruit	phala	'bras bu
generality	pradhāna	spyi
giving	dāna	sbyin pa
great compassion	mahākaruṇā	snying rje chen po
Great Exposition School	vaibhāṣika	bye brag smra ba
Great Seal	mahāmudrā	phyag rgya chen po
ground	bhūmi	sa
Hearer	śrāvaka	nyan thos
high status	abhyudaya	mngon mtho
Highest Yoga Tantra	anuttarayogatantra	rnal 'byor bla med kyi rgyud
illusory body	māyādeha	sgyu lus
individual emancipation	pratimokṣa	so sor thar pa
inference	anumāṇa	rjes dpag
inherent establishment	svabhāvasiddhi	rang bzhin gyis grub pa
initiation	abhiṣeka	dbang
innate	sahaja	lhan skyes

English	Sanskrit	Tibetan
Joyous Land	tuṣita	dga' ldan
Knowledge Woman	vidyā	rig ma
Land of Controlling Others' Emanations	paranirmitavaśavartin	gzhan 'phrul dbang byed
Land of Liking Emanation	nirmāṇarati	'phrul dga'
Land of the Thirty-Three	trāyastriṃśa	sum bcu rtsa gsum
Land Without Combat	yāma	'thab bral
liberation	mokṣa	thar pa
lineage	gotra	rigs
lord	īśvara	dbang phyug
love	maitri	byams pa
Mādhyamika	mādhyamika	dbu ma pa
manifest enlightenment	abhisaṃbodhi	mngon byang
manifest knowledge	abhidharma	chos mngon pa
Mantra Vehicle	mantrayāna	sngags kyi theg pa
matrix of a One-Gone-Thus	tathāgatagarbha	de bzhin gshegs pa'i snying po
meditative equipoise	samāhita	mnyam bzhag
meditative stabilization	samādhi	ting nge 'dzin

English	Sanskrit	Tibetan
mental and physical aggregates	skandha	phung po
merit	puṇya	bsod nams
method	upāya	thabs
Method Vehicle	upāyayāna	thabs kyi theg pa
migrator	gati	'gro ba
mind of enlightenment	bodhicitta	byang chub kyi sems
Mind-Only School	cittamātra	sems tsam
natural nirvāṇa	svabhāvanirvāṇa	rang bzhin myang 'das
Nature Truth Body	svabhāvikakāya	ngo bo nyid sku
nonaffirming negative	prasajyapratiṣedha	med dgag
obstructions to liberation / afflictive obstructions	kleśāvaraṇa	nyon mong pa'i sgrib pa
obstructions to omniscience	jñeyāvaraṇa	shes bya'i sgrib pa
omniscience	sarvākārajñāna	rnam pa thams cad mkhyen pa
path	mārga	lam
path of accumulation	saṃbhāramārga	tshogs lam
path of meditation	bhāvanāmārga	sgom lam

ENGLISH	SANSKRIT	TIBETAN
path of no more learning	aśaikṣamārga	mi slob lam
path of preparation	prayogamārga	sbyor lam
path of seeing	darśanamārga	mthong lam
patience	kṣānti	bzod pa
perfection	pāramitā	pha rol tu phyin pa
Perfection Vehicle	pāramitāyāna	phar phyin theg pa
Performance Tantra	caryātantra	spyod rgyud
person	pudgala	gang zag
phenomenon	dharma	chos
Pledge Seal	samayamudrā	dam tshig gi phyag rgya
predisposition	vāsanā	bag chags
proliferations	prapañca	spros pa
repetition	jāpa	bzlas brjod
requiring interpretation / interpretable	neyārtha	drang don
Scriptural Division of the Knowledge Bearers	vidhyādhārapiṭaka	rig 'dzin gyi sde snod
Seal	mudrā	phyag rgya
Secret Mantra Vehicle	guhyamantrayāna	gsang sngags kyi theg pa

English	Sanskrit	Tibetan
selflessness	nairātmya	bdag med
selflessness of persons	pudgalanairātmya	gang zag gi bdag med
selflessness of phenomena	dharmanairātmya	chos kyi bdag med
sentient being	sattva	sems can
sets of discourses	sūtrānta	mdo sde
Sky-Goer	ḍākinī	mkha' 'gro
Solitary Realizer	pratyekabuddha	rang sangs rgyas
special insight	vipaśyanā	lhag mthong
stage of completion	niṣpannakrama	rdzogs rim
stage of generation	utpattikrama	bskyed rim
substantial existence	dravyasat	rdzas su yod pa
suchness	tathatā	de kho na nyid
Superior	āryan	'phags pa
suspicion / doubt	saṃśaya / vicikitsā	the tshom
Sūtra School	sautrāntika	mdo sde pa
Sūtra-Autonomy-Middle Way School	sautrāntika-svātantrika-mādhyamika	mdo sde spyod pa'i dbu ma rang rgyud pa
symbolic being	samayasattva	dam tshig pa
tenet / system of tenets	siddhānta	grub mtha'

English	Sanskrit	Tibetan
three refuges	triśarana	skyabs gsum
Truth Body / Body of Attributes	dharmakāya	chos sku
ultimate truth	paramārthasatya	don dam bden pa
uncompounded	asaṃskṛta	'dus ma byas
Universal Monarch	cakravartin	'khor sgyur
unusual attitude	adhyāśaya	lhag bsam
valid cognition	pramāṇa	tshad ma
vehicle	yāna	theg pa
Victor	jina	rgyal ba
view of the transitory collection	satkāyadṛṣṭi	'jig tshogs la lta ba
wind	prāṇa	rlung
wisdom	prajñā	shes rab
Wisdom Knowledge Woman	jñānavidyā	ye shes kyi rig ma
Wisdom Seal	jñānamudrā	ye shes kyi phyag rgya
Wisdom Truth Body	jñānadharmakāya	ye shes chos sku
wrong view	mithyādṛṣṭi	log lta
Yoga Tantra	yogatantra	rnal 'byor rgyud
yoga with signs	sanimittayoga	mtshan bcas kyi rnal 'byor

English	Sanskrit	Tibetan
yoga without signs	animittayoga	mtshan ma med pa'i rnal 'byor
Yogic-Autonomy-Middle Way School	yogācāra-svātantrika-mādhyamika	rnal 'byor spyod pa'i dbu ma rang rgyud pa

Bibliography

In the first section the titles are arranged alphabetically according to the English, followed by the Sanskrit and Tibetan; in the second section, by author. Here and in the notes, for works found in the Tibetan canon "P" refers to the *Tibetan Tripiṭaka: Peking Edition kept in the Library of the Otani University, Kyoto,* edited by Daisetz Teitarō Suzuki (Tokyo, Kyoto, Japan: Tibetan Tripiṭaka Research Foundation, 1955–1961). "Toh" refers either to *A Complete Catalogue of the Tibetan Buddhist Canons,* edited by Prof. Hakuji Ui et al. (Sendai, Japan, 1934) or to *A Catalogue of the Tohoku University Collection of Tibetan Works on Buddhism,* edited by Prof. Yensho Kanakura *et al.* (Sendai, Japan, 1953); TBRC W23703 (PDF of: Delhi: Karmapae Chodhey, Gyalwae sungrab partun khang, 1977). "Co ne" refers to the *co ne bstan 'gyur;* TBRC W1GS66030 (*co ne dgon chen*: *co ne*, 1926). The English titles are usually abbreviated.

1. Sūtras and Tantras

All Secret Tantra
sarvarahasyanāmatantrarāja
thams cad gsang ba rgyud kyi rgyal po
P114, vol. 5 (Toh. 481)

Appearances Shining as Vajras
snang ba rdo rjer 'char ba
(Not found in either P or Toh.)

Brief Explication of Initiations
śekhoddeśa
dbang mdor bstan pa
P3, vol. 1 (Toh. 361)

Chapter of the True One Sūtra
satyakaparivartasūtra
bden pa po'i le'u'i mdo
(Not found in either P or Toh.)
Compendium of All the Weaving Sūtra
sarvaidalyasaṃgraha
rnam par 'thag pa thams cad bsdus pa
P893, vol. 35 (Toh. 227)
Compendium of the Principles of All Ones-Gone-Thus
sarvatathāgatatattvasaṃgrahanāmamahāyānasūtra
de bzhin gshegs pa thams cad kyi de kho na nyid bsdus pa zhes bya ba theg pa chen po'i mdo
P112, vol. 4 (Toh. 479)
Compendium of Wisdom Vajras
jñānavajrasamuccaya
ye shes rdo rje kun las btus pa
P84, vol. 3 (Toh. 447)
Condensed Perfection of Wisdom Sūtra
sañcayagāthāprajñāpāramitāsūtra
shes rab kyi pha rol tu phyin pa sdud pa tshigs su bcad pa
P735, vol. 21 (Toh. 13)
Detailed Rite of Amoghapāsha
amoghapāśakalparāja
don yod pa'i zhags pa'i cho ga zhib mo'i rgyal po
P365, vol. 8 (Toh. 686)
Eight Thousand Stanza Perfection of Wisdom Sūtra
aṣṭasāhasrikāprajñāpāramitāsūtra
shes rab kyi pha rol tu phyin pa brgyad stong pa'i mdo
P734, vol. 21 (Toh. 12)
Expression of the Ultimate Names of the Wisdom-Being Mañjushrī
mañjuśrījñānasattvasya paramārthanāmasaṃgīti
'jam dpal ye shes sems dpa'i don dam pa'i mtshan yang dag par brjod pa
P2, vol. 1 (Toh. 360)
Guhyasamāja Tantra
sarvatathāgatakāyavākcittarahasyaguhyasamājanāmamahākalprāja
de bzhin gshegs pa thams cad kyi sku gsung thugs kyi gsang chen gsang ba 'dus pa zhes bya ba brtag pa'i rgyal po chen po
P81, vol. 3 (Toh. 442–3)

Hevajra Tantra
hevajratantrarāja
kye'i rdo rje zhes bya ba rgyud kyi rgyal po
P10, vol. 1 (Toh. 417–8)
Introduction to the Forms of Definite and Indefinite Progress Sūtra
niyatāniyatagatimudrāvatāra
nges pa dang mi nges par 'gro ba'i phyag rgya la 'jug pa
P868, vol. 34 (Toh. 202)
Kālachakra Tantra
paramādibuddhoddhṛtaśrīkālacakranāmatantrarāja
mchog gi dang po'i sangs rgyas las byung ba rgyud kyi rgyal po dpal dus kyi 'khor lo
P4, vol. 1 (Toh. 362)
Kāshyapa Chapter Sūtra
kāśyapaparivartasūtra
'od srung gi le'u'i mdo
P760. 43, vol. 24 (Toh. 87)
Little Saṃvara Tantra
tantrarājaśrīlaghusaṃvara
rgyud kyi rgyal po dpal bde mchog nyung ngu'i rgyud
P16, vol. 2 (Toh. 368)
Meeting of Father and Son Sūtra
pitāputrasamāgamasūtra
yab dang sras mjal ba'i mdo
P760. 16, vol. 23 (Toh. 60)
Ornament of the Vajra Essence Tantra
vajrahṛdayālaṃkāratantra
rdo rje snying po rgyan gyi rgyud
P86, vol. 3 (Toh. 451)
Paramādya Tantra
śrīparamādyanāmamahāyānakalparāja
dpal mchog dang po zhes bya ba theg pa chen po'i rtog pa'i rgyal po
P119, vol. 5 (Toh. 487)
Questions of Subāhu Tantra
subāhuparipṛcchānāmatantra
dpung bzang gis zhus pa zhes bya ba'i rgyud
P428, vol. 9 (Toh. 805)

Saṃpuṭa Tantra
saṃpuṭanāmamahātantra
yang da par sbyor ba zhes bya ba'i rgyud
P26, vol. 2 (Toh. 381)

Sūtra of the Wise Man and the Fool
damamūkonāmasūtra
mdzangs blun zhes bya ba'i mdo
P1008, vol. 40 (Toh. 341)

Sūtra Revealing the Secret
gsang ba lung bstan pa'i mdo
(Not found in either P or Toh.)

Vairochanābhisaṃbodhi Tantra
mahāvairocanābhisaṃbodhivikurvati-adhiṣṭhānavaipulyaparyāya
rnam par snang mdzad chen po mngon par rdzogs par byang chub pa rnam par sprul ba byin gyis rlob pa shin tu rgyas pa mdo sde'i dbang po rgyal po zhes bya ba'i chos kyi rnam grangs
P126, vol. 5 (Toh. 494)

Vajraḍāka Tantra
vajraḍākaguhyatantrarāja
rdo rje mkha' 'gro gsang ba'i rgyud kyi rgyal po
P44, vol. 3 (Toh. 399)

Vajrapāṇi Initiation Tantra
vajrapāṇyabhiṣekamahātantra
lag na rdo rje dbang bskur ba'i rgyud chen mo
P130, vol. 6 (Toh. 496)

Vajrapañjara Tantra
ḍākinīvajrapañjaramahātantrarājakalpa
mkha' 'gro ma rdo rje gur zhes bya ba'i rgyud kyi rgyal po chen po'i brtag pa
P11, vol. 1 (Toh. 419)

Vajrashekhara Tantra
vajraśekharamahāguhyayogatantra
gsang ba rnal 'byor chen po'i rgyud rdo rtse mo
P113, vol. 5 (Toh. 480)

Viṣhṇu Tantra
khyab 'jug gi rgyud
(Not found in either P or Toh.)

White Lotus of the Excellent Doctrine
saddharmapuṇḍarīkasūtra
dam pa'i chos pad ma dkar po'i mdo
P781, vol. 30 (Toh. 113)

2. Other Works

Abhayākaraguptapāda (*'jig med 'byung gnas kyi sbas pa*)
Clusters of Quintessential Instructions, Commentary on the Saṃpuṭa Tantra
saṃpuṭatantrarājaṭīkā-āmnāyamañjari
yang dag par sbyor ba'i rgyud kyi rgyal po'i rgya cher 'grel pa man ngag gi snye ma
P2328, vol. 55 (Toh. 1198)
Alaṃkakalasha
Commentary on the Vajra Garland Tantra
vajramālāmahāyogatantraṭīkāgambhīrārthadīpikā
rnal 'byor chen po'i rgyud dpal rdo rje phreng ba'i rgya cher 'grel pa zab mo'i don gyi 'grel pa
P2660, vol. 61 (Toh. 1795)
Ānandagarbha (*kun dga' snying po;* tenth century)
Commentary on the Guhyasamāja Tantra
guhyasamājamahātantrarājaṭīkā
rgyud kyi rgyal po chen po dpal gsang ba 'dus pa'i rgya cher 'grel pa
P4787, vol. 84 (Toh. 1917)
Illumination of the "Compendium of Principles"
sarvatathāgatatattvasaṃgrahamahāyānābhisamayanāmatantravyā-khyātattvālokakarī
de bzhin gshegs pa thams cad kyi de kho na nyid bsdus pa theg pa chen po mngon par rtogs pa zhes bya ba'i rgyud kyi bshad pa de kho na nyid snang bar byed pa
P3333, vol. 71–2 (Toh. 2510)
Āryadeva (*'phags pa lha;* second to third century C.E.)
Four Hundred / Treatise of Four Hundred Stanzas
catuḥśatakaśāstrakārikā
bstan bcos bzhi brgya pa zhes bya ba'i tshig le'ur byas pa
P5246, vol. 95 (Toh. 3846)
Lamp Compendium of Practice
caryāmelāpakapradīpa
spyod pa bsdus pa'i sgron ma
P2668, vol. 61 (Toh. 1803)
Asaṅga (*thogs med;* fourth century)
Five Treatises on the Grounds
Grounds of Yogic Practice / Actuality of the Grounds
yogācārabhūmi
rnal 'byor spyod pa'i sa

P5536–8, vol. 109–10 (Toh. 4035–7)
Compendium of Ascertainments
nirṇayasaṃgraha
gtan la dbab pa bsdu ba
P5539, vol. 110–11 (Toh. 4038)
Compendium of Bases
vastusaṃgraha
bzhi bsdu ba
P5540, vol. 111 (Toh. 4039)
Compendium of Enumerations
paryāyasaṃgraha
rnam grang bsdu ba
P5542, vol. 111 (Toh. 404)
Compendium of Explanations
vivaraṇasaṃgraha
rnam par bshad pa bsdu ba
P5543, vol. 111 (Toh. 4042)
Ashvaghoṣha (*rta dbyangs;* third or fourth century)
Fifty Stanzas on the Guru
gurupañcāśikā
bla ma lnga bcu pa
P4544, no. 81 (Toh. 3721)
Twenty Stanzas on the Bodhisattva Vow
bodhisattvasaṃvaraviṃśaka
byang chub sems dpa'i sdom pa nyi shu pa
P5582, vol. 114 (Toh. 4081)
Bhavabhadra
Commentary on the Vajraḍāka Tantra
śrīvajraḍākanāmamahātantrarājasya vivṛti
rgyud kyi rgyal po chen po dpal rdo rje mkha' 'gro zhes bya ba'i rnam par bshad pa
P2131, vol. 50 (Toh. 1415)
Buddhaguhya (*sangs rgyas gsang ba*)
Condensation of the "Questions of Subāhu Tantra"
subāhuparipṛcchānāmatantrapiṇḍārtha
dpung bzang gis zhus pa'i rgyud kyi bsdus pa'i don
P3496, vol. 78 (Toh. 2671)
Condensation of the "Vairochanābhisaṃbodhi Tantra"
vairocanābhisaṃbodhitantrapiṇḍārtha

rnam par snang mdzad mngon par rdzogs par byang chub pa'i rgyud kyi bsdus pa'i don
P3486, vol. 77 (Toh. 2662)
Word Commentary on the Vairochanābhisaṃbodhi Tantra
vairocanābhisaṃbodhivikurvitādhiṣṭhānamahātantrabhāṣya
rnam par snang mdzad mngon par byang chub pa rnam par sprul pa'i byin gyis brlabs kyi rgyud chen po'i bshad pa
P3487, vol. 77 (Toh. 2663)
Butön Rinchendrub (*bu ston rin chen grub*, 1290–1364)
Condensed General Presentation of the Tantra Sets, Key Opening the Door of the Precious Treasury of Tantra Sets
rgyud sde spyi'i rnam bzhag bsdus pa rgyud sde rin po che'i gter sgo 'byed pa'i lde mig
Collected Works, Part 14 pha (New Delhi: International Academy of Indian Culture, 1969), (Toh. 5167)
Extensive General Presentation of the Tantra Sets, Jeweled Adornment of the Tantra Sets
rgyud sde spyi'i rnam par gzhag pa rgyud sde rin po che'i mdzes rgyan
Collected Works, Part 15 *ba* (New Delhi: International Academy of Indian Culture, 1969), (Toh. 5169)
Medium Length General Presentation of the Tantra Sets, Illuminating the Secrets of All Tantra Sets
rgyud sde spyi'i rnam par gzhag pa rgyud sde thams cad kyi gsang ba gsal bar byed pa zhes bya ba
Collected Works, Part 15ba (New Delhi: International Academy of Indian Culture, 1969), (Toh. 5168)
Chandrakīrti (*zla ba grags pa*)
Commentary to "Supplement to the Middle"
madhyamakāvatārabhāṣya
dbu ma la 'jug pa'i bshad pa
P5263, vol. 98 (Toh. 3862)
Supplement to the Middle
madhyamakāvatāra
dbu ma la 'jug pa
P5262 and 5261, vol. 98 (Toh. 3861)
Devakulamahāmati (*lha rigs kyi blo gros chen po*)
Commentary on the Difficult Points of the Vajrapañjara Tantra
ḍākinīvajrajālapañjaratantrarājasya pañjikāpauṣtika

rgyud kyi rgyal po mkha' 'gro ma rdo rje dra ba'i dka' 'grel de kho na nyid rgyas pa
P2326, vol. 54 (Toh. 1196)
Dharmakīrti (*chos kyi grags pa*)
Seven Treatises on Valid Cognition
Commentary on (Dignāga's) "Compilation of Valid Cognition"
pramāṇavarttikakārikā
tshad ma rnam 'grel gyi tshig le'ur byas pa
P5709, vol. 130 (Toh. 4210)
Ascertainment of Valid Cognition
pramāṇaviniścaya
tshad ma rnam par nges pa
P5710, vol. 130 (Toh. 4211)
Drop of Reasoning
nyāyabinduprakaraṇa
rigs pa'i thigs pa zhes bya ba'i rab tu byed pa
P5711, vol. 130 (Toh. 4212)
Drop of Reasons
hetubindunāmaprakaraṇa
gtan tshigs kyi thigs pa zhes bya ba rab tu byed pa
P5712, vol. 130 (Toh. 4213)
Analysis of Relations
saṃbandhaparīkṣāvṛtti
'brel pa brtag pa'i rab tu byed pa
P5713, vol. 130 (Toh. 4214)
Principles of Debate
vādanyāyanāmaprakaraṇa
rtsod pa'i rigs pa zhes bya ba'i rab tu byed pa
P5715, vol. 130 (Toh. 4218)
Proof of Other Continuums
samṭānāntarasiddhināmaprakaraṇa
rgyud gzhan grub pa zhes bya ba'i rab tu byed pa
P5716, vol. 130 (Toh. 4219)
Durjayachandra (*mi thub zla ba*)
Commentary on the Difficult Points of the Hevajra Tantra
kaumudīnāmapañjikā
kau mu dī zhes bya ba'i dka' 'grel
P2315, vol. 53 (Toh. 1185)

Gyaltshab Darma Rinchen (*rgyal tshab dar ma rin chen*, 1364–1432)
Explanation of (Āryadeva's) "Four Hundred": Essence of Eloquence
bzhi brgya pa'i rnam bshad legs bshad snying po
Blockprint in the Dalai Lama's library; place and date of publication unknown.
Indrabodhi (or Indrabhūti)
Commentary on the Difficult Points of the Vajrapañjara Tantra
ḍākinīvajrapañjaramahātantrarājasya pañjikāprathamapaṭalamukhabandha
rgyud kyi rgyal po mkha' 'gro ma rdo rje gur gyi dka' 'grel zhal nas brgyud pa
P2324, vol. 54 (Toh. 1194)
Jamyang Shaypa (*'jam dbyangs bzhad pa*, 1648–1721)
Great Exposition of Tenets / Explanation of "Tenets": Sun of the Land of Samantabhadra Brilliantly Illuminating All of Our Own and Others' Tenets and the Meaning of the Profound [Emptiness], Ocean of Scripture and Reasoning Fulfilling All Hopes of All Beings
grub mtha' chen mo / grub mtha'i rnam bshad rang gzhan grub mtha' kun dang zab don mchog tu gsal ba kun bzang zhing gi nyi ma lung rigs rgya mtsho
New Delhi: Ngawang Gelek Demo, 1973
Great Exposition of the Middle / Decisive Analysis of (Chandrakīrti's) "Supplement to (Nāgārjuna's) 'Treatise on the Middle'": Treasury of Scripture and Reasoning, Thoroughly Illuminating the Profound Meaning [of Emptiness], Entrance for the Fortunate
dbu ma la 'jug pa'i mtha' dpyod lung rigs gter mdzod zab don kun gsal skal bzang 'jug ngog
New Delhi: Ngawang Gelek Demo, 1973
Jangkya Rölpay Dorjay (*lcang skya rol pa'i rdo rje*, 1717–1786)
Presentations of Tenets / Clear Exposition of the Presentations of Tenets, A Beautiful Ornament for the Meru of the Subduer's Teaching
grub pa'i mtha'i rnam par bzhag pa gsal bar bshad pa thub bstan lhun po'i mdzes rgyan
Varanasi: The Pleasure of Elegant Sayings Printing Press, 1970
Jinadatta (*rgyal bas byin*)
Commentary on the Difficult Points of the Guhyasamāja Tantra
guhyasamājatantrapañjikā
dpal gsang ba 'dus pa'i rgyud kyi dka' 'grel
P2710, vol. 63 (Toh. 1847)

Jñānakīrti (*ye shes grags pa*)
Abridged Explanation of All the Word of the Sugata
tattvāvatārākhyasakalasugatavacastātparyavyākhyāprakaraṇa
de kho na nyid la 'jug pa zhes bya ba bde bar gshegs pa'i bka' ma lus pa mdor bsdus ste bshad pa'i rab tu byed pa
P4532, vol. 81 (Toh. 3709)

Jñānapāda (*ye shes zhabs*)
Engaging in the Means of Self-Achievement
ātmasādhanāvatāra
bdag sgrub pa la 'jug pa
P2723, vol. 65 (Toh. 1860)

Jñānashrī (*ye shes dpal*)
Eradication of the Two Extremes in the Vajra Vehicle
vajrayānakoṭidvayāpoha
rdo rje theg pa'i mtha' gnyis sel ba
P4537, vol. 81 (Toh. 3714)

Kalkī Puṇḍarīka (*rigs ldan pad ma dkar po*)
Stainless Light
vimālaprabhānāmamūlatantrānusāriṇīdvādashasāhasrikālaghukāla-chakratantrarājaṭīkā
bsdus pa'i rgyud kyi rgyal po dus kyi 'khor lo'i 'grel bshad rtsa ba'i rgyud kyi rjes su 'jug pa stong phrag bcu gnyis pa dri ma med pa'i 'od ces bya ba
P2064, vol. 46 (Toh. 845)

Kalsang Gyatsho, Seventh Dalai Lama (*bskal bzang rgya mtsho,* 1708–1757)
Explanation of the Rite of the Guhyasamāja Maṇḍala
gsang 'dus dkyil 'khor cho ga'i rnam bshad
New Delhi, Tanzin Kunga, 1972

Könchog Jigmay Wangpo (*dkon mchog 'jigs med dbang po,* 1728–1791)
Precious Garland of Tenets / Presentation of Tenets, A Precious Garland
grub pa'i mtha'i rnam par bzhag pa rin po che'i phreng ba
Dharamsala: Shes rig par khang, 1969

Kṛṣhṇapāda (*nag po zhabs*)
Explanation of the Vajrapañjara Tantra
ḍākinīvajrapañjaranāmamahātantrarājakalpamukhabandha
mkha' 'gro ma rdo rje gur zhes bya ba'i rgyud kyi rgyal po chen po'i rtag pa'i rgyal po'i bshad sbyar
P2325, vol. 54 (Toh. 1195)

Longchen Rabjam (*klong chen rab 'byams / klong chen dri med 'od zer,* 1308–1363)
Precious Treasury of the Supreme Vehicle
theg pa'i mchog rin po che'i mdzod
Gangtok: Dodrup Chen Rinpoche, 1969 (?)
Treasury of Tenets, Illuminating the Meaning of All Vehicles
theg pa mtha' dag gi don gsal bar byed pa grub pa'i mtha' rin po che'i mdzod
Gangtok: Dodrup Chen Rinpoche, 1969 (?)

Longdol Ngagwang Losang (*klong rdol bla ma ngag dbang blo bzang,* 1719–94)
Terminology Arising in Secret Mantra, the Scriptural Division of the Knowledge Bearers
gsang sngags rig pa 'dzin pa'i sde snod las byung ba'i ming gi grang
The Collected Works of Longdol Lama Parts 1 and 2. New Delhi, International Academy of Indian Culture, 1973

Losang Chökyi Gyaltshan (*blo bzang chos kyi rgyal mtshan,* 1570–1662)
Presentation of the General Teaching and the Four Tantra Sets
bstan pa spyi dang rgyud sde bzhi'i rnam par bzhag pa'i zin bris
Collected Works, vol. 4. New Delhi: Gurudeva, 1973

Maitreya (*byams pa*)
Ornament for the Great Vehicle Sūtras
mahāyānasūtrālaṃkārakārikā
theg pa chen po'i mdo sde'i rgyan gyi tshig le'ur byas pa
P5521, vol. 108 (Toh. 4020)
Ornament for the Clear Realizations
abhisamayālaṃkāra
mngon par rtogs pa'i rgyan
P5184, vol. 88 (Toh. 3786)

Mātṛcheta and Dignāga (*phyogs kyi glang po*)
Interwoven Praise
miśrakastotra
spel mar bstod pa
P2041, vol. 46 (Toh. 1150)

Nāgārjuna (*klu sgrub*)
Collections of Reasoning
Treatise on the Middle / Fundamental Treatise on the Middle, Called "Wisdom"
prajñānāmamūlamadhyamakakārikā / madhyamakaśāstra

dbu ma rtsa ba'i tshig le'ur byas pa shes rab ces bya ba
P5224, vol. 95 (Toh. 3824)
Sixty Stanzas of Reasoning
yuktiṣaṣṭikākārikā
rigs pa drug cu pa'i tshig le'ur byas pa
P5225, vol. 95 (Toh. 3825)
Treatise Called "The Finely Woven"
vaidalyasūtranāma
zhib mo rnam par 'thag pa zhes bya ba'i mdo
P5226, vol. 95 (Toh. 3826)
Seventy Stanzas on Emptiness
śūnyatāsaptatikārikā
stong pa nyid bdun cu pa'i tshig le'ur byas pa
P5227, vol. 95 (Toh. 3827)
Refutation of Objections
vigrahavyāvartanīkārikā
rtsod pa bzlog pa'i tshig le'ur byas pa
P5228, vol. 95 (Toh. 3828)
Praise of the Nonconceptual
nirvikalpastava (?)
rnam par mi rtog par bstod pa
(Not found in P or Toh.)
Precious Garland of Advice for the King
rājaparikathāratnāvalī
rgyal po la gtam bya ba rin po che'i phreng ba
P5658, vol. 129 (Toh. 4158)

Pabongkhapa Jampa Tandzin Trinlay Gyatsho (*pha bong kha pa byams pa bstan 'dzin 'phrin las rgya mtsho,* 1878–1941)
Miscellaneous Notes from Jonay Paṇḍita's "Explanation of the Great Exposition of Secret Mantra"
rje btsun bla ma co ne paṇḍi ta rin po che'i zhal snga nas sngags rim chen mo'i bshad lung nos skabs kyi gsung bshad zin bris thor tsam du bkod pa
Collected Works, Vol. 2. New Delhi: Chophel Legdan, 1972

Padma Karpo (*pad ma kar po,* 1527–1592)
General Presentation of the Tantra Sets, Captivating the Wise
rgyud sde spyi'i rnam gzhag mkhas pa'i yid 'phrog
Collected Works, Vol. 11. Darjeeling: Kargyud Sungrab Nyamso Khang, 1974

Rāhulashrīmitra (*sgra gcan 'dzin dpal bshes gnyen*)
Clarification of Union
yuganaddhaprakāśanāmasekaprakriyā
zung du 'jug pa gsal ba zhes bya ba'i dbang gi bya ba
P2682, vol. 62 (Toh. 1818)
Ratnākarashānti (*shānti pa / rin chen 'byung gnas zhi ba*)
Commentary on the Difficult Points of the Hevajra Tantra
hevajrapañjikāmuktikāvalī
dgyes pa'i rdo rje'i dka' 'grel mu tig phreng ba
P2319, vol. 54 (Toh. 1189)
Commentary on (Dīpaṅkarabhadra's) "Four Hundred and Fifty"
guhyasamājamaṇḍalavidhiṭīkā
dpal gsang ba 'dus pa'i dkyil 'khor gyi cho ga'i 'grel pa
P2734, vol. 65 (Toh. 1871)
Handful of Flowers, Explanation of the Guhyasamāja Tantra
kusumāñjaliguhyasamājanibandha
gsang ba 'dus pa'i bshad sbyar snyim pa'i me tog
P2714, vol. 65 (Toh. 1851)
Presentation of the Three Vehicles
triyānavyavasthāna
theg pa gsum rnam par bzhag pa
P4535, vol. 81 (Toh. 3712)
Ratnarakṣhita
Commentary on the Difficult Points of the Saṃvarodaya Tantra
saṃvarodayamahātantrarājasya padminīnāmapañjikā
sdom pa 'byung ba'i rgyud kyi rgyal po chen po'i dka' 'grel
P2137, vol. 51 (Toh. 1420)
Samayavajra (*dam tshig rdo rje*)
Commentary on the Kṛṣhṇṣshnaya Tantra
kṛṣṇayamāritantrarājāprekṣaṇapathapradīpanāmaṭīkā
gshin rje gshed nag po'i rgyud kyi rgyal po mngon par mthong ba lam gyi sgron ma zhes bya ba'i rgya cher bshad pa
P2783, vol. 66 (Toh. 1920)
Shākyamitra (*shā kya'i bshes gnyen*)
Ornament of Kosala, Commentary on the "Compendium of Principles"
kosalālaṃkāratattvasaṃgrahaṭīkā
de kho na nyid bsdus pa'i rgya cher bshad pa ko sa la'i rgyan
P3326, vol. 70–71 (Toh. 2503)

Shaṃkarapati (*bde byed bdag po*)
Praise of the Supra-Divine
devātiśayastotra
lha las phul du byung bar bstod pa
P2004, vol. 46 (Toh. 1112)
Shāntarakṣhita (*zhi ba 'tsho,* eighth century)
Work on the Establishment of the Principles
tattvasiddhināmaprakaraṇa
de kho na nyid grub pa zhes bya ba'i rab tu byed pa
P4531, vol. 81 (Toh. 3708)
Shāntideva (*zhi ba lha,* eighth century C.E.)
Engaging in the Bodhisattva Deeds
bodhisattvacaryāvatāra
byang chub sems dpa'i spyod pa la 'jug pa
P5272, vol. 99 (Toh. 3871)
Shraddhākaravarman
Introduction to the Meaning of the Highest Yoga Tantra
yogānuttaratantrārthāvatārasaṃgraha
rnal 'byor bla med pa'i rgyud kyi don la 'jug pa bsdus pa
P4536, vol. 81 (Toh. 3713)
Shrīdhara (*dpal 'dzin*)
Innate Illumination, Commentary on the Difficult Points of the Yamāri Tantra
yamāritantrapañjikāsahajāloka
gshin rje gshed kyi rgyud kyi dka' 'grel lhan cig skyes pa'i snang ba
P2781, vol. 66 (Toh. 1918)
Sönam Tsemo (*bsod nam rtse mo;* 1142–1182)
General Presentation of the Tantra Sets
rgyud sde spyi'i rnam par gzhag pa
(sGang tog, 'Bras ljongs sa ngor chos tshogs, 1969)
Tagtshang Sherab Rinchen (*stag tshang lo tsā ba shes rab rin chen,* b.1405)
Explanation of the Treatise "Freedom from Extremes through Understanding All Tenets": Ocean of Eloquence
grub mtha' kun shes nas mtha' bral grub pa zhes bya ba'i bstan bcos rnam par bshad pa legs bshad kyi rgya mtsho
Photographic reprint in the possession of Khetsun Sangpo; place and date of publication unknown
Tripiṭakamāla
Lamp for the Three Modes

nayatrayapradīpa
tshul gsum gyi sgron ma
P4530, vol. 81 (Toh. 3707)
Tsongkhapa Losang Dragpa (*tsong kha pa blo bzang grags pa,* 1357–1419)
Door of Entry to the Seven Treatises, Dispelling the Mental Darkness of Seekers
sde bdun la 'jug pa'i sgo don gnyer yid kyi mun sel
(Toh. 5416)
Great Exposition of Secret Mantra / The Stages of the Path to a Victor and Pervasive Master, a Great Vajradhara: Revealing All Secret Essentials
rgyal ba khyab bdag rdo rje 'chang chen po'i lam gyi rim pa gsang ba kun gyi gnad rnam par phye ba
P6210, vol. 161 (Toh. 5281)
Great Exposition of the Stages of the Path Common to the Vehicles / Stages of the Path to Enlightenment Thoroughly Teaching All the Stages of Practice of the Three Types of Persons
skyes bu gsum gyi nyams su blang ba'i rim pa thams cad tshang bar ston pa'i byang chub lam gyi rim pa
P6001, vol. 152 (Toh. 5392)
Vajragarbha (*rdo rje snying po*)
Commentary on the Condensation of the Hevajra Tantra
hevajrapiṇḍārthaṭīkā
kye'i rdo rje bsdus pa'i don gyi rgya cher 'grel pa
P2310, vol. 53 (Toh. 1180)
Vinayadatta (*'dul bas byin*)
Rite of the Great Illusion Maṇḍala
gurūpadeśanāmamahāmāyāmaṇḍalopāyika
sgyu 'phrul chen mo'i dkyil 'khor gyi cho ga bla ma'i zhal snga'i man ngag ces bya ba
P2517, vol. 57 (Toh. 1645)
Vīryavajra (*dpa' bo rdo rje*)
Commentary on the Saṃpuṭa Tantra
sarvatantrasyanidānamahāguhyaśrīsaṃpuṭanāmatantrarājaṭīkāratnamālā
rgyud thams cad kyi gleng gzhi dang gsang chen dpal kun tu kha sbyor zhes bya ba'i rgyud kyi rgyal po'i rgya cher bshad pa rin chen phreng ba zhes bya ba
P2329, vol. 55 (Toh. 1199)

Index

01/14